HOLY HESYCHIA

THE STILLNESS THAT KNOWS GOD

HOLY HESYCHIA
THE STILLNESS THAT KNOWS GOD

(Book One *of* IN DEFENCE OF THE HOLY HESYCHASTS)
by
SAINT GREGORY PALAMAS

Translated and with a Commentary by Robin Amis

PLEROMA

PLEROMA PUBLISHING

Southover, Wells, BA5 1UH, U.K.

www.pleromabooks.co.uk

for

PRAXIS RESEARCH INSTITUTE, INC.

A non-profit Corporation registered in the State of Massachusetts

Reg. No. 043-110-773

www.praxisresearch.net

This edition copyright © Praxis Research Institute, 2016
Edited by A.N. Walker

This edition is a substantial revision, with additional material, of the work
previously published by Praxis Institute Press in 2002 as *The Triads: Book One*

British Library Cataloguing-in-Publication Data
A record is available from the British Library

ISBN 978 0 9955 1030 2

O Star of Orthodoxy,
support of the Church and its teacher,
O comeliness of ascetics, and incontestable champion
of those who speak of theology,
Gregory wonder-worker,
the pride of Thessalonica
and preacher of grace,
pray without ceasing
for the salvation
of our souls.

Greek Orthodox Troparion to Saint Gregory Palamas

ACKNOWLEDGEMENTS
from *The Triads: Book One*

We acknowledge our gratitude to the many people who have helped us complete this translation and discover in the English language the unique Christian philosophy of this late Byzantine saint. In particular we wish to recognise the assistance of David Vermette, Dr. Seymour Simmons, of Alex Kosmatopoulos, Greek poet and translator of Mallory's Morte d'Arthur into Greek, as well as certain monks of the Athonite monastery of Osiou Gregoriou, particularly Father Damianos and Father Artemius.

We would also like to acknowledge the critical edition of John Meyendorff's French translation, 'Defense des saints hesychastes', as well as Nicholas Gendle's English translation of selections from the Triads.

Finally I must acknowledge the help of my wife, Lillian Amis, both for her tolerance of my long hours of silence devoted to this task, and for not being afraid to comment openly on the text wherever it was necessary.

Robin Amis

CONTENTS

PREFACE ix

TRANSLATOR'S INTRODUCTION *by* Robin Amis 1

HISTORICAL INTRODUCTION *by* David Vermette 17

IN DEFENCE OF THE HOLY HESYCHASTS *by* St Gregory Palamas

Part 1: First Question & Answer 25

Part 2: Second Question & Answer 49

Part 3: Third Question & Answer 61

COMMENTARY ON THE TRIADS *by* Robin Amis

Part 1: SPIRITUAL KNOWLEDGE
First Discipline: Discerning Two Different Kinds of Knowledge 109

Part 2: SPIRITUAL PRACTICE
Second Discipline: Entry into the Heart 137

Part 3: SPIRITUAL ILLUMINATION
Third Discipline: Illumination and the Charismatic Light 155

AFTERWORD *by* Lillian Delevoryas Amis 209

NOTES 217

FURTHER READING 235

PREFACE

In Defence of the Holy Hesychasts, which is also known as *On Those Living the Hesychast Life in Sanctity*, was composed in three separate volumes, each book containing three parts, hence the whole work is commonly referred to as *The Triads*. Within it, Saint Gregory Palamas presents an exposition of the great teachings of the Fathers on stillness, inner prayer, the uncreated light, deifying grace, and the distinction between God's essence and energies.

The first edition of this work, published as *The Triads: Book One* in 2002, was translated and edited by Robin Amis. He subsequently revised the translation and wrote the additional Commentary, working on the project until his death in 2014. This edition is the fruit of that work and now contains his *Commentary on the Triads*, which represents the insights he gathered from numerous visits to Mount Athos, and from guiding students in the practical discipline of achieving inner stillness in ordinary life.

He felt that this text was crucial, as he recognised in it an expression of what he had been trying to do throughout his life – to convey those glimpses of the extraordinary behind the veil of appearances and to share with others an authentic and effective way of reaching that light. In Palamas's classic exposition of the way of inner stillness, *hesychia*, he found a clear description of such a way, not only corresponding to his own experience but also grounded in the tradition he had ultimately found in the Orthodox faith. He hoped that producing this book would bring to the awareness of his readers the possibility of finding the way into their interior world, in turn opening the door to the heart which leads to the experience of God.

TRANSLATOR'S INTRODUCTION

Robin Amis

Saint Gregory Palamas was a scholar, a monk and then a bishop. He was also a hesychast, a practitioner of inner stillness, or *hesychia*, taught by the Early Fathers of the church as a way of opening the heart and mind to God. In those days, the mainstream of Christian spirituality was still centred around the ascetic exercises first recommended by St Paul.[1] For the hesychasts, many of them living away from people or in monastic communities, these exercises were taken as a complete way of life – the Christian equivalent of the practices of monks and hermits in Eastern religions. Hesychasm is a form of Christian practice which was developed to bring alive the reality of God's presence in personal experience. The word *hesychia*, stillness, is found in the sayings of the Desert Fathers and by the fourth century was further described by St John Chrysostom, St Gregory of Nyssa and St Basil the Great. In the seventh century St John of Sinai, known as John Climacus in the East after his work *The Ladder of Divine Ascent*, was one of the first to systematically set out hesychasm as the practice of hesychia. St Symeon the New Theologian added to this exposition in the tenth century. When St Gregory Palamas wrote *In Defence of the Holy Hesychasts* in the fourteenth century, he was following a tradition that was even then over a thousand years old and which is still practised today, nearly seven hundred years later. This is a living tradition, hallowed by time and proven in practice and by the fruits of those who follow its aim.

It has been said that the Christian ideal has not been tried and found wanting – it has been found difficult, and left untried.[2] The writings of Palamas give the lie to this by showing that the practice of Christianity was certainly tried and succeeded, but the complete teaching of the successful form never reached the West, except to small groups of people. Yet today it still survives, hidden within the Eastern churches. The truth is that Christianity has been repeatedly tried and has repeatedly succeeded, but that is has failed to spread from those successive small beginnings without being so distorted that it becomes almost ineffective. There is indeed an effective form of Christianity that has not yet been tried in the West. In this respect, the Triads of St Gregory Palamas, written in order to establish the theological foundation of hesychasm, may still play an important part and help us now personally find the stillness that knows God.

Background to *In Defence of the Holy Hesychasts*

The Eastern Roman Empire (which was re-named as the 'Byzantine' Empire a century after its fall) in which St Gregory Palamas lived was a state in decline. Civil wars from within and foreign invasions from without had eroded the glory of earlier centuries. In succession, Arabs, Slavs, Latins (Western Europeans) and Turks had chipped away at the dying Empire, the last vestige of Ancient Rome and the Greco-Roman culture that had been transformed by Christianity many centuries before.

This book presents St Gregory's major work, which was probably the greatest book of the final era of that great civilisation whose premature death is still being worked out not only in the Balkans but throughout the Western world, since Constantinople, 'the second Rome', was one half of the original core of our modern Western civilisation. From my own studies, it now seems clear that the splitting of the original Roman Empire into two different halves eventually led to two separate developments – two incomplete and in some ways very different civilising influences. One half led to the development of the 'naked intellect', taking the form of a rationalism that then led to the triumph of materialism.

With the collapse of the Western Empire, Rome fell into a true dark age as barbarians fought for dominance and the West fell beyond the civilising influence of the Eastern Empire. It lost touch with the works of the Early Fathers and the storehouse of ancient Greek philosophy which continued to be the staple of education in the East. When the works of ancient philosophy were re-introduced to the West from the twelfth century onwards, particularly via the Arab translation schools of Spain, western education began to develop in a direction where formal intellect became dominant. It was this that led to humanism and from that to the narrow sensory form of western science with its power over the world and its lack of understanding of human character. It was in the Eastern Empire that Christianity preserved the inner character of the apostolic churches, of the Desert Fathers and the monasticism that arose from them, and so produced a vast number of ascetic saints. We know the boundaries of the Eastern Empire – combining the intellectual rigour of classical Greece, the religious fervour of the Middle East, and the splendour that was Rome, it comprised Greece, the Balkans, and present-day Turkey, Syria, the Lebanon, Palestine and Egypt. By the time of Palamas, in the early fourteenth century, the Byzantine Empire had managed to hold on to its capital, Constantinople, and still held some scraps of territory in Greece and the Greek islands. But by then much of it had already died, and within a century the once glorious empire fell into a half-millennium of subjection.

I shall seek to show that the forgotten civilisation of the Eastern Empire, for all its political confusions, contained on the religious side a tradition and civilising power that the western half of Europe never knew in full. A tradition whose strength, transfused now into a world fallen into division, corruption, aimless moral emptiness and rampant iniquity, might yet restore not only an ailing Christian church, but also civilisation itself.

Another Way of Knowing

The theology of St Gregory Palamas was directly involved with the struggle against the scholastic/rationalist approach to knowledge that had already begun to change the doctrine of the Western churches during his lifetime. The scholastic rationalism was the result of introducing elements of pre-Christian philosophical thought into theology, which led to the disputes about how God might be known. It also seems that it was this intellectual divergence from the original doctrine of the Church and the teachings of the Early Fathers that has led to the subsequent decline of the Christian religion in the West. During this change, a teaching about a God who is repeatedly described as inaccessible to the senses and inexplicable to reason becomes inexplicably rationalised and 'made sensible'.

It was Palamas who probably best exposed the flaws in this approach by defining the traditional way in which God can be known. His approach to this issue is neither based on sensory observation nor intellectual analysis, although it does require an understanding that there can exist another way of knowing, different from that of modern scientific and rationalistic thought. But his answer has until now been little understood in the West. This concept is so far from modern thinking that it may be difficult for those who are immersed in the materialist world-view to see the truth of Palamas's argument.

This failure of knowledge was not only a failure to clarify belief, it was also a failure of European thought, from the time of Palamas time until now, to account for certain elements of human inner experience. Certainly, its outcome has now shaped life in the West for more than seven hundred years. The enduring value to us now of *In Defence of the Holy Hesychasts* is that Palamas tells us a great deal about the nature of Christian practice. He relates in methodical detail not only the nature of inner experience, but also the practical way to attain it. The book is the summation, the last line of defence and the encapsulation of the first millennium of Christian culture – the culture that is the origin from which, more than any other source, our modern civilisation sprang.

More recent researches have helped us to understand the significance of early Christian practice and the reality of its outcome. One set of clues was found by taking account of the understanding that just as language shapes thought, so the outer and inner forces that shape our life also shape our language. In this way the language of hesychast monks like St Gregory Palamas was shaped by lives driven by the search for God and the striving for repentance, *metanoia* – change of heart and mind. Their language distinguished theological ideas, philosophical terms and psychological states which were developed to a fine point and which might nevertheless be overlooked at first glance, if they are seen merely as intellectual formulations rather than as practical methods.

Relying on Appearances

The fact that language shapes thought underlies the method which, in this translation, systematically translates key words in a way that will reveal our understanding of how Palamas and the hesychasts of his time once thought. In the translations of this work that have been available until now, not only *nous* (usually translated as mind or intellect) but certain other Greek words have been given multiple meanings, varying according to the context. There were obviously good reasons for some of these variations – for example, they would fit more easily into modern thought. Yet in fact some of them seem to produce certain confusions in the reader.

As we worked on this text it began to appear that the confusions themselves, once understood, were showing us one of the most important conclusions to be drawn from the text. They revealed how different our contemporary thought is from that of the first Christian millennium, giving glimpses of a fundamental divergence between two very different ways of seeing the world. Contrasting these two world-views showed that they influenced perception itself, presenting the world to the *psyche* (soul) in two ways that appear remarkably different one from the other.

Under the influence of the normal contemporary world-view, the way things appear to the senses is taken as the very nature of those things in themselves. This means that any difference in how they appear to us is taken to be a difference in their nature. That is to say that different appearances of one thing are mistakenly seen as if they were different things, subject to different laws, in direct contradiction to the millennia-old philosophical understanding that apparent differences are not real,[3] they are only differences caused when the same thing is seen in different ways. Philosophical insights of this kind, which helped to shape our civilisation in the past, have little influence over people today.

A Different Translation

As far as I know, this translation of Book One of *In Defence of the Holy Hesychasts* is still the only complete translation into English. Its source is the same text[4] as Nicholas Gendle's partial translation in the Classics of Western Spirituality series.[5] The focus of this translation is to bring to light the detailed spiritual teaching which Palamas presents, more or less unremarked elsewhere, alongside material which Meyendorff, the translator of the book into French, described as 'polemical.'[6]

Studied in this way, the book itself is then found to reveal unexpected characteristics of the culture that gave it birth. An understanding of these characteristics as they are understood in practice to this day, particularly on Mount Athos, transforms and clarifies the meaning of the translated text. In this light, behind the so-called polemical character of the text, lies a clear description of the practical methods of spirituality, the rigorous discipline of the hesychast culture of the Eastern Church. It can now be clearly seen as a genuine treatise on knowledge and truth from the viewpoint of that different culture, and we can see that the polemical element serves, in a way commonly used by authors of that time, as a mask intended to cover some of their deeper teachings.

In this translation, certain words of psychological meaning have been left in the original Greek, particularly *nous* and *psyche*, which in our times are both translated in many different ways, some of these differences being reflected in the Meyendorff translation. Wherever possible throughout this new translation these particular words are simply transliterated into English as nous and psyche.

An Unexpected Conclusion

In essence, the unexpected conclusion from the translation of this book was that over the past thousand years or so, alongside the advance of science and technology, there has been a general deterioration in our deeper understanding of ourselves and the world, a deterioration in which the vast majority of people have begun to think of things not as they can be understood, but simply as they appear at first glance. These factors not only suggest that there has been a change which has been in some way harmful to our humanity, but they also give pointers to ways in which this damage might be undone.

This possibility of a cure is one of the reasons for raising the issue in a book such as this. These observations link to the special way this translation approaches the ideas of nous and psyche. Rendering these words in the way used here provides a number of clues to the deeper meaning of the text and I am already convinced that this deeper meaning has the most practical significance.

Nous and Psyche

In rediscovering the Christian spiritual psychology of the first millennium one has first to be aware of the precise terms in which it was first expressed. The two words nous and psyche are central to any understanding of this profound psychology. However, they have been so often mistranslated that to understand them correctly not only gives us a new key to the meaning of the text of the Triads, but also helps us to better understand the Christian religion itself.

The word *psyche* is usually translated into English as soul. Its root meaning was life or breath. So when we talk about the immortality or salvation of the soul, we are talking about the psyche. But there is a strange divergence in our understanding of the Christian idea of soul, and this divergence shows in the modern usage of this word where it serves as the root of the word psychology. In this sense we understand psyche as being concerned with how we think and how we feel. And the Early Fathers, the church, and Palamas himself, also used it in the same context. Psyche is concerned with – but not limited to – thought and feeling, memory, imagination, and desire. In the original Greek of the Bible, psyche as the animating power of our physical life, psyche as the soul that inherits immortality, and psyche as the inner content of our lives are one and the same thing. The word psyche encompasses the following aspects of human life:

1. Soul: the immortal part of man, the object of salvation.
2. Breath, or life: that which departs the dying body.
3. Mind: inner processes now attributed loosely to mind, including thoughts, feelings, desires, imaginings, and all the psychological content of our lives.

The confusion in the translation of this word, in which one word is given different meanings, is in fact symptomatic of a confusion of thought. To say that psyche has these different meanings is equally to say that today we attribute the different qualities of psyche to different things, that we are blind to the relation between them. In the West, the word 'soul' has become a debased and vague term. The psyche, in its original biblical sense, has now separated into two distinct conceptual fields and in order to encapsulate the full meaning of the word psyche as understood by traditional Christianity we will have to combine the meanings of five English words – soul, life, breath, psyche and mind. The words soul, life and breath form one field; the words psyche (as in modern psychology), and mind (as in the mind-body dichotomy) comprise the other field. Due to this divergence, there is little or no connection between the concept of psychic health and the concept of the eternal animating principle known as soul. This dissociation points to the deep spiritual sickness in Western man.[7]

The promise of immortality is realised in the psyche and the change that leads to this attainment is a change in the psyche. So Christian truth is directly concerned with the psyche, and Christian teachings also contain a strong element of psychology. Understanding psyche in its original sense opens up to us the active part we can play in our own transformation – instead of the soul simply being a passive recipient of something that comes from outside of us, the psyche can be recognised as an actor in its own fate, and we can thus participate more practically in the daily struggle for perfection.

When the soul endowed with intelligence firmly exercises her freedom of choice in the right way, and reins in like a charioteer the incensive and appetitive aspects of her nature, restraining and controlling her passionate impulses, she receives a crown of victory; and as a reward for her labours, she is granted life in heaven by God her Creator.[8] (St Anthony the Great)

The Nous

The human nous, although it encompasses the notion of mind, is not intellect in the modern sense of the word, as it is often translated. It also includes the awareness within the psyche. The nature of the nous is that it is the part of the psyche that watches the other parts of the psyche. I wrote about it in an earlier book: 'The nous is the background to the whole drama of inner Christianity. In that inner view of the Christian drama the whole struggle between truth and illusion occurs in this hidden place but is imaged out on the visible world. Whenever we believe the illusions of our mind, truth lies bleeding. When we remember a truth so that illusion is put to flight, trumpets sound in heaven – for even heaven is found through the nous. When we share our illusions with others, the Devil has found allies on the field of battle, and when we accept the invented concept as a divine truth, the angels are put to flight and the field is left to dishonour. When nous is made pure and empty of the debris of battle, there is 'a new heaven and a new earth' (Revelation 21:1). Then we have begun to 'put on the new man, which is renewed in knowledge after the image of him that created him' (Colossians 3:10). Only then will the kingdoms of man become a Kingdom of God in this world.'⁹

In the writings of Palamas, the word nous applies both to the nous as an intangible 'thing', a capacity of the psyche, and to the activity of the nous, of which perhaps the most important is the attention. In general, attention has several levels:

1. Inattention: no attention is given, so we do not notice what is going on inside us or out.
2. Mechanical or hypnagogic attention: this could also be called alternating attention; one pole is inside us and the other outside and it jumps from one to the other. This attention is caught on one set of contents, and progresses from content to content – thought to thought, or feeling to feeling, or from thought to feeling etc, by association and according to laws that are not under our control, until it is freed by inner disturbance, or the same outwardly until it evokes some reaction in us which drags us inside ourselves again.
3. Open attention: in this state we can be aware of many things at once, inside us and outside. This is true 'doubled attention,' or circular attention according to St Gregory and St Dionysius. It is only in this state that we can choose, for it is only in this state that we can 'see things going on and influence them'.

To achieve such attention it is necessary to work for precision, beginning with greater precision in the way we handle these ideas.

By clarifying the meaning of nous and psyche as they were used in the time of Palamas and in the religious world he inhabited, I hope to introduce the reader to an early form of Christianity in a way that shows how that ancient form of faith can fit in with certain modern forms of thought. Today it is clear that this ancient and partially psychological interpretation of the gospel teaching can still awaken us to the true and universal aim of human life – once known as salvation – and the different kind of knowledge of how this could be obtained. The practice of this ancient teaching will convey and help develop certain beneficial human qualities, including a more constant form of attention, and will give us a quite different experience of life.

After thirty years of exploration into ancient and modern forms of Christian spirituality, it is now clear to me that for most of the first thirteen or so centuries of the church, certainly in the Eastern church, a major role was played by this therapeutic interpretation of the gospel teaching of Christianity, a teaching in which the Greek word psyche had a broader scope than its modern usage. Indeed, those early Christians formed a true science of the soul – an 'inner science' which described the nature of the psyche and the part it played in the pursuit of salvation. In the Christian world, this was the first psychology.

By the time of Palamas, this knowledge had been practised by thousands of men and women over many centuries of striving for a more genuine form of worship, even – as the text we are discussing will make abundantly clear – for a true illumination. These people were taught by those generations of saints who are known today as the 'Early Fathers' (a generic term that also includes Mothers), and their way provided knowledge and working methods to help them achieve their aim in acquiring hesychia, with the hope of illumination and ultimately deification, or theosis: to become Christian in action as well as intention. The result was an inner science that although it may be compared to such disciplines as Zen or Yoga, is nevertheless significantly different.

Yet today, through the accidents of history, this ancient tradition is much less known in the West than systems taught by Asiatic religions. Even so, the methods of this 'therapeutic mysticism,' developed over a span of nearly two thousand years, are still being transmitted in remote locations and can still reach and transform human beings in ordinary life as well as under monastic conditions. We say this because we have found by experience that practising this inner form of Christian teaching can be highly effective for modern individuals who are seriously seeking inner, or spiritual development, while still living with the responsibilities of family and career.

Christianity in a Time of Inner Blindness

Inner blindness in most people is also blindness to God, and we live in a time of inner blindness that has overshadowed the West for so many centuries that unless we clearly see the evidence to the contrary – as could happen by studying Palamas in depth – the hiding of our inner life, and the veneer of pretence that covers it over will seem normal to us.

Perhaps the most important thing about this book by Palamas lies in its practical usefulness at such a time. In arguing against the cold intellectual religion of the rationalists, it teaches a form of Christianity which transforms the inner life and leads to inner illumination. Palamas describes what was long ago lost to the Western church during the change that divided it from the East – the Christian keys that can unlock the inner life. At the same time he does so in a way that gives us clues that I have attempted to relate to modern thought and the modern states of mind that have subsequently arisen from that early humanism.

In one way, the difference between the Eastern and Western churches seems linked to the differences between the monastic and contemplative traditions of these two branches of the one church. To the mind trained in a Western way, this difference appears to be only conceptual, but to the mind trained in the Eastern church it goes much deeper. In fact, the Western tendency to see it as conceptual is itself symptomatic of the divergence which long ago led to a true 'Balkanisation of the mind' – demonstrated by the fundamental psychological differences between these two 'sides' of our modern European civilisation. Among other things, because of these differences, each side of this divide, East and West, continually misunderstands, underestimates and mistrusts the other.

The difference at root arises from different concepts of spirituality, a difference which was most clearly expressed over six hundred years ago during the great watershed debate in Constantinople between Barlaam the Calabrian and St Gregory Palamas. Here the fundamental differences surfaced between the Western intellectual model of the divine, in the Aristotelian sense in which God is assumed or inferred as if an ideal, on the one hand, and on the other, the hesychast experience of God whose activity (Gr. *energeia*) may be felt or inwardly perceived as a presence.

The Western view of theology is a paradox in which the same Western attitude so well revealed in the debate between Barlaam and Palamas first made of theology a purely theoretical study, and then rejected it for lack of factual content. Saint Isaac the Syrian suggests that people choose knowledge over faith because: *When lack of grace dominates a man then for him, knowledge is greater than faith.*[10] Palamas, spokesman for the hesychasts of Mount Athos, defined the difference by saying that the Fathers of the church did not theologise like Aristotle, but like the Apostles. In the Eastern church, theology is a description of a special kind of experiential knowledge and the theologian is one who possesses such knowledge through direct personal experience. It is for this reason that certain saints are described as 'equal of the Apostles'.

The Eastern church, by the Ninth Ecumenical Council of 1351, affirmed that Palamas carried the debate and his doctrine was recognized as Orthodox theology. The Western church instead describes his 'monstrous errors',[11] and accuses him of a 'resurrection of polytheism.' In the West, the victory is thus credited to Barlaam, and ever since then the two churches have looked at the world from two 'different places' in the universe. From this we can see how differing views, given the authority of a church, can lead to different psychological attitudes and a different society. With the Renaissance, the intellectual view fought by Palamas became so deeply entrenched that the Reformation, fleeing from the result of this return to the rule of verbalised law, in which sins could be forgiven by a printed paper,[12] turned further into intellectualism and so sowed the seeds of today's flight from faith.

Hesychasm encapsulates both an Orthodox belief and a practical spiritual path. As a belief, it implies a wholly experimental idea of a contemplative path, not cold and theoretical but practical and experiential. As a practical path its essence is the gospel concept of a purity of heart in which its theological teachings are confirmed in experience.

In the fourth Century, Evagrius of Pontus equated *gnosis* (noetic knowledge) with *theoria*, or contemplation, but it must be understood that the very concept of contemplation differs in meaning between Eastern and Western churches. The Eastern view is that: *'The union of someone who has been divinised to the light which comes from above occurs when all noetic activity ceases.' This union is not the product of a cause, nor is it just a relationship, for these are both results of activity in the nous; the union occurs as a result of interior separation, but it is not itself a separation.*[13] The Orthodox liturgy incorporates a line from the Psalms which refers to a God who cannot be known 'in essence,' but whose actions on us can be known when we are sensitised and made able to register them, in the phrase: *For with thee is the fountain of life; in thy light shall we see light.* (Psalm 36:9) In practice, the communications of God to us can then also be known, though not easily, but this knowledge is derived from neither the intellect nor the senses, and knowledge so gained is thus open to question by those who place the activity of human intellect above the activity of divine grace. Palamas expresses this by saying that God cannot be known in essence, but can be known by His energies and known, as energy is known in physics, by the actions to which it gives rise – by the way God acts in us. St Theophan, a master of this tradition in the nineteenth century, says the same: *The Holy Spirit is known by its activity in the personality.*

Constant frictions have arisen in theology because interpretations of the Bible can be made to support ideas that appear to be mutually exclusive. For instance, the idea that we cannot know God can be derived from the realisation that: *You cannot look on the face of God and live.* The hesychasts, by contrast, assert that we can know God through the grace of his illuminating light, which Palamas termed uncreated energy. This idea and aim is still reflected in the theology of Athonite monks. As Archmandrite George Kapsanis, Abbot of the Holy Monastery of Gregoriou wrote: *A God who does not deify man can have no interest to man.*[14]

Palamas speaks of what he calls 'true theology', and it must be understood here that to the hesychast mystic, theology is not an intellectual study but experiential, and is based on the effort to live according to spiritual reality. True theology is therefore never speculative. It is concerned with what is revealed to us and with what we can learn from this about what can be seen and what cannot be seen. All else has an admixture of speculation.

Palamas begins Part Three of the present work with these words: *The opponents of the hesychasts not only lack the knowledge that comes from spiritual practice, but even ignore what they learn from their experience of life, the only thing that is certain and irrefutable. Moreover, they absolutely refuse to listen to the words of the fathers. 'Puffed up with futile pride', as the Apostle says, 'in their fleshly mind they busy themselves with things they have not seen.' They are so far from the right way that, while they openly criticise the saints, they cannot even agree between themselves about anything. That is why they choose to speak about illumination, although they actually consider that any illumination which is accessible to the senses is an illusion, and at the same time, say themselves that all divine illumination is accessible to the senses. For instance, they claimed that all illuminations that occurred among the Jews and their prophets, under the Old Covenant before the coming of Christ, were only symbolic. But they also say that the illumination on Tabor at the time of the Saviour's transfiguration and the one when the Holy Spirit descended, and all similar phenomena, were clearly perceptible to the senses. Again, according to them, knowledge is the only illumination that transcends the senses, so they claim that this is superior to the light. Thus they believe that knowledge forms the end of all contemplation.*

He speaks here of a theoretical understanding, formed in what St Paul calls the carnal state of mind, and the pride that this leads to, and how this leads to the idea that human knowledge is above the divine knowledge. This rationalist form of 'spirituality' is essentially different from that of hesychasm, and it is this which has, over the centuries, led the Western world into the spiritual desert of intellectualism. In concluding the passage quoted above, Palamas writes: *They do not possess the firmness and simplicity of truth, but fall easily into contradiction. Ashamed at the accusation of their own conscience, they seek, like Adam, to hide themselves in complication, conundrums and ambiguities about different meanings of words.*

The hesychast teaching, still followed in locations such as the Holy Mountain, has existed since before the present Western forms of contemplation were defined and differs in having an experiential basis. Its teachings relate to certain key passages about inner peace that are found in the Gospel, such as that in the Gospel of John: *Peace I leave with you, my peace I give unto you: not as the world giveth, give I unto you. Let not your heart be troubled, neither let it be afraid.* (John 14:27)

Hesychasm is a Method, Not a Goal

We need to understand that the hesychast teaching of inner peace is not the final goal. The final goal is something spiritual for which the methods of inner peace form stepping-stones. Hesychasm is the main method of inner transcendence used in the thousand-year-old traditions preserved in the monasteries of Mount Athos. The basic principle is that the nous must be still, must be in a state of hesychia, before we can transcend the psyche.

St Gregory Palamas, the great spokesman of hesychasm, said: *Deification is beyond every name. This is why we who have written much about hesychia have never until now dared to write about deification.*[15] The goal of the process is deification (Gr. *theosis*), the awakening of the divine in each of us. When the activity of nous is suspended, one perceives by the action of the Spirit – a kind of direct consciousness instead of consciousness reflected by the nous. The following passage, from Part Three, section 18 of the present work states it thus: *Do you see now that in place of the nous, eyes, and ears, they acquire the incomprehensible Spirit? It is through Him that they see, hear and understand. For if all their noetic activity has come to rest, how could the angels and men like angels see God except by the power of the Spirit? This is why their vision is not sensory – they do not receive it by the senses. Neither is it an act of noetic perception, since they do not find it in thoughts, nor in the knowledge that comes from them. They only discover it after all noetic activity ceases. So it is not the product of either imagination or discursive reason, neither is it an opinion, nor a conclusion reached by syllogistic argument. In separating from the activity of the psyche, we find the peak of pure prayer – which is also purity of heart – and the nous does not acquire this simply by raising itself up by means of negation.*

According to the teaching of the fathers, every divine command and every sacred law holds purity of heart as its aim. Every mode and aspect of prayer is crowned by pure prayer. Every thought which strives from below towards Him Who is transcendent and separate from the world, comes to a halt once it has gone beyond all created things.

Re-emergence of an Original Faith

It seems as if the original form of the Christian faith is now beginning to reach the Western world, and if this is so, it is necessary to see the importance of this event in the historical pattern – an event which has a true social significance. The re-emergence of the inner tradition of the Fathers is also the recovery of what was once an important part of the mainstream of the church.

Until recently, only a small proportion of these works were available in the West. Many are still inaccessible outside monasticism and many others survive only in one or two ancient copies. It is particularly difficult to rediscover the parts of these teachings specifically intended for non-monastics. Even now, when modern scholarship has at last restored to us some of the most important of the forgotten texts of this Christian tradition, it is almost too late, since theological and psychological terms have been translated into the empty phrases that have brought Christianity into disrepute with so many people. It is hoped that presenting this great work of St Gregory Palamas might play a small part in restoring that part of our heritage which can, in turn, revitalise the psyche of modern man.

HISTORICAL INTRODUCTION
David Vermette

The Hesychast Controversy

Sometime in the early 1300s, Barlaam, a monk and scholar, came to the Byzantine capital to test his intellectual mettle against the learned minds of that city. Although he was Orthodox, and born Greek, Barlaam was nevertheless a representative of the western intellectualism of this period. At the same time, he was an opponent of the theology of Thomas Aquinas, and some historians have suggested that he was influenced by the 'nominalism' of such western figures as the Oxford Franciscan William of Ockham, but this is largely conjecture.

In the 1330s, Barlaam was appointed by John Kantakouzenos, the Grand Domestic (an office akin to Prime Minister) and future Emperor of Byzantium, to a position at the great University of Constantinople. One of Barlaam's first intellectual opponents was the famous Byzantine historian and scholar Nicephoras Gregoras. Gregoras roundly defeated him in a public debate by revealing the limitations in Barlaam's knowledge of Aristotle. It was after this humiliation that Barlaam stirred up a controversy with the hesychast monks, thinking, perhaps, that they would provide an easier target. After spending some time in hesychast hermitages in Constantinople and near Thessaloniki, Barlaam began to make known his opposition to what he imagined to be the errors of the hesychast monks. Whatever personal motives Barlaam may have had for his vigorous opposition to the hesychast teaching of the time, there is little doubt that he was genuinely shocked by what he learned from the monks with whom he had contact, so great was the division in theology and practice between East and West even then. Because the heritage of the Desert Fathers had never been fully assimilated by the Western church, Barlaam found himself confronted by 'a different Christianity,' a Christianity that to someone of his training appeared heretical and even ridiculous.

Because of the differing concepts of knowledge between Eastern and Western churches, a difference which forms the main subject of the Part One of the present work, Barlaam's opposition to the hesychasts fell mainly in the domain of what might be termed theological epistemology. Following the usual western approach, Barlaam began with the assumption that God was simple, unitary, and without division. Consistent with his opposition to the hyper-rationalism of Thomas Aquinas, Barlaam reasoned, in the western way, that since God Himself was utterly transcendent and could not be known by rational means, He could only be known through His creation. On this basis, the hesychast's claims to 'know' God in an intimate way, particularly through participation in the Uncreated Light, were clearly deluded. He was willing to admit that the light they perceived might be an angel or some natural phenomenon – some part of the created order – but it could not be God. It could only be God if it was of the essence of God. But God's essence was invisible and unintelligible, incommunicable to human beings.

From the Athonite point of view, for which Saint Gregory became chief spokesman, Barlaam's account created too great a chasm between God and humanity. Had God Himself not come down to Earth in the great mystery of the Incarnation? Did not the tradition of the Fathers speak of a divinisation in which the purified and illuminated Christian became, in the words of St Peter himself, sharers of the Divine nature? In the hesychast view, Barlaam's notion was closer to the Platonic conception of 'the One' or 'the Good,' a naked abstraction, as opposed to the Christian God who chose to reveal Himself as a person. It also smacked too much of a Neo-platonic dualism in which 'spirit' and 'matter' were strictly opposed to one another. Patristic teaching emphasises the deification of the whole person, including the body. From his monastic seclusion on Mount Athos, Gregory Palamas first wrote privately to Barlaam, trying to correct his misconceptions about hesychasm. Evidently failing to get an appropriate response, and meeting increased and continuing opposition, Gregory wrote this great theological and apologetic work, the Triads *In Defense of the Holy Hesychasts*, first on Mount Athos and later in Thessaloniki. Between 1340 -41 the council of the Mount Athos communities composed and signed a text against Barlaamism which has since become known as the *Hagiorite Tome*. This document is now included in the great compendium of esoteric Christian texts, the *Philokalia*. (see *The Declaration of the Holy Mountain in Defense of Those who Devoutly Practise a Life of Stillness*, in the *Philokalia*, Vol. 4)

The controversy was by now a matter of public debate and so the need arose for a formal resolution. A council was convened under the auspices of the reigning Emperor, Andronicus III. It met at St Sophia in Constantinople on June 10, 1341. Both Barlaam and Palamas were present and debated the questions openly. The council decided the issues in favour of Gregory. His personal Christian qualities can be seen from the fact that, after the debate, Gregory and his friends greeted and congratulated Barlaam for a job well done. Barlaam returned to Italy shortly after this event. He converted to Roman Catholicism and was appointed Bishop of Gerace. History last glimpses Barlaam toward the end of his life giving Greek lessons to the young Petrarch. He quickly leaves the historical stage of the 'hesychast controversy,' although his position was taken up by other contestants.

Just five days after the June 1341 Council, the Emperor Andronicus III, a supporter of Palamas, died. This precipitated a period of civil war, with two main parties vying for the throne of Byzantium. As happened frequently in Byzantine history, theology became entangled in politics, with Palamas becoming identified with the political faction of John VI Kantakouzenos. In this highly charged atmosphere, the controversy surrounding the hesychasts continued, despite the findings of the council. A second council met in Constantinople in August 1341, and Palamas again won the day, but political winds were, temporarily, blowing in contrary directions. In this second phase of the conflict, Palamas's main opponent was Gregory Akindynus, a Bulgarian Slav. Akindynus, an acquaintance of Palamas, had originally tried to mediate between Barlaam and the Athonite, but, being convinced by the former's arguments, emerged as a chief representative of the 'anti-Palamite' group. After 1346, his former opponent Nicephoras Gregoras championed Barlaam's ideas. Although a friend of Palamas's patron, John Kantakouzenos, Gregoras remained a bitter, and almost fanatical opponent of the hesychast monks until his death in 1360.

Associated with a political faction in civil war, Palamas was arrested and imprisoned on the orders of the Ecumenical Patriarch in 1343. Despite the findings of the two previous councils, he was excommunicated in 1344. As the tide turned and the political and military fortunes of John Kantakouzenos (crowned co-emperor in May 1346) began to rise, the eventual rehabilitation of Gregory Palamas and the vindication of the traditions for which he stood became inevitable. In February 1347 the anti-Palamite Patriarch of Constantinople, John Kalekas, was deposed. His place on the Patriarchal throne was assumed by a hesychast, Isidore, an old friend of St Gregory's from his days in Thessaloniki. Palamas was freed from prison immediately and his Orthodoxy re-established. In May 1347, he was appointed Archbishop of Thessaloniki. Civil war was still raging in that city, so he was unable to take his seat as Archbishop until 1350. The end of the controversy came in 1351 when a final Council convened on May 28 of that year in Constantinople, to which Palamas hastily travelled from Thessaloniki. Yet again, the perspective he represented carried the day. On August 15, 1351, in a ceremony at St Sophia in Constantinople, a formal tomos was read vindicating the hesychast position. The tomos was signed by both co-emperors, and presented to the Ecumenical Patriarch. To all intents and purposes since then, the position of Saint Gregory has been the accepted theology of the Orthodox Church.

Saint Gregory served as Archbishop of Thessaloniki until he departed this life in 1359. His homilies during this period emphasise social justice, as the saint had a special concern for healing the wounds of this city after a period of war and division: *Blessed are the peacemakers: for they shall be called the children of God.*(Matthew 5:9) A final noteworthy episode in Palamas's life finds him taken prisoner by Turkish pirates, who held him for ransom. During his captivity he engaged the members of the Sultan's family in conversation regarding the tenets of Islam, and is reported to have expressed his hope for understanding between Christians and Muslims. This mirrors the saint's tolerance towards members of the Roman Church, with whom he enjoyed a friendly correspondence – an open-mindedness which far exceeded that of many of his Byzantine contemporaries – even those who were much closer to Rome theologically than was Saint Gregory. Gregory Palamas died on November 27, 1359. He was officially glorified as a Saint by the Ecumenical Patriarch Philotheus, his disciple and friend, in 1368, a mere nine years after his death.

The Triads

The real fact is that *In Defence of the Holy Hesychasts*, written 1337-9, is only secondarily a polemical or apologetic work. In the form of an argument against the westernising views of Barlaam the Calabrian and his supporters, Saint Gregory presents an exposition of the great teachings of the Fathers on stillness, inner prayer, the Uncreated Light, deifying grace, and the distinction between God's essence and His energies. The book was composed in three volumes, each of which contains three parts, hence it is commonly referred to as the Triads. This book presents the first volume of that work, and was published for the first time in the English language in 1995 as *The Triads: Book One*.

Beyond the very 'Byzantine' mode of expression, the text presents special difficulties to the modern reader. For instance, reading the modern literature on the subject, it could appear as though hesychasm were invented in the fourteenth century. There is no doubt that this epoch represented one of the most important of the periodic revivals of the inner teaching of the Early Fathers, a teaching that is not an adjunct to Christianity, but is at its very heart. It must be made clear that Saint Gregory Palamas and his Athonite contemporaries did not envision themselves as theological innovators. Saint Gregory, even in drawing his distinction between essence and energies, was merely making explicit what was implicit in the teachings of earlier Fathers. Even the breathing techniques and psychosomatic methods which are often closely associated with fourteenth Century hesychasm were probably of much earlier origin. St John Climacus (in the sixth century) and St Hesychius the Priest (eight or ninth century) both recommend combining the Prayer of the Name of Jesus with the breath. It is unlikely that they were speaking in metaphors.

The central difficulty in researching the history of the teaching represented by St Gregory Palamas is that of relying on documentary evidence for an unwritten tradition. Notably, the eminent historian Sir Steven Runciman, a supporter of Mount Athos in our own times, begins his account of *The Great Church in Captivity* with the recognition that: *The Orthodox Faith of Eastern Christendom ... has always preferred to cling to esoteric and unwritten tradition.* This is the nature of its orthodoxy, so although it is easy to view Gregory as a relatively isolated figure from an obscure world of the past, addressing problems of interest to scholars who study long-dead empires, the fact is that Gregory Palamas is one link – albeit a very important link – in the long line of succession of the Fathers which, according to the contemporary abbot of the Athonite Monastery of Simonopetra, "comes forth from the action of the Holy Spirit".

This line of succession still exists today, and, as experience shows, these words from the fourteenth century come to life only when one begins to come under the influence of this succession – and this is particularly the case with most Westerners, who are the heirs more of Barlaam than of Palamas. Under this influence, we read the Triads not as a relic of theological controversies of the past, but as a living document that speaks of a timeless present which you and I can enter, with God's help.

A document such as this necessitates a double translation. It must not only be rendered from Greek into English, but also translated from an artefact of a past culture to an experiential record of a timeless teaching – something that it represents so eloquently to those who have ears to hear.

IN DEFENCE OF THE HOLY HESYCHASTS

Saint Gregory Palamas

IN DEFENCE of the HOLY HESYCHASTS

PART ONE: FIRST QUESTION & ANSWER

FIRST QUESTION

I have heard it said by certain people that monks too must study worldly wisdom and that unless they learn this it is impossible for them to avoid ignorance[1] and false beliefs. Even if they have achieved the highest level of dispassion, they say we cannot acquire perfection and sanctity without seeking education everywhere, but above all from Hellenic education,[2] for that too is a gift from God,[3] just as much as was the knowledge granted to the prophets and apostles through revelation.

These people say that this kind of education gives the psyche a knowledge[4] of created things and enriches the faculty of noetic knowledge,[5] which is the highest of all the powers of the psyche.[6] Not only does it drive out all evils from the psyche, since every passion has its origin and foundation in ignorance, but it also leads men to the knowledge of God, for God can only be known through the intermediary of His creatures.

I was not at all convinced when I heard these views, for my small experience of monastic life had shown me that the opposite was true. But I did not know how to answer them, because these people claimed with pride: *We not only concern ourselves with the mysteries of nature, we measure the celestial cycles, and study the opposed motions of the stars, their conjunctions, phases, and ascendants, and consider what they mean, and we take great pride in all this. Since the inner principles of these phenomena are found in the original and creative nous of the divine, and the images of these principles exist in our psyche, we try our hardest to understand them and to overcome our ignorance about them by methods such as distinction, syllogistic reasoning and analysis.[7] We do this because, in this life and after it, we wish to be conformed to the likeness of the Creator.*

Unable to answer these arguments, I remained silent towards these people but now I beg you, Father, to instruct me in what I should say to defend the truth, so that I may, as the Apostle says, be ready to give an account of the faith that is in us.[8]

FIRST ANSWER

⇥ 1.1 ⇤

Brother, according to the teaching of the Apostle: *It is well for the heart to be established in grace.*[9] But how can one describe in words the Good which is beyond words? For this, you must depend on God for a grace that does not come to the nous of those who show off their wisdom, thinking that they know everything. Therefore, in this case you can only give thanks to God, for He has given you this grace, which does not come to the mind of those who think they know all in the wealth of their wisdom.

So, if you do not have an answer for these people, even while knowing that they do not know the truth, you should not be distressed. Your own conviction has a firm foundation in experience,[10] so you will remain absolutely firm and unchanging and be constantly sustained on a foundation of truth. As for those who rely on logical proof, they will certainly change their minds, through no action on your part. For every word argues with some other word,[11] so that each word can become the object of dispute, and as a result it is impossible to discover the purpose of their words. Because of this the Hellenists, as well as those wise ones[12] who followed their teachings, have been clearly shown to be forever refuting one another's statements. They allow each other to be refuted simply by apparent superiority in verbal argument.

⇥ 1.2 ⇤

It is my opinion that you can give a sufficiently appropriate reply to those who apply their lives to profane philosophy and seek knowledge in worldly education, and who are so enthusiastic in their praise for it. Simply tell them, 'my excellent friends, in this way you will gain no more knowledge than ignorance'. Those who seek human glory, and give everything to obtain it, are more likely to gain dishonour than glory, since you can never please the whole world. Even those who seek knowledge from those who are wise about appearances will gather this much, since those sages say the same themselves,[13] though more from ignorance than from knowledge, for their opinions differ and fight against each other and each has more enemies than supporters.

The danger is that one will not find the reasons of these opinions within the nous of the Creator.[14] The Apostle indeed asks us: *Who has known the mind of the Lord?*[15] It is a failure of their reason[16] that profane wisdom cannot recover any of their images from within the psyche. The knowledge that expects to find the image of God in worldly wisdom is false knowledge. The psyche does not become in any way like Truth itself when it obtains this worldly wisdom. As this knowledge cannot lead it to truth, the boasting of those who flatter themselves that they possess truth by this means is futile. So let them listen to Paul when he calls worldly wisdom 'carnal'[17] and speaks of it as the *knowledge which puffs up*,[18] and as a *mind of flesh*?[19] How could the wisdom of the flesh provide the image of the divine to the psyche? *Consider*, he says, *that among those who have been called, not many are wise according to the flesh, nor are many of them mighty, nor are many of them wellborn.*[20] Noble birth does not make the psyche noble, nor does physical strength make it strong, nor does the wisdom of the flesh add any wisdom to our thinking.

Indeed, the beginning of wisdom is to become wise enough to discern and then prefer what is truly useful, heavenly and spiritual – that which comes from God, leads to God and make as God those who acquire it – from what is useless, earthly and base.

⇥ 1.3 ⇤

Nevertheless, as these people recognise for themselves, we have within us the images of reasons[21] which are also within the Creative Nous. So what is it that, since the beginning, has disabled these images? Is it not because of sin, and also our ignorance and disregard of the commandments? Why do we need to be taught to see this divine image, even though it is already inscribed within us? Is it not because the passionate part of the psyche, aroused to do evil, has corrupted them, disrupting the vision of the psyche and leading it astray from the original beauty?

In the light of this, if we want to keep our divine image and our knowledge of the truth intact,[22] we must therefore abstain from sin, we must know the law and commandments by the practice of them, and we must persevere in all the virtues, and return towards God through prayer and true contemplation. For without purity one would not be any less mad, nor any the wiser, even by studying natural philosophy from Adam to the end. Yet even if you were to know this natural philosophy, if you purify and strip away the bad habits and imperfect doctrines from your psyche, you will gain the wisdom of God, which has overcome the world. Then you will enter joyfully into eternity[23] with *God, the only wise one.*[24]

The doctrines to which I refer have nothing to do with the size or movement of the heavens and the celestial bodies, nor the effects these bring about. They are not concerned with the earth and what is around it, nor the metals and precious stones in its interior, nor in the phenomena produced by holding the breath.[25] It is the Hellenic heresy that concentrates all its enthusiasm and interest on those who research the science of such things. Indeed, the Stoics define this sort of science as the aim of contemplation.

⇥ I.4 ⇤

And now you tell us that today certain people ridicule the aim recommended to Christians, on the basis that the inexpressibly good things we have been promised for the age to come[26] are too modest a goal! Instead, they seek to introduce speculative science, which is all they know, into the church of those who practise the wisdom of Christ. They say that those who do not possess scientific knowledge are ignorant and imperfect beings; that everyone must give themselves entirely to Hellenic studies and disregard the teachings of the gospels. So, because he totally ignored those sciences, by their mockery they distance themselves from him who said: *Become perfect.*[27] *If one is in Christ, one is perfect,*[28] *and we preach to the perfect.*[29]

As for me, when I spoke of the purity that brings salvation, I did not simply mean stripping away worldly ignorance, for I know that there is a blameless ignorance and there is a culpable knowledge. So it is not that kind of ignorance that must be stripped away, but their ignorance of God and the divine doctrines, the ignorance of which our theologians have forbidden. If you conform to the rules prescribed by our theologians, and make your whole way of life better, you will become filled with the wisdom of God and in this way you will become an image and likeness of God in reality. Then you will have attained perfection simply by obeying the gospel commandments. Saint Dionysius, who wrote *The Ecclesiastical Hierarchy,* clearly defined this conformity to the doctrine of this Hierarchy when he said: *Divine Scripture teaches us that we will only obtain the likeness of and union with God through the most loving observance of the holy commandments and by the doing of sacred acts.*[30]

If these words are not true, if a person really could rediscover and perceive the divine image within, transform his character for the better and rid his soul of the shadows of ignorance simply through worldly education, then the wise ones of the Greeks would have been more closely conformed to God. They would have seen God better than did the fathers who came before the Law, and the prophets who were under the Law, of which most were called to this honour while they lived a simple life! Did not John, the highest peak of the prophets,[31] spend all his life from earliest infancy in the desert? Is he not the person whom all those who abandon the world wholeheartedly follow as their model? This is absolutely clear. Then where in the desert were the schools of that futile philosophy which those people call 'saving'? Where were the voluminous books, and where are those who fill the whole of their lives reading them and persuading others to do the same? Do we find in those books the rules of the solitary and virginal life of the holy hermits, with a written description of the struggles they have undergone, so as to encourage the reader to imitate them?

⇥ 1.5 ⇤

I will leave aside the man who was the *greatest among the children of women.*[32] Even though he was raised to such a height, he was not in the least concerned with this education which some people now say leads to God, he had not even read the sacred books. So I leave all that aside! But why then did *He who is before all ages,*[33] who appeared after him, and *came into the world to bear witness to the truth,*[34] *to renew the image,*[35] and to make it rise again to the Archetype, why did He not effect this return by worldly methods? Why did He not say 'if you would be perfect, obtain a worldly education. Be quick to learn the sciences and the ways of nature and created things?'[36] Why did He say instead: *Sell all that you possess, give to the poor,*[37] *take up the cross,* and *make every effort to follow me?*[38] Why did He not teach the proportions, the angles, the phases and conjunctions of the planets in their wanderings? And why did he not solve our physical problems and difficulties in order to remove the darkness of ignorance from our souls?

Why is it that the disciples that He called were fishermen, illiterates, countrymen, and not those wise ones? Was it not to *confound the wise ones of the age,* as Paul said?[39] Would He confound those who, according to these people, led us to Him? Why did He *make their wisdom foolish*?[40] Why has He *judged it good to save those that believe by the foolishness of preaching*?[41] Is it not because *the world did not know God by its wisdom*?[42] And what have they learned, these people of whom you speak?

For the Word of God came in the flesh. The light arose from *He who was made for us wisdom coming from God,*[43] for He was *the light which gives light to every man who comes into the world.*[44] For, according to the chief of the Apostles: *The day has dawned, and the morning star has risen in our hearts,*[45] in the hearts of believers. But these people need a special wick[46] that will light their way out of the philosophies and knowledge of the world. This is what will lead them to the knowledge of God. Yet instead, they advise other men to grow old in vain, sitting beside a smoking lamp,[47] and tell them to cease purifying themselves in stillness through the control of thoughts, and to abandon the unceasing prayer which lifts us up to God.

⇥ I.6 ⇤

Has it never occurred to them that it was by desiring the Tree of Knowledge, then tasting it, that we were driven out of the place of delights? Because we did not want to *cultivate and watch over it*[48] according to the commandment, we gave ourselves up to the evil advisor, who entered by deception and seduced us with the beauty of the knowledge of good and evil. And today, for those who do not wish to cultivate and watch over their hearts according to the teaching of the fathers, he promises exact knowledge of the celestial spheres, moving and symmetrical, and of their properties. This knowledge too is both good and evil; it is good in its nature, but the intention of those who use it modifies it in one direction or another.

More importantly, I will say here that the practice and the blessings of different languages, the power of rhetoric, historical knowledge, the discovery of the mysteries of nature, the different methods of practising logic, the different viewpoints of mathematical science, the varied forms and measures of immaterial science – all these things are at different times both good and evil. This is not only because the way they appear is a result of the thoughts of those who use them, so that they easily take a form shaped by their point of view, it is also because their study is a good thing only to the measure that through it one develops clarity of vision in the eye of the psyche.[49]

So it is bad for one who dedicates himself to this study to continue it until old age. The better solution is to become briefly involved, then to move our efforts onto something that is a higher good and very much more certain. Disregard for such study also brings great compensation from God.[50] This is what the 'Second Theologian'[51] said about Athanasius the Great, that the benefit gained from his secular studies was that he learned to define what he judged it good to disregard. In his own words, whether he rejected or possessed this knowledge, he preferred Christ, and he enjoyed everything else equally.

⇥ 1.7 ⇤

But the Evil One, who is always looking for ways of wickedly turning us aside from what is higher, casts spells[52] in our psyches then weaves them unfailingly with the ties that are most dear to men of vanity. To some he suggests vistas of deep and diverse knowledge, while to others he suggests wealth, false fame or carnal pleasures; his purpose being that we spend our whole lives seeking these things, and never have enough strength left to set our hand firmly to the education which purifies the psyche.

The fear of the Lord is the beginning of knowledge,[53] it is this which brings to birth unceasing prayer to God in compunction,[54] and in fulfilment of the gospel commandments. Once reconciliation with God is re-established through prayer and fulfilment of the commandments, then fear becomes love. The sorrows of prayer, transformed into joy, lead to the appearance of the flower of illumination. Then, like a perfume from this flower, knowledge of the mysteries of God is given to those who can retain it. This is education in true knowledge. A man devoted to the love of vain philosophy, engrossed in its figures and its theories, never sees even the beginning of this, which is the fear of God. How can this enter his psyche? Even if it could, how would it be able to live in a psyche that is surrounded, bewitched, and enclosed by varied and conflicting arguments, at least until it says goodbye to all these things and gives itself entirely to the School of God, at last giving itself wholly to His love by following the commandment.[55] This is why it is good that the fear of God is the beginning of wisdom and divine contemplation. This fear cannot dwell in the psyche with any other feeling, it clears them all out. Then it polishes the psyche by prayer, making it like a tablet ready to be imprinted by the gifts of the Spirit.[56]

⇥ 1.8 ⇤

This is also why Basil the Great recalled the words of Pharaoh to Israel: *You are idle, you are idle, that is why you say, 'Let us go and sacrifice to the Lord',*[57] adding this commentary: *This is a good way to take it easy. Let us use it to pass the time! Indeed, the worst form of leisure is that of the Athenians, who forever passed their time in the discussion of novelties,*[58] *a pastime, which some people imitate today and in doing so, spend their lives in pleasing the wicked spirits.*[59]

Nobody has said that Basil the Great's words about this were no more than flights of rhetoric. We also recall what he said in explaining the proverb of

Solomon, which advises us: *To know wisdom and instruction; to perceive the words of understanding.*[60] The great Basil continued: *Now certain men who devote their time to geometry, discovered by the Egyptians, or astrology, venerated by the Chaldeans, or who are in general interested in numbers and the clouds of meteorology, have scorned the study of the divine words. Many of them, because of their enthusiasm for these things, have grown old searching in vain. Therefore one must apply discernment to the studies one makes, seeking out useful studies and rejecting what is foolish or harmful.*[61] Do you see? He calls these worldly studies and the knowledge that comes from it, vain, harmful, and foolish. Nevertheless, as you said, certain people claim that this knowledge is the aim of contemplation and consider it beneficial.

Basil, writing to Eustathius of Sebaste, laments that he had passed the greater part of his life studying these sciences. He says: *As for me, I have devoted a long time to vanity and wasted nearly all my youth on the fruitless effort I gave myself in learning the sciences of a wisdom made foolish by God.*[62] *But one day, as if emerging from a deep sleep, I realised the uselessness of the wisdom of the princes of this world, which came to nothing.*[63] *I wept for a long time for my pitiful life, and prayed to be given instruction on what to do.*[64] And have you heard his names for the education and knowledge which certain people today vainly seek to promote? They are called 'vanity', 'fruitless effort', 'wisdom gone mad', 'wisdom that comes to nothing', 'wisdom of this age and of the princes of this age', 'wisdom which obscures the life and way that is true to God'. This is why this lover of true wisdom repented of what he had formerly devoted himself to, in which he found no guidance for entering into true wisdom.

⇥ 1.9 ⇤

Today, there are those who even go beyond such careless presumption. They say that a lifelong focus on Hellenic education is no obstacle to perfection. They do not hear the words of the Lord which say the opposite: *Hypocrites! You know how to read the signs of the sky. How can you not recognise the time of the Kingdom?*[65] For the time of the eternal Kingdom is come, the God who gives it is present among us. If they truly seek the renewal of the nous, why do they do not return to Him in prayer to receive the ancient dignity of the free man? Instead, they turn to those who have not been able to free themselves. Yet the Brother of God clearly said: *If any of you lacks wisdom, he should ask God, who gives to all, and it will be given to him.*[66]

Is it possible that the knowledge which comes from worldly wisdom drives out of the psyche all the bad things that originate from ignorance, when even knowledge from the gospel teaching cannot do so? *For it is not the hearers of the law who shall be saved, says Paul, but those who fulfil it.*[67] The Lord said that he who knows the will of God and does not obey it will be more heavily punished,[68] than he who does not know it. Do you not see that knowledge alone achieves nothing? And why speak only of knowledge of what we should do, or of knowledge of the visible world or of the invisible? No, even a knowledge of God, Who created all this, will not achieve anything on its own.

What will we gain from the divine doctrine if we do not live a life pleasing to God, that way of life which our Lord came to plant on earth?[69] It is John, the theologian with the golden mouth who says this. Moreover, not only is there no benefit from this kind of knowledge, it will also cause the greatest harm to people, so those who hold these points of view are also its victims. What is meant by: *He who comes with the wisdom of words, empties of power the cross of Christ?* [70] And: *He who does not speak with the persuasive words of human wisdom;*[71] and: *He who knows nothing save Jesus Christ, and him crucified?*[72] What does Paul say to the Corinthians? *Knowledge puffs up.*[73] Do you see? The summit of evil, the crime most natural to the devil, pride, was born of knowledge. But if this is so, how can it be possible that all the passions result from ignorance? Does knowledge purify the psyche? Paul says: *Knowledge puffs up, but love builds up.*

Do you see? There exists a kind of knowledge that is without love. It does not purify the psyche in any way, but kills it, as it lacks the love that is the head, the body, and the very root of all virtue. So how could this knowledge, which sustains nothing of worth since to sustain is the property of love, allow us to be made in the image of Him who is good? Then how could this form of the knowledge that, as the Apostle said, *puffs up pride* belong to the domain of faith, instead of that of nature? If even knowledge like this 'puffs up pride', how much more will that which we have been speaking of do the same? For it is natural, it arises from the *old man.*[74]

In fact, worldly education serves natural knowledge. It can never become spiritual unless it is allied to faith and love of God, and it can never become spiritual unless it has been regenerated not only by love, but also by the grace that comes from love. Then, it becomes different from what it was, new and deiform, pure, peaceful, tolerant, persuasive, full of words which sustain those who listen to them, and full of good fruits. It is this form that is called *the wisdom from on high,*[75] or *the wisdom of God,*[76] as it is in some sense spiritual. Because it is subject to the wisdom of the Spirit, it knows and receives the gifts of the Spirit.

As for the other wisdom, it is earthly, sensual and devilish, says the brother of God.[77] Therefore it does not receive the gifts of the Spirit, because it is written *the natural man does not receive the gifts of the Spirit.*[78] This other wisdom regards such gifts of the Spirit as foolishness, as delusions or false judgement. It seeks to completely suppress the greater part of them, carries on an open struggle to render them in the sense of its own subjectivity and, insofar as they are able, to introduce false doctrine. It even skilfully approaches certain of these gifts to use them for its own ends, as sorcerers do with foods sweet to the taste.[79]

⇥ I.IO ⇤

Thus the knowledge that comes from worldly education is not only different, it is opposed to true and spiritual knowledge. Yet it seems that some people are not only misled themselves, they also seek to mislead those who listen to them. They speak as if there is only one kind of knowledge and claim that this constitutes the aim of contemplation. Now here is a fact which will reveal to you something of the terrible depth of evil into which the worldly philosophers have fallen. The Evil One and his philosophers, who derive their skill in doing evil from him, have stolen one of our most useful teachings and use it as dangerous bait. Thus they identify our injunction *be attentive to yourself*[80] with their motto *know yourself.*[81]

But if you try to find out what their aim is with this precept, you will find a pit of godlessness. They teach the transmigration of the psyche, saying that you cannot know yourself and so be faithful to the teaching unless you know the body to which you were previously attached, the place where you dwelt, what you did there, and what you heard there. They say that one learns these things through obedience to the evil spirit, who deceptively whispers such things to us in secret! This, then, is where they with their 'know yourself' lead those who cannot clearly perceive the deception and so think they speak just as our fathers spoke!

This is why Paul and Barnabas, while not unaware of the thoughts of the Evil One and his initiates, absolutely disapproved of the woman who said: *These men are the servants of the most-high God.*[82] What words can one say more pious than these? But they knew about the one who tries to make himself appear like an angel of light.[83] They knew that his servants pretend to be *ministers of righteousness*[84] and that they reject the true word because it is not suited to a lying mouth.

So even when we hear these Hellenists saying pious words, we do not think that they venerate God. We do not number them among our teachers, because we know they have stolen these words of ours. This is why one of them said about Plato: *Who is Plato, if not Moses speaking in Greek?*[85] So we know that if they have something beneficial, they have obtained it from us without fully understanding it. On examination, we also understand that they give it a different meaning. And if one of the fathers says the same thing as one of these worldly men, the similarity is only in words. The meanings are quite different. In fact, according to Paul, the one has *the nous of Christ*,[86] while at best, the others express human reasoning. *As far as the heavens are from the earth, so far is my thought from yours, says the Lord.*[87]

Moreover, even if these people sometimes had a thought in common with Moses, Solomon and their imitators, how will this be useful? What man who is sound of mind and who belongs to the Church could draw the conclusion that their teaching comes from God, or could even say that these heretics who appeared after Christ had received their doctrines from God, simply because they had not muddled all the truth after they received it from the Church? *Every good and perfect gift is from on high, coming down from the Father of lights,* said the disciple of the light.[88]

But even if the heretics receive living gifts which are not deformed, how will the worldly man, himself a heretic, offer them to others without deforming them? A living being, even if deformed, is at least alive, but a god who does not create out of nothing, who did not exist before our psyches, nor before what they call matter without form, how could this be God? In the words of the prophet: *The gods who did not make the heavens and the earth shall perish from the earth and from under the heaven*[89] and with them, those who say they are gods.

As for those people they call 'theologians' or 'teachers', and think that they can borrow theological terms, is it necessary even to mention them? Should we keep away from *the true light, which gives light to everyone coming into the world*[90] and wait for the terrible shadows of ignorance to illumine us, with the excuse that, as with serpents, there is something useful for us? For the flesh of serpents is only useful to us if they have been killed, cut up, and used with reason as a remedy against their own bites.[91] Those who kill them in this way turn a part of these snakes against themselves, just as if they killed a new Goliath with his own sword, a Goliath who had taken up arms, *who had set himself against us, who had defied the armies of the living God,*[92] yet this army was educated in divine things by fishermen and unlettered men.

⫸ I.12 ⫷

We do not prevent anyone from acquainting himself with worldly education if he wishes, at least if he has not adopted the monastic life. But we do not advise anyone to devote himself to this, and we expressly warn against any expectation of gaining accurate knowledge of divine things from it, since it is not possible to extract any teaching about God from such an education. For *God has made it foolish*, not that He created it that way, for how could light produce darkness? But He made it into folly, so that it could not be confused with His wisdom.

Pay attention here! For if we say this, we also appear to say that the Law given by Moses was abolished and made foolish by the appearance of the Law of grace. But since the Law is not abolished, because it comes from God, the wisdom of the Hellenists has certainly been rendered foolish, because that does not come from God. Even though nothing exists which does not come from God, the 'wisdom' of the Hellenists is a false wisdom. Even though the nous which discovered it, being a nous, comes from God, this wisdom in itself and to the extent that it has been diverted from its proper end which is the knowledge of God, should not be considered as wisdom, but rather as a miscarriage of wisdom, wisdom against reason, wisdom gone mad. This is why the Apostle Paul said that it has been made foolish, not of itself, but because it seeks the things of this age and does not know the pre-eternal God, nor wish to know Him.

After asking, *where is the disputer of this world?* Paul immediately adds: *Has not God made foolish the wisdom of this world.*[93] This means that, in appearing on its own, it appears to have acted without true knowledge, so that it was not really wisdom despite the name we give it. For if it had been wisdom, how would it have become foolish, and that by an act of God and His wisdom appearing on earth? For, according to the great Dionysius: *The higher good does not oppose the lower good.*[94] As for me, I would also say that noetic things are not weakened by one another, and I would add that all beautiful things see their own beauty strengthened by the appearance of the higher Beauty. How could this not be so, now that very Power, the Source of Beauty, has appeared? We will not say that the 'second lights,'[95] by which I mean those natures that are above this world, have been made useless by the first Light Who illuminates them. Nor will we say that our reason and our intelligence, although very much lower than those lights, but lights nevertheless, have become darkness on the appearance of the divine light, since this has come *to light every man who comes into the world*.[96] But whoever opposes this Light, be they angel or man, becomes darkness, because he separates from it by his own free will and so finds himself abandoned by the Light.

⊁ I.13 ⊀

This is how such wisdom, by opposing the wisdom of God, became folly. If it had been capable of discerning and announcing the wisdom of God through his creatures, if it had revealed what was hidden, if it had been an instrument of truth driving out ignorance, if it had participated in the Object of His message as well as its Cause, how would it have been made folly by the self-same One who gave this wisdom to creation? How could the blow that such wisdom received not be anything other than the means by which the wisdom of God was in fact seen on the face of the world? How would He who has established peace in the whole world, and for each creature in particular, not fight against it when, on the one hand He was the source of true wisdom and, on the other hand, by His arrival He had struck at this wisdom of foolishness, as well as at those who had received it?

Yet it was necessary that this wisdom was there, not to be made foolish, but to be accomplished according to the ancient Law. Paul wrote about this: *Do we thus abolish the Law? Never! On the contrary, we confirm the Law*.[97] The Lord invites us to look closely at this, for it contains eternal life.[98] He also said: *If you had believed Moses, you would have believed in me*.[99]

Do you see the extraordinary agreement of the Law with grace? For this reason, when the true Light appeared, the Law became still better, because its hidden beauty was revealed. But this is not so with the wisdom of the Greeks. It was clothed in elegant words, both attractive and persuasive, so that it hides its foolishness; but once its foolishness was revealed it became worse than ever and justly earned the name of folly. Neither is it a case of divine folly, which is the mystical[100] name given to the wisdom of God,[101] it was not acting above reason, but foolishly, due to a lack of knowledge of the truth, since it had abandoned the aim appropriate to simple human wisdom. Not only did it abandon this truth, but it strayed in the opposite direction, and persisted in falsehood and presented that as truth. Thus, it sought to slander truth as if the truth were lies, and set the creation against the Creator.[102] Even today, its action consists in turning the scriptures of the Spirit against the Spirit, against spiritual works, and against spiritual men.

⇥ I.14 ⇤

The foolish philosophy of the worldly wise neither comprehends nor reveals the wisdom of God. How could it be otherwise, when the world did not know God by it?[103] But Paul, in saying elsewhere that *knowing God, they did not glorify Him as God*[104] he, the heir and disciple of Peace, who finds that the supernatural Peace in us is given by Christ alone, is not arguing with himself, but is simply saying that if they have come to conceive of God, they have done so in a fashion that is not appropriate to God. They have not worshipped Him as the Creator of all things, as the Almighty, as the one whose vision extends over all, or as the unique Being, without beginning and uncreated.

This is why these sages have been abandoned by God ever since the time when they lived, as Paul has again shown when he said: *God gave them over to their reprobate mind,*[105] *because they adored creation instead of their Creator,*[106] by rolling in the mire of base and shameful passions. Even worse, they decreed laws and composed writings that act in harmony with the daemons and pander to the passions. Do you see that the philosophy of these philosophers was foolish from its beginning and by its very nature? Its folly was not acquired from outside itself.

Because it opposed the simplicity of the gospel preaching, and because it did not have the truth, what had first been rejected by heaven was made foolish again when it came to earth. This is why the man who gives his attention to that philosophy, hoping to be led by it to obtain the knowledge of God or to receive purification for his psyche, experiences the same ills as it does, and becomes foolish. The clear proof that he finds himself in this situation, the one and only proof, is that he does not accept in faith and simplicity the traditions which have reached us from the holy fathers, even while knowing that these traditions are better and wiser than those which come from human investigation and reasoning, and that they are demonstrated by works, instead of being proven by words. All those who have not only received these traditions but have also reaped their fruits by experience really know in themselves that *the foolishness of God is wiser than men.*[107] They all know this, and can bear witness to it.

⇥ I.15 ⇤

But this is only the first proof that these philosophers are in fact fools. The second is even more important. The power of that reason rendered foolish and non-existent wages war against those who accept these traditions in simplicity of heart, and so it scorns the words of the Spirit, as do men who neglect them and so have set creation against the Creator. It turns against the mysterious activities of the Spirit, which acts better than reason in those who live according to the Spirit, and attacks the Spirit by attacking such men.

The third proof, which is even more evident, is that these wise ones without wisdom claim that – like the prophets – they are made wise by God. However, Plato, writing in praise of such men in the central part of his tribute to them, states clearly that they embraced the light of delirium as a principle: *And he who comes to compose poetic works without the inspiration of daemons, will be imperfect both in himself and his works, and the work of the man who is self-possessed is eclipsed by that of the madman.*[108] It was also Plato who, having begun to speak about the nature of the world through the mouth of Timaeus, vows to say nothing which is not dear to the gods.[109] But how can a philosophy which is dear to the daemons be beloved of God and come from God? As for Socrates, a daemon accompanied and initiated him and it appears to be true that it was a daemon who said to him that he was the wisest of all.[110] Homer exhorted a goddess to use him as her medium when he sang of Achille's murderous anger. He allowed the daemon to take him over as an instrument, representing the goddess as the source of his own wisdom and eloquence.[111]

For Hesiod it was not enough to be subject to the action of one daemon, since he is the author of the *Theogony.*[112] That is why he drew to himself exactly nine at the same time, sometimes from Pieria, sometimes from Mount Helicon.[113] And, in effect, *he was filled with all kinds of wisdom* which they had given him and meanwhile, *he puts the pigs out to pasture on the mountainside and eats the laurels of Helicon.* Another god played with the inner strength of one of these sages. Yet another said about himself: *I have been tamed by a muse who makes prophecies.* Another claimed that the whole choir of the Muses would dance together in his psyche, and also that the daughter of the seven stars of Pieria gave him his teaching on the seven zones, the seven planets and their characteristics. He claimed that Urania, the daughter of Zeus, taught him the rest of astrology, and whatever else he knew concerning the things of earth was taught by other gods, regarded by these people as guardians of things here below.

→ I.16 ←

Then do you wish to make us say that those who speak freely about themselves in this way possess the wisdom of God? Certainly not. What matters is that we are concerned for ourselves and the true wisdom, which will not enter a psyche that is full of craftiness and friendly to daemons. Indeed, if wisdom has previously entered, it flies away whenever the psyche turns towards evil.

For a holy and disciplined spirit will flee from deceit, and will rise and depart from foolish thoughts[114] said Solomon, who possessed the wisdom of God and wrote a book on the subject. Is there anybody who lacks understanding more than people who boast that they are initiated into the mysteries of the daemons and who attribute the origin of their own wisdom to them? What we say now is not said about philosophy in general, but only about the philosophy of such people. If in fact, according to Paul, we cannot at the same time *drink the cup of the Lord and the cup of the daemons,*[115] how could someone possess the wisdom of God and still be inspired by daemons? That is not possible. Absolutely not! And since, as Paul said elsewhere: *In the wisdom of God, the world did not know God,*[116] then be careful! It is not the wisdom of these unwise sages that he has named the *wisdom of God*, but that which the Creator breathed into creatures.

Whoever has recognised this wisdom as a message from God has recognised the God that it proclaims. Such a person possesses the true knowledge of created things and so he possesses the wisdom of God. He becomes expert in the wisdom of God. It is this knowledge of created things, says the great Dionysius: *That should lead true philosophers to be uplifted to He who is the cause not only of all beings but also of the very knowledge which one can have of these beings.*[117]

⤐ I.17 ⤙

Therefore, if a true philosopher ascends to the creative Cause, he who does not ascend is no true philosopher. He does not possess wisdom, but only a sort of false imitation of true wisdom, and this is not wisdom, but the negation of all wisdom. And how could we name the negation of wisdom the *wisdom of God*? Besides, the daemonic nous is a good thing in as much as it is nous,[118] but becomes bad whenever it is misused. While it is better than us at knowing the measurements of the world, the orbits, conjunctions, and definitions of moving bodies, it is a nous-less nous, full of darkness, since it does not use its knowledge in a way that pleases God.

In the same way, this Hellenic wisdom thinks it can base itself on the Wisdom of God found in created things, by which God transforms the corruption of a being through the birth of another being, to show that God is not the Lord of all things, nor the Creator of the universe! But it does not see that everything always has an origin! This 'wisdom' therefore turns aside from the veneration of the true God. According to the same Dionysius the Great, *it makes unholy use of divine things to oppose God*,[119] and so becomes a foolish and senseless wisdom. How could this be the wisdom of God?

This is why Paul shows us that wisdom has two forms, saying: *In the wisdom of God, the world has not known God through wisdom.*[120] Do you not see that he spoke on the one hand of wisdom which is of God, and on the other, simply of wisdom, which causes ignorance of God? This last is what the Greeks discovered. It is different from that of God, and is demonstrated by the double use of the word 'wisdom'. What does this sage of God say further on? *We teach the wisdom of God.*[121]

Do the Greeks agree with Paul, or does Paul agree with them? Not at all, which is why he excludes the possibility of any such agreement and says: *We speak wisdom among them that are perfect; yet not the wisdom of this world, nor of the princes of this age, that come to naught.*[122] This is a wisdom *which none of the princes of this world have known.*[123] This latter wisdom is found in us in Christ Jesus, *who has been made by God for our wisdom.*[124] As to the other wisdom, it was not in these people but in the creatures they were studying. They investigated it all their lives and reached a certain conception of God, for nature and creation give great opportunities for this. The daemons, in a thoroughly daemonic way, do not hinder this. Indeed, how could one have taken them for gods if the thought of God had never entered human reason?

⇥ 1.18 ⇤

By examining the nature of the objects of sense perception these people have arrived at a certain concept of God, but not at an understanding truly worthy of Him and appropriate to His blessed nature. *For their foolish heart was darkened*[125] by the hideous intrigues of wicked daemons who passed on their teachings to them. Indeed, if a correct concept of God had appeared in the thought of these philosophers, how would they have believed it when the daemons presented their polytheistic teaching? How could anybody take daemons for gods? Yet, entangled in this foolish wisdom and education deprived of inspiration, they maligned both God and nature. They gave rulership to nature, at the same time depriving God of His sovereignty, at least as far as they are concerned. They attributed the Divine Name to daemons. So far were they from finding the knowledge of created things – the object of their desire and zeal – that they claim inanimate things have a psyche and are part of a psyche higher than our own;[126] that beings without reason might have reason since they could receive a human psyche; that the daemons are greater than we, and – what sacrilege! – that the daemons are our creators. They not only classified matter and all of what they call the World Soul, with everything else uncreated or causeless, as co-eternal with God, but also anything noetic which is not clothed in the density of a body, even our own psyches.

Are we therefore going to say that those who believe this philosophy have the wisdom of God, or even normal human wisdom? I hope that none of us would be mad enough to say this, for, as the Lord said, *a good tree does not produce bad fruit.*[127] As far as I am concerned, I do not think that this 'wisdom' is even worthy to be called 'human'. It is so inconsistent that it describes the same things at the same time as both animate and inanimate. It says both that they have and that they lack reason. And it says that things whose nature is without sensibility, and which have no sensory organs, could contain our psyches![128] Paul sometimes speaks of this wisdom as *human wisdom*, as when he says: *My preaching does not rest on the persuasive words of human wisdom.*[129] And again: *We do not speak in words which teach human wisdom.*[130] But he also thinks it right to call those who have acquired this wisdom, *wise according to the flesh,*[131] or *wise men become fools,*[132] the disputants of this age,[133] and their wisdom is qualified by him in similar terms. It is *wisdom become folly*, the *wisdom which has been done away, empty deceit,*[134] the *wisdom of this age*, and it belongs to *the princes of this age, who are coming to an end.*[135]

⇥ I.19 ⇤

For myself, I listen to the father who says: *Woe to the body which does not get nourishment from outside itself, and woe to the psyche which does not receive grace from above itself.* For the body will perish once it has been turned into a lifeless being and the psyche will be caught up with daemonic life and daemonic thoughts when it turns away from what is proper to it.

But if someone says that philosophy, in the sense that it is natural, is a gift from God, then they speak the truth, without contradicting us. But this does not lighten the accusation that weighs on those who misuse philosophy and lower it to an aim that is against its nature. For they make their own condemnation even heavier when they use God's gift in a way that is not pleasing to God. Even the nous of daemons was created by God, and so it naturally has understanding, but we do not hold that its activity comes from God, even if the possibility of action comes from Him. Therefore one can properly call that kind of reasoning unreasonable.[136] The nous of the worldly sages is also a divine gift, to the measure to which it naturally possesses a wisdom capable of reasoning. But when it puts forward doctrines like these, it has been perverted by the devil's wiles, which have transformed it into foolish wisdom that is wicked and unaware.[137] So if someone tells us that the desire and knowledge of the daemons themselves is not entirely bad – since they desire to exist, to live, and to think – here is the best reply for me to give: there is no need to argue against us because we say, with the brother of the Lord, that Hellenic wisdom is daemonic[138] because it arouses quarrels and contains almost every kind of false teaching, and because it is alienated from its appropriate aim, that is, from the knowledge of God. At the same time we recognise that, even in this state, it may participate in the good in a remote and indistinct manner. We should remember that nothing evil is evil because it exists, but only when it deviates from the activity appropriate to it, and so from the aim belonging to that activity.

> ⇥ I.20 ⇤

So what should be the work and goal of those who seek the wisdom of God in creatures? Is it not to acquire truth and to glorify the Creator? This is evident to everyone, but the knowledge of those worldly sages deviates from both these aims. So, is there anything that may be of use in this philosophy? Certainly there is great therapeutic value in substances obtained from the flesh of serpents,[139] so doctors consider that the antidote drawn from them has no equal. Yet when poison is prepared with deceitful purpose, the sweetest food is used to hide its deadly nature. Likewise, there is some benefit to be had even from the words of the worldly wise, the same as there is in a mixture of honey and hemlock. But those who seek to separate the honey from the mixture must take care that they do not drink the deadly residue by mistake.

If you examine the problem, you will see that most of the harmful heresies originate in this way. This is what happened with those who make an icon of knowledge, the 'iconognosts', who claim that man receives the image of God as knowledge, and that it is this knowledge that conforms the psyche to God. But, as it was said to Cain: *If you make your offering correctly, without dividing correctly* ...[140] Very few are able to divide well and one may only divide well when the sense of the psyche is trained to discern good from evil. But why do we need to run these dangers in vain, when it is possible to contemplate the wisdom of God in his creatures not only without danger, but with profit? When hope in God has liberated life from every care, this naturally impels our psyche to understand God's creatures; then it will be filled with admiration, will deepen its understanding, and continually glorify the Creator. By this miracle the psyche will be led forward to what is above and, according to St Isaac: *It finds treasures which cannot be expressed in words.*[141] It is then that it uses prayer as a key, penetrating with this into mysteries which, as St Paul teaches: *No eye has seen, no ear has heard, nor the heart imagined,*[142] and which are revealed by the Spirit only to those who are worthy.

⇥ I.21 ⇤

Do you now see which is the shortest way that now leads us with least danger and most profit to these supernatural and heavenly treasures? If you begin with worldly wisdom, on the other hand, it is first necessary to kill the serpent, in other words overcome the pride that comes to you from this wisdom. How difficult this is! No wonder it is said that *the arrogance of philosophy has nothing in common with humility.* After you have overcome it, you must separate and throw away the head and tail,[143] for these things are the extremities, and they are evil in the highest degree. By the head, I mean manifestly wrong opinions concerning things noetic, divine, and primordial. By the tail, I mean illusions about created things. As to what lies between, that is, discourses on nature, you must separate out harmful ideas by using the abilities in critical analysis and observation belonging to your psyche, just as pharmacists purify the flesh of serpents with fire and water.

However, to do all this, and make good use of what has been properly set aside, much effort and much judgement will be required! Nevertheless, if you put to good use that part of the secular wisdom that has been clearly separated from the rest, no harm can result, for now by its nature it will have become an instrument for good. Even so, it cannot in the strict sense be called a gift of God and a spiritual thing, for it is derived from the order of nature. It is not sent from on high. This is why Paul, who is wise concerning all things divine, calls it 'carnal', saying: *Consider that among us who have been chosen, there are not many of us who are wise according to the flesh.*[144] Who could make better use of this wisdom than those Paul calls externally wise? Yet even though they have this wisdom in their nous, he calls them *wise according to the flesh.* The term is appropriate!

⇥ I.22 ⇤

In lawful marriage, the pleasure whose aim is procreation cannot truly be called a gift of God, because it is physical and given us by nature, not by grace, even though that nature has been created by God. In the same way, the knowledge derived from exterior education, even if it is well used, is a gift of nature and not of grace: it is given by God to everyone without exception. It is a part of our nature, and we can develop it by practice. This last point – that nobody acquires it without effort and practice – is clear proof that it is a natural and not a spiritual gift. It is our sacred wisdom that is properly called a gift of God, it is not a gift of nature. Even simple fishermen who receive this wisdom from on high become, as Gregory the Theologian says, sons of thunder, whose word encompasses the very bounds of the universe.[145] By this grace, even publicans are made merchants of souls and even the burning zeal of persecutors who receive it is transformed. Saul became Paul[146] and turned away from the earth *to attain the third heaven and hear indescribable things.*[147] We too can become conformed to the image of God by this grace, so that we will continue in this form after death.

As to natural wisdom, it is said that Adam possessed it in abundance, more than any of his descendants, although he was the first of all those who failed to safeguard our conformity to the divine image. On the other hand, the worldly philosophy existed to serve this sacred wisdom[148] before the advent of Him who came to recall the psyche to its primordial beauty. But why were we not renewed by it before the advent of Christ? Why did we need, not a teacher of philosophy, an art which passes away with this age so that it is said to be *of this age*,[149] but One who *takes away the sin of the world*[150] and who gives a true and eternal wisdom – even though this appears to be *foolishness*[151] to the short-lived and corrupt wise men of this world? It is the lack of this which makes truly foolish those who do not bind it to their nous. Do you see clearly that it is not the study of worldly sciences that brings salvation, nor does it purify the knowledge within the psyche, nor make it into a likeness of the divine Archetype?

I will draw an appropriate conclusion from what I have previously said on the subject. If a man who turns toward the prescriptions of the law to seek purification gets no help from Christ, even though the Law has clearly been given by God, then neither will learning the worldly sciences help. Then will it not also be true that Christ will be of no help to someone who turns to the rejected philosophy of the worldly men to gain purification for his psyche? It is Paul, the spokesman of Christ, who tells us this and bears witness to it.

⊁ 1.23 ⊬

Now, brother, this is what you must say to those who give too much importance to worldly wisdom. In the passages we have transcribed below we shall show them in another way how futile and trivial this appeared to our holy fathers, particularly to those who have experienced it.

Gregory, Bishop of Nyssa, from *Contemplation on the Formation of the Body*:
This is the law of the spiritual sheep: never to heed the voice which speaks outside the Church and, as the Lord said, never listen to the voice of a stranger.[152]

Gregory, Bishop of Nyssa, from *Letter to Eupatros*:
Your zeal for reading about worldly matters proves to me that you do not care about the divine sciences.[153]

Basil the Great, from *Commentary on the Fourteenth Psalm*:
We have discovered two meanings to the word 'truth.' One refers to understanding the ways leading to the blessed life, the other is the proper understanding of many of the phenomena of the world. The first truth contributes to our salvation. It is present in the hearts of the perfect, who transmit it unchanged to those around them. But if we do not know the truth about the earth and the sea, the stars, their movement, and their speed, this will not prevent anybody from reaching the promised beatitude.

Dionysius the Great, from the second book of *The Ecclesiastical Hierarchy*:
In the teaching of the divine scriptures, assimilation to and union with God is only accomplished through the most loving observance of the revered commandments and by the doing of sacred acts.[154]

Chrysostom, from *Commentary on the Gospel of Saint Matthew*:
What in the past the externally wise could not imagine even in their dreams, fishermen and unlettered men have told us with full certainty. Having renounced the earth, they speak of all that can be found in the heavens. They bring us a new life and a new existence, a freedom, a bondage, a new world and everything different, but not in the manner of Plato, or Zeno, or of those who composed the laws. The very personality of these last has shown us that an evil spirit and a primitive daemon which turns against our nature instructed their souls. As for the fishermen, they teach us about such knowledge of God that no philosopher had ever succeeded in bringing to mind. So the knowledge of these philosophers is in the past and has disappeared for good reason, for these are the doctrines of daemons; it has disappeared into disrepute, the object of mockery, of less value than cobwebs. Unlike our own doctrines, it is presumptive, full of shadows and futility.[155]

Saint Gregory the Theologian, from *Homily 16*:
The first wisdom is a life praiseworthy and purified by God, a life on the way to being purified by the Most Pure and the Most Luminous One, by Him who asks of us only one sacrifice – purification. The first wisdom is to scorn

the 'wisdom of words' that takes the form of verbal refinements and deceitful and misleading contradictions. This first is the wisdom which I praise, it is this which I seek, the wisdom by which fishermen, after having overcome the 'wisdom reduced to nothing', have captured the entire universe in the net of the gospels, with their perfect and concise words.

Saint Cyril, from *Commentary on the Ninth Psalm*:
Those who have practised the worldly, daemonic and animal wisdom boast about themselves and plunge those with limited intelligence into the fire. They make them the sons of Gehenna. They speak in favour of lying and with their glib tongues they make their ruse attractive. They succeed in fooling many people who are taken with the advice of these charlatans, and who then fall into their nets. All their counsels are snares and entanglements to trap those without education.[156]

Gregory, Bishop of Nyssa, from *Commentary on Ecclesiastes*:
See the syllogistic demonstration of Ecclesiastes! It says that much knowledge accompanies much wisdom, and that an increase of sorrow follows an increase of knowledge. So the acquisition of the many superfluous sciences of those in the world, as well as the highest human wisdom and knowledge acquired by pain and long hours, do not bring anything necessary or useful, nor anything that earns eternal life for those who have dedicated so much zeal to these things. Instead, it earns them even greater pain. So we must say goodbye to all that, be vigilant in chanting, in prayers, and in supplications addressed to our own Creator, our God and our Master, attach ourselves firmly, and commit our time to Him. In order that our useless occupations may not condemn us to even a brief delay in the school of vanities, we must lift up our hearts and nous to the incomprehensible height of the divine majesty with the help of this kind of exercise. By participation and communion in which we abandon ourselves to the inexpressible glory – to the measure that it may be contemplated and imagined – we must fix our attention on the beauty of the sun of glory, and allow it to illumine us men inwardly and outwardly. Then we will be filled with inexpressible divine joy.[157]

PART TWO: SECOND QUESTION & ANSWER

SECOND QUESTION

You have done well, Father, to have brought up these quotations from the saints concerning my question. In listening to you resolve my uncertainty, I have enjoyed this evidence of the truth. But one thought keeps creeping into my mind. Since every word argues with every other, as you yourself have said, would it not also be possible to argue against your own words? Yet I know that the testimony of works is indisputable, and I have heard that the saints say just what you say, so I will think no more about this. If someone is not convinced by the saints, how would he be capable of faith? How would he not also reject the God of the saints? For it was He who said to the Apostles, who said it to the saints that followed them, that *he who rejects you rejects me*[1] that is, he rejects truth itself. And how should those who reject the truth reach agreement with those who seek the truth?

I ask you now, Father, to hear my explanation of each of the other arguments which I have understood are put forward by these men who spend their lives occupied with Hellenic education. I also ask you to tell me whatever you judge best about them, and to add the opinion of the saints on the subject. These people say, in effect, that we are wrong when we wish to confine our nous within our body. Instead, they say, we must at all costs shift it out of our body. They severely criticise some of our people and write against them, under the pretext that our people encourage beginners to look into themselves and to introduce their nous into themselves by means of breathing practices. They say that the nous is not separate from the psyche, so how can we bring into ourselves something that is not separate from us but is part of our psyche? Then they add that these friends of ours speak of introducing divine grace into themselves through the nostrils. But I know that this is an attempt to malign us, for I have not heard our people say anything like this.[2] I must conclude that their conduct is equally misleading in other areas, since those who make false accusations also distort reality. So, Father, please teach me: why do we try so hard to bring our nous into ourselves? Why do we not think that it is wrong to confine it in our body?

SECOND ANSWER
⇥ 2.1 ⇤

Brother, have you not heard that the Apostle says: *Your body is the temple of the Holy Spirit which is in us,*[3] and also, *Ye are the temple of God?*[4] For God Himself says: *I will dwell in them, and will walk in them, and I will be their God.*[5] Then why should anybody who is endowed with a nous think it improper to bring their nous into a body whose very nature it is to be the dwelling place of God? How then would God have caused the nous to inhabit the body in the first place? Was He also wrong? The truth is, brother, that these words apply more properly to those heretics who claim that the body is an evil thing made by the Wicked One.[6] As for us, we believe it is a bad thing for the nous to be caught up in carnal thoughts. But it is not in itself wrong for the nous to be in the body, since the body is not evil.[7] This is why those who joined to God with their life cry out to God with David: *My soul thirsteth for thee, my flesh longeth for thee,*[8] and *my heart and my flesh rejoice in the living God.*[9] And with Isaiah: *My bowels shall sound like a harp for Moab*; and, *Thou hast renewed my inward parts as an earthen wall;* [10] and also: *We have conceived, O Lord, because of thy fear, and have been in pain, and have brought forth the spirit of thy salvation.*[11]

Because we trust in this Spirit, we will not fall. It is those who speak the language of here below who will fall, those who say falsely that the words and life of heaven are just like those on earth. For if the Apostle, too, calls the body 'death', in these words: *Who will deliver me from this body of death?*[12] – it is because material and corporeal thought really takes its form from the body. Accordingly, to contrast it with spiritual and divine thinking, he rightly calls it body and not simply body, but *body of death.* A little earlier he had shown more clearly that he does not accuse the flesh itself, but that sinful desire which overcame it later because of the fall; *I am sold to sin*[13] he says. But he who is sold is not a slave by nature. And again: *For I know that in me, that is, in my flesh, nothing good dwelleth.*[14] He does not say, do you see, that it is the flesh which is evil, but what dwells in it. What is evil is not the fact that the nous lives in our body, but an evil power: *The law which is in our members, which struggles against the law of my mind.*[15]

⇥ 2.2 ⇤

This is how we overcome this *law of sin*.[16] We expel it from the body, and in its place we introduce supervision[17] by the nous, and by this authority we bring each power of the psyche, and every member of the body[18] that responds to it, under the rule of the nous. For the senses, we determine the object and the scope of their actions and this work of the law is called *self-control*.[19] From the passionate, desiring part of the psyche, we obtain the best state of being, which bears the name of *love*.[20] We also improve the rational part, by eliminating all that prevents the thoughts from turning towards God. That part of the law we name *watchfulness*.[21] So one who has purified his body by self-control, one who by divine love has made his wilfulness and his desires a means of virtue, one who presents to God a nous purified by prayer, then receives and sees in himself the grace promised to those whose hearts are pure. He can then say with Paul: *For God, who commanded the light to shine out of darkness, hath shined in our hearts, to give the light of the knowledge of the glory of God in the face of Jesus Christ.*[22]

But, he says, *we have this treasure in earthen vessels.*[23] In consequence, in order to know the glory of the Holy Spirit, we carry the light of the Father, in the person of Jesus Christ, in earthen vessels, that is to say, in our bodies. So will our nous be without nobility if we too keep our own nous within the body? Who could argue with this, save a man who is spiritually asleep and whose nous is without divine grace?

⇥ 2.3 ⇤

The psyche is one, yet it has many powers and its natural instrument is the body, which is given life in accordance with the psyche. But what instrument does this power of the psyche, which we call the 'nous', use when it is active?

Nobody has ever supposed that the nous resides in the fingernails, in the eyelids, in the nostrils or the lips. Everyone agrees it is found inside us, but some hesitate to be specific. Some claim the nous is primarily in the belly and some place the nous in the brain as if in a kind of acropolis. Others consider that its vehicle is the very centre of the heart, the place within the heart that is free of natural breath.[24] With this we agree and can also say from exact experience that our reason is not inside us as if in a container, because it is incorporeal. Nor is it outside us, because it is part of us. So the natural organ of the nous is the heart, and we learn this not from a man, but from the very Creator of man, who taught: *It is not what enters, but what comes out of the mouth, that defiles a man;*[25] saying further, *those things which proceed out of the mouth come forth from the heart.*[26] Macarius the Great did not say otherwise: *The heart directs and governs all other organs of the body. When grace endows the heart, it rules over all the members and all the thoughts. For there, in the heart, the nous abides as well as all the thoughts of the psyche and all its hopes.*[27]

So our heart is the seat of reason,[28] and the primary organ of the power of nous. Consequently, as long as we seek to monitor and rectify our reason by strict watchfulness, how else would we watch it, if we do not gather our nous back within – scattered without as it is by the senses? How could we monitor our reason, if we did not bring it back to the interior of this same heart that is the seat of our thoughts? This is why Macarius, so justly called 'the blessed,' immediately goes on to say *grace itself writes upon their hearts the laws of the Spirit.*[29] Where? In the governing organ, the throne of grace, where we find the nous as well as all the thoughts of the psyche, that is to say, in the heart. Do you see now how very necessary it is for those who decide to maintain watchful stillness[30] to turn back their nous and confine it to the body, and above all within the deepest part of the body, which we call the 'heart'?

⇥ 2.4 ⇤

If, as the Psalmist says, *the king's daughter is all-glorious within,*[31] why do we search for her outside? And if, as the Apostle says, *God sent forth the Spirit of his Son to cry in our hearts, Abba, Father,*[32] how is it that we too do not pray with the Spirit in our hearts? And if, as the Lord of the prophets and apostles teaches, *the Kingdom of Heaven is within us,*[33] then whoever focuses the energy of his nous outside of himself, how could he not also find himself outside the kingdom of heaven? For *the upright heart,* says Solomon, *seeks knowledge,*[34] which he calls elsewhere, *noetic and divine.* All the fathers who seek to gain this knowledge say that: *A spiritual nous is inevitably wrapped in spiritual understanding. Whether it is in us or not, we must never stop seeking this understanding.*[35]

Do you see that if we desire to combat sin and acquire virtue, to find the reward of the struggle for virtue, which is noetic understanding, the pledge of that reward,[36] we must bring the nous back into the body and into itself? The opposite, to look for noetic visions by making the nous 'go out', not only into sense perceptions, but out of the body itself – that is the greatest of the Hellenic errors, the root and source of all corrupt doctrine.

Such doctrines breed stupidity and come from foolish presumption, an invention of daemons. This is why those who speak by daemonic inspiration find they are beside themselves, not knowing what they are saying. As for us, we not only return the nous to our body and into the heart, but also within itself.

⇥ 2.5 ⇤

Then there are those who say that the nous is not separate from the psyche but is interior to it, consequently they question how we can possibly recall it into ourselves. It seems that these people are ignorant of the fact that the essence of the nous is one thing, its activity another. Or rather, they are well aware of this, but willingly side with the deluded and avoid the question. Such men, sharpened to contradiction by dialectic, do not accept the simplicity of the spiritual teaching. As the great Basil says: *They invert the force of truth with opposing arguments of false knowledge,*[37] *aided by the persuasive arguments of sophistry.*[38] Such people judge themselves worthy to judge spiritual things[39] and even teach them, even though they are not themselves spiritual! Do they not see that in fact the nous is not like the eye which sees other visible objects but cannot see itself?

The nous operates in one way in its function of exterior observation, this is what the great Dionysius calls the movement of the nous *along a straight line.*[40] It has another way in which it comes back to itself, then acts from itself when it becomes aware of itself. This movement the same father calls *circular.*[41] This is the most excellent and appropriate activity by which the nous comes to transcend itself and become united to God. *For the nous,* says St Basil, *when it is not dispersed, returns to itself, and thereby ascends towards the contemplation of God,*[42] as if by an infallible road. Notice how he says 'dispersed?' What is dispersed without therefore needs to be collected and bound within. Dionysius, the most reliable witness of the spiritual realm, says that this movement of the nous is not subject to any error.[43]

⇥ 2.6 ⇤

The Father of Lies always desires that people will be led astray by their own faults, abandon the spiritual ascent, and so fall into fulfilling his plan for them. Until now, as far as we know, he had not yet found a partner to take the lead in guiding others to this goal by fine talk. But now, as you tell me, it seems he has accomplices who have even written treatises towards this end, and who seek to persuade men, even those who have embraced the higher life of hesychasm, that it would be better to keep the nous outside the body during prayer.[44] Such people do not even respect the clear and authoritative words of John, who writes in his Ladder of Divine Ascent: *The hesychast is one who strives to confine his incorporeal soul within its bodily home.*[45] Our spiritual fathers have passed the same teaching down to us, and rightly so.

For naturally, if the hesychast does not keep the inner life within the bounds of the body, if he makes a division on account of its natural form, if the outer and distinct is not properly aligned towards the essence of nous, then as long as this natural form has life, the image of life appropriate to the union of its parts is not complete.[46]

⇥ 2.7 ⇤

You see, brother, how John Climacus has shown that it is enough to examine the matter in a human, let alone a spiritual way, to see that when you decide truly to belong to yourself – to be in accord with the interior man, to be a monk[47] who is worthy of the name – then it is absolutely necessary to recall and keep the nous within the body. On the other hand, especially with beginners, it is not inappropriate to teach them to observe themselves and to send their nous back into themselves by way of the inward breath. A man of understanding would not forbid the use of sure methods to bring the nous back within itself to someone whose attention wanders.

Those who are beginning to undertake this struggle find that their nous, escapes as soon as it is collected. It is therefore necessary for them to bring it back into themselves almost continually. In their inexperience they do not realise that nothing in the world is more difficult to observe nor more mobile than the nous, which is why certain teachers recommend controlling the inward and outward movement of the breath, and holding it briefly.[48] In this way they will be able to hold their nous steady by watching their breath until, by the grace of God, they might progress, having withdrawn the nous from what is around it, having purified it, and in doing so might truly become capable of returning it to *unified recollection.*[49, 50]

At the same time, we can say that this control of the breathing is a spontaneous result of the attentiveness of the nous. The in and out movement of the breath becomes peaceful during intense reflection, especially in those who practice stillness in body and in thought. In effect, people like this practise a spiritual sabbath, insofar as they cease all personal activity. They strip from the awareness of the psyche all changeability, all imaginings, all sense perceptions, and, in general, all voluntary activity of the body. Even involuntary acts, like breathing, are restrained as far as possible.

⇥ 2.8 ⇤

For those who have made progress in hesychasm, all this occurs without painful effort, and without the need to think about it, for the complete entry of the psyche within itself necessarily and spontaneously produces it. But with beginners, none of these things happens without a struggle. As patience is a fruit of love, *for love bears all,*[51] and we have been taught to practise patience with all our strength to come to love, so it happens in this also. But why say any more about it? Those who have experience can only laugh when contradicted by the inexperienced. Their teacher is not words, but work and the experience that comes from their own efforts. It is this last which bears useful fruit, and it is this which renders barren the comments of the critics.

One of the great doctors teaches that, *since the transgression,*[52] *the inner man is a likeness of the outer.*[53] Thus, the man who seeks to turn his nous back into itself need not propel it in a straight line, but into the infallible circular motion.[54] How will he not gain great profit in this if, instead of letting his eye roam hither and thither, he should fix it on his breast or navel as a point of concentration?[55] In this way, letting his posture take the outward form of a circle, he will not only collect himself, but will shape himself to the interior movement of the nous that he seeks to have his nous follow. In addition, by taking this attitude in his body, he will return the power of the nous, which otherwise drains out through the sight, back into the interior of the heart.

If the power of the animal intelligence[56] is situated at the centre of the belly,[57] where the law of sin exercises its rule and is given pasture, why should we not establish there *the law of the nous,*[58] which opposes this power, armed with prayer? Then the evil spirit, who has been driven away by the *font of regeneration,*[59] will not return to install himself there with seven other spirits more evil than himself, and so making *the latter state worse than the first.*[60]

⇥ 2.9 ⇤

Attend to yourself,[61] says Moses,[62] meaning, to yourself as a whole, not just a part while neglecting the rest. How? With the nous, evidently, for we cannot be attentive to ourselves as a whole with any other power. Therefore keep this guard over your psyche and body, it will easily deliver you from the evil passions of both body and psyche.

So attend to yourself, take a grip on yourself, be aware of yourself, or rather mount guard over yourself, take command, master yourself![63] For this is how you will make the unruly flesh submit to the Spirit, so that *there will never again be a wicked word in your heart.*[64]

If the spirit of him who rules – that is, the evil spirits and harmful passions – rises within you, as Scripture says, *do not leave your place.*[65] In other words, do not cease watching over any part of your psyche nor any member of your body. In this way, you will become impervious to the spirits that attack you from below, and you will be able to present yourself with confidence to He who *tries the hearts and the reins,*[66] because you will have tried yourself, and as Paul says: *If we would judge ourselves, we would not be judged.*[67] You will then have the blessed experience of David, and will say to God: *The shadows are no longer dark, thanks to you, and night for me will be as clear as day, for you have taken possession of my reins.*[68] In effect, David is saying, *not only have you made all the desires of my psyche your own, but if there is a spark of desire in my body it has returned to its source, it is bound to you by its origin, raised and united to you.*

Those who abandon themselves to sensual and corrupting pleasures exhaust the whole desire of their psyche on the flesh, so that they become entirely flesh. It is then, as the Scripture says, that the Spirit of God cannot dwell in them. But in the case of those who have elevated their nous to God and exalted their psyche through divine longing, their flesh too is transformed and elevated.[69] Then it participates in the divine communion and becomes the dwelling and possession of God. It is no longer the seat of enmity towards God, and no longer possesses any desires opposed to those of the Spirit.

⇥ 2.10 ⇤

Between the flesh and the nous, what is the most direct link for that spirit which arises in us from below?[70] Is it not the flesh that, as the Apostle said, does not shelter anything good until the law of life has come to live in it? It is thus on account of this most powerful reason that we must never relax our focus on it. So how do we make sure that it becomes our own, so that we do not lose it?

Unless we train ourselves in our external posture so as to keep watch over ourselves, how can we prevent the Evil One from rising up in us, we who do not yet know how to reject spiritual evil by spiritual means? And why speak only of novices, when the most perfect adopt this posture during prayer and so attract to themselves the benevolence of God? Some of them lived after Christ, but others preceded His coming. Elias himself, the most perfect of those who had seen God, leaned his head on his knees and so with a great struggle gathered his nous into himself, bringing to an end a drought of many years.[71]

So it would seem, brother, that those of whom you speak appear to suffer from the disease of the Pharisees. They do not wish to observe and purify the interior of the vessel,[72] which is to say, their hearts. They disregard the tradition of the fathers and seek to take precedence over everybody like new teachers of the law. Yet they themselves disdain the form of prayer that the Lord had commended in the case of the publican, and they advise others not to practise this form of prayer. But in the Gospel, the Lord actually said: *He didn't even dare to raise his eyes to heaven.*[73] Those who seek to turn their vision back into themselves in their prayer correctly imitate the publican. Some people call them 'omphalopsychics',[74] intentionally maligning them as if they were adversaries. Yet who among them ever said that the psyche was in the navel?

⇥ 2.11 ⇤

These people clearly use slander as a way of presenting themselves. More than this, they openly insult those worthy of praise, while pretending that they are simply correcting their mistakes. It is not on account of the hesychast life or of the truth that drives them to write, but their vanity. It is not their desire to lead people towards watchfulness, but to lead them away from it.[75] They endeavour by all these means to discredit the work of watchfulness, as well as those who devote themselves to it, finding an excuse for this in the practices which are linked to it.

These people would be ready to teach that *the law of God is within the stomach,*[76] on hearing those who approach God exclaiming, *my stomach resonates like a harp,*[77] and *my innards are renewed as a wall of bronze,*[78] as if they too were 'coeliopsychics'.[79] They slander without distinction anybody who employs physical symbols to represent, define, or study things that are noetic, divine, or spiritual. But the saints do not suffer at all by this. Instead, they receive praises and crowns without number in heaven, while these people wait outside the sacred veil, and can do no more than ponder the shadows of the truth.[80] One is deeply afraid that they will pay for this by eternal judgement, not only because they set themselves apart from the saints, but because they attacked them with their words.

⇥ 2.12 ⇤

You know the Life of Symeon the New Theologian, almost from beginning to end his life was a miracle, since God glorified him by means of supernatural miracles. You may also know his writings, and if you describe these as 'words of life' you are not at all mistaken. You know of Saint Nicephorus, who spent long years in the desert, in *hesychia*,[81] and later lived in the most deserted parts of the Holy Mountain, allowing himself no respite. It was he who transmitted the practice of watchfulness to us, having collected it from all the writings of the fathers. These two saints evidently taught the practical method to those who have chosen this way, practices which, as you report to us, some people now oppose. But why speak only of the saints of the past? These men who testified a little time before us, and who are recognised as having possessed the power of the Holy Spirit, have passed these things on to us out of their own mouths. For example, that theologian called the 'True Theologian,' the most reliable of the witnesses of the real mysteries of God, was celebrated in our time. I speak of Theoleptus,[82] the Bishop of Philadelphia, who was truly inspired by God,[83] who illumined the whole world like a chandelier. And Athanasius, who for many years graced the patriarchal throne and whose tomb was honoured by God. And Nilus, originally from Italy, who emulated Nilus the Great, Seliotis, and Ilias, who were in no way inferior to him. Then there were Gabriel and Athanasius, who had the gift of prophecy.

It is about all these that I would speak, and about many others who were before them, with them, and after them. They encouraged and inspired those who wish to maintain this tradition. At the same time, these new teachers of hesychasm wish to admonish us, not from experience, but as part of their boasting, since they do not know even a trace of hesychia. These people seek to reject the same tradition, to distort it, to make it appear despicable, all without giving any benefit to those who hear them.

Speaking for ourselves, we have personally communicated with some of these saints, and they were our teachers. So what does this matter? Do we count as nothing those who have received the teaching of experience and of grace, in order for us to bow before those who are given to teach only by their pride and their search for verbal dispute. That will not be, never! And you, keep yourself away from these people and apply yourself wisely to David, when he says: *Bless the Lord, O my soul, and all that is within me, bless His holy name.*[84] Let yourself be convinced by the fathers, and listen to their advice on how to make your nous return within you.

*The heart
directs and governs
all other organs of the body.
When grace endows the heart,
it rules over all the members and all
the thoughts. For there, in the heart,
the nous abides as well as all
the thoughts of the psyche
and all its hopes.*

PART THREE: THIRD QUESTION & ANSWER

THIRD QUESTION

I understand better now, Father, that the opponents of the hesychasts not only lack the knowledge that comes from spiritual practice, but even ignore what they learn from their experience of life, the only thing that is certain and irrefutable. Moreover, they absolutely refuse to listen to the words of the fathers. *Puffed up with futile pride*, as the Apostle says, *in their fleshly mind they busy themselves with things they have not seen.*[1] They are so far from the right way that, while they openly criticise the saints, they cannot agree between themselves about anything. That is why they choose to speak about illumination, although they actually consider that any illumination which is accessible to the senses is an illusion and at the same time say themselves that all divine illumination is accessible to the senses. For instance, they claimed that all illuminations that occurred among the Jews and their prophets under the Old Covenant before the coming of Christ were only symbolic. But they also say that the illumination on Tabor at the time of the Saviour's Transfiguration, and the one when the Holy Spirit descended and all similar phenomena, were clearly perceptible to the senses. Again, according to them, *knowledge*[2] is the only illumination that transcends the senses, so they claim that this is superior to the light. Thus they believe that knowledge forms the end of all contemplation.

Next, I shall briefly describe to you what our opponents claim to have heard from those they confer with. I beg you to help me, and to accept that I have never heard anything like this among the hesychasts, and cannot persuade myself that these people could have heard such things from one of our people. But they claim that they entered the school of the hesychasts under false pretence without any intention of accepting their teaching. They wrote that these masters suggested that they should completely abandon sacred Scripture as if it were something wicked, and apply themselves to prayer alone. They claim that these teachers say that prayer drives out evil spirits, which merge with the very being of people and when this happens they become emotionally inflamed, leap about in delight, all without their psyches undergoing any change. Then they see sensory lights, and have come to think that the sign of divine things is a clear white colour and that evil things are a fiery yellow.

They wrote that their teachers of hesychasm spoke in this way, while they themselves said that all this is daemonic. And if anyone contradicts any of their opinions, they say that this is a sign of passion, which in turn is a mark of delusion.[3] They throw numerous reproaches in the faces of their adversaries and in their writings they trace the many convolutions and perfidies of the serpent, turning back upon themselves in many ways. They use many ruses, and interpret their own words in different and contradictory manners. They do not possess the firmness and simplicity of truth, but easily fall into contradiction. Ashamed at the accusation of their own conscience, they seek to hide themselves like Adam, clothing themselves in complication, conundrums and ambiguities about different meanings of words. I therefore pray, father, that you will clarify our opinion of their views.

THIRD ANSWER

⇥ 3.1 ⇤

They describe vices alongside virtues and their impious words appear to be so close to pious words that a small addition or subtraction is enough to easily transform one into the other so that the meaning of the words is completely changed. This is why nearly all false opinions wear the mask of truth and will deceive anyone who does not notice the small additions or omissions. This is the dangerous means used by the evil daemon, so skilled in the art of deception. Telling a lie close to the truth, he invented a double ruse; the small distance is not noticed by most people, who easily take a lie for the truth, or the truth for a lie when it is close to it. In both cases this completely separates us from the truth.

Initiated in this art, the followers of Arius who opposed the definition of faith declared at Nicea with the one they had made at Nike,[4] treated with contempt that which *rightly divided the word of Thy truth*.[5] Arius himself was deceptive when he managed to concelebrate and take communion with those who had repudiated him in favour of the Church. But the great Alexander, having discovered the deception but unable to clearly reveal it, turned to God in prayer, following which that infamous man was justly delivered to a shameful death. He was truly carried away by his own lunacy.

⇥ 3.2 ⇤

This, brother, is the ruse most often used by those who speak as you describe, and beginners in hesychasm are indeed advised to avoid too much reading. They are advised instead to give themselves to the prayer of a single thought[6] until unceasing prayer becomes the normal state of their thinking,[7] even if they have physically moved on to another occupation. Novices will find the same counsel given by Saint Diadochos, Philemon the Great, Nilus, so rich in things divine, John, the author of the *Ladder*, as well as many fathers now living. This is not because reading is either useless or wrong. But those people added this word 'wrong,' and by doing this, they made the good advice of the fathers seem to be something that is actually harmful.

Among other things, we know that all the saints have shown by their words and their actions that prayer drives out evil spirits and passions. All the wise men think this and teach it, but none of them ever said that these evil spirits had become merged with our essence. By making this arbitrary addition, those who spoke to you made the aim of our efforts seem wrong.

The great Basil himself said that the heart should 'leap' as if bounding with enthusiasm for love of the Good. Athanasius the Great said that this was a sign of grace. The author of the *Ladder* plainly teaches from experience that we come out of prayer as if with a body of flame when we have met God with a pure nous. He says that without the presence of light in prayer, without the sweetness it brings to the psyche, then prayer is corporeal or 'Judaic'. Several others, notably Saint Isaac, have clearly shown that a reflection of joy will appear on the faces of those who pray, and not only as a result of inner prayer but also when united in psalmody.

The principle [8] behind all of this is the need to improve the reasoning psyche[9] yet these critics of the saints you speak about have rejected what is praiseworthy and have made it the object of blame. Having twisted the sure testimonies of sacred and divine illumination, they have hidden behind small details that favour their accusations and, alas, attempt to make the inexperienced think that the divine is in reality daemonic. But above all, they are convinced that *he who is hidden in the eternal shadows*[10] produces some light, although in a deceptive way. Yet they do not admit that God transcends all illumination and all light, nor do they say that He fills with a noetic light all reasoning natures according to their capacity.

⇥ 3.3 ⇤

For me, knowledge is called light only to the measure to which it is communicated by the divine light, but you tell me our opponents claim that knowledge is the only intelligible illumination. According to the words of the great Paul: *For God, who commanded the light to shine out of darkness, has shined in our hearts, to give the light of the knowledge of the glory of God.*[11] In his turn, the great Dionysius said: *The presence of the noetic light unifies those it illumines and reintegrates them in a single and true knowledge.*[12] Do you see? The light of knowledge is communicated by the presence of the light of grace, and liberates us from the ignorance that fragments us. This father called the light 'noetic,'[13] while the great Macarius, clearly concerned with those who receive the light of grace in the form of knowledge, says it is *perceptible to the nous.*[14] He says that you will see by its effects if the noetic light that has shone in your psyche comes from God or Satan. Elsewhere, after having called the glory which had appeared on the face of Moses 'immortality', although it illumined a mortal face, and showing how it appears in the psyche as soon as we truly love God, Macarius said: *As the visible eyes see the visible sun, so it is with the eyes of their psyche that these men see the noetic light which reveals itself and will shine from their bodies at the moment of Resurrection, to make them resplendent with eternal light.*[15]

As for the light of knowledge, we may never say that it is 'noetic'. On the contrary, that light sometimes acts like a noetic light. At the same time, the nous sees it as an intelligible light through its noetic sense. When it enters reasoning psyches, it liberates them from the ignorance which bound them to their state, bringing them back from diverse opinion to unified knowledge. This is why the cantor of the Divine Names, when he begins to sing the luminous names of the Good, teaches us that: *The Good is described as the light of the nous because it illuminates the nous of every supra-celestial being with the light of the nous and because it drives from souls the ignorance and the error squatting there.*[16]

So the knowledge which comes after ignorance has been driven out is one thing, while the noetic light which makes this knowledge appear is another. This is why the noetic light is manifestly present in the *supra-celestial nous,* which is to say, in that which has transcended itself. How can we describe the supra-celestial light which transcends the nous as 'knowledge,' except by metaphor? To put it another way, only the rational psyche could purify itself of the ignorance due to its natural state, which that great doctor described as 'ignorance' and 'illusion'.

⇥ 3.4 ⇤

Yes, even the human nous, and not only that of the angels, when it is victorious over the passions, may transcend itself and so become angelic. The nous will then find the light, and will become worthy of a supernatural vision of God. It does not see the essence of God, but it sees God by a revelation that is both appropriate to and consistent with God himself. Such a revelation does not happen through negation.[17] One really sees it, and this seeing is superior to negation, for God is not only beyond knowledge, He is even beyond unknowing.

The revelation itself is also truly a mystery, the more divine and extraordinary since divine manifestations, even if they are symbolic, remain unknowable in their transcendence. In fact, they appear according to a law which is neither that of divine nature nor of human nature – being, as it were, for us and yet beyond us – so that there is no name which can properly describe them. This was well demonstrated when, in reply to Manoah's question: *What is your name?* God replied: *It is marvellous.*[18] Yet this vision, being not only incomprehensible but also un-nameable, is no less marvellous for that.

Moreover, although this vision is above negation, the words that describe it are inferior to the negative way. The latter progresses by using examples and analogies, which is why we most often add the word 'like' to the words we use to express it. This is in order to make a closer likeness, since the vision itself is indescribable and beyond all name.

⇥ 3.5 ⇤

When the saints[19] contemplate this divine light within themselves, they see it by the divinising communion of the Spirit, with the mysterious accompaniment of inspired illuminations. It is then that they see the garment of their deification by the grace of the Word, as their nous is glorified and filled with a brilliance of extraordinary beauty. In the same way, when on the mountain, the divinity of the Word glorified with divine light the body that was bound to Him. For He Himself has given the glory which the Father gave Him to those who are obedient to Him. As the Evangelist says: *He willed that they should be with Him and contemplate His glory.*[20]

But how could this happen physically since He himself was no longer bodily present after His ascension into heaven? Therefore it must necessarily happen in a noetic way as the nous went beyond the heavens and became the companion of Him who ascended into heaven for us. At this point it unites itself to God in a clear yet inexplicable way and contemplates supernatural and mysterious visions filled with all the spiritual knowledge of the sublime light. However, it no longer contemplates the sacred symbols accessible to the senses, nor any more is it the variety of the Holy Scriptures which are known. Here the nous is made beautiful by the creative and original Beauty, and illumined by the light of God.

In the same way, according to the one who revealed and interpreted their *Hierarchy,*[21] the sublime orders of the supra-celestial beings are arranged in a hierarchy not only according to their relation to the original experience and knowledge, but also to the light first seen in the sublime triadic initiation. Not only did they gain participation in and contemplation of the glory of the Trinity, but also of the light of Jesus that was revealed to the disciples on Tabor.[22] Judged worthy of this vision, they receive a true initiation, for that light is also a deifying light. They truly come closer to Him and receive their first communion from His deifying radiance. This is why the truly blessed Macarius called this light the food of supra-celestial beings. And here is what another theologian says: *In spiritually celebrating this light, the whole divine order of heavenly beings gives us clear proof of the love which the Logos bears towards us.*[23]

And the great Paul, at the moment of meeting the invisible and heavenly visions in Christ, was 'ravished'[24] and found himself beyond the heavens, yet his nous did not actually need to move to a different place. He did not need to change his position to pass beyond the heavens. For this 'ravishing' denotes an entirely different mystery, known only to those who have felt it. And it is not necessary to say today what we have heard on the subject from the fathers who have had this experience, for we do not wish to expose them to slander. But what has now been said will be enough to show very clearly, to those who are not convinced, that there is a noetic illumination visible to those who have purified their heart which is completely different from knowledge, yet may bring knowledge.

➤ 3.6 ◄

As you yourself have told us, these people have said that the illuminations described in the Old Testament have a symbolic character. They have clearly shown that there is a holy illumination of which this is a symbol. Saint Nilus[25] teaches that most of these are symbols of this illumination, saying: *When the nous has put off the old self and shall put on the new one, born of grace, then it will see its own state in the time of prayer resembling sapphire or the colour of heaven; Scripture calls this 'the Place of God',[26] that the elders saw on Mount Sinai.*[27] In the same way, we hear Saint Isaac say to us: *The nous, when grace acts on it, sees its own purity in prayer, like the celestial colour which the community of Israel called the Place of God when it appeared to them on the mountain.*[28]

Do you see how these illuminations are symbols of what can happen now in pure hearts? And John Chrysostom explained the words of the Apostle: *For God, who commanded the light to shine out in darkness, hath shined in our hearts.*[29] According to him, the Apostle shows that the glory of Moses shone in us even more strongly, for it has shone in our hearts just as it did on the face of Moses. He also tells us: *At the beginning of creation, He spoke and there was light. Today He did not speak, but he Himself has become our light.*[30] So, if the light at the beginning of creation or that which shone on the face of Moses was a limited form of knowledge, the illumination which occurs in our hearts would also be knowledge, but greater because it has been developed. Thus, since the light was not knowledge, but a radiance appearing on his face, the radiance it produces in us is also not knowledge, but a radiance of the psyche appearing to the purified nous. So there is one light that is visible to the eyes and necessarily sensible, and another that is noetic since it acts within us, and thus can only be seen by the eyes of the nous.

⇥ 3.7 ⇤

Yet that light was not simply a light of the senses, although it appeared on the face of the prophet. According to Saint Macarius, in fact, the saints of the present day receive in their psyches the same glory that appeared on the face of Moses. This same father also called this light the *glory of Christ*, and regarded it as being above the senses, although it appeared accessible to sense. With a small addition, he puts forward this word of the Apostle: *All of us who, with face uncovered, contemplate the glory of the Lord, that is to say, his noetic light, as if in a mirror, are transformed in the same image from glory to glory, that is to say by the increase in the light which is in us and which, under the influence of the divine light, becomes ever more distinct.*[31]

What does Saint Diadochos say? *You should not doubt that when the nous begins to regularly feel the action of the divine light it becomes so completely translucent that it sees the abundance of its own light vividly. When the strength of the psyche makes it mistress of the passions, it becomes all light.*[32] And what does the divine Maximos say? *The human nous would not have the strength to raise itself to apprehend divine radiance if it were not for God himself who draws it up and illumines it with divine brightness.* [33]

What does Nilus, that illustrious pillar of truth, say, along with Basil the Great? *All human knowledge is simply study and practice, while the knowledge coming from the grace of God is justice and mercy. The first of these can be acquired by the passionate, while the second is only received by those who have conquered the passions and whose radiant nous illumines them even outside the time of prayer.*[34]

Do you now understand, brother, that when the nous is freed from passions it sees itself during prayer as a light, and shines with divine light? So listen again with care to the truly blessed Macarius, who the most divine Nilus called a chosen vessel, and who said, in the *Chapters* paraphrased by Metaphrastes: *The perfect illumination of the Spirit is not only a noetic revelation, but a certain and continuous illumination of hypostatic light in the psyche.* This is well confirmed by passages such as: *He who commanded the light to shine in the heart of darkness has shone in our hearts*[35] and *enlighten my eyes, lest I sleep the sleep of death,*[36] and again, *send out thy light and thy truth, let them bring me to thy holy mountain.*[37] There is also this: *The light of your countenance is come upon us as a sign,*[38] and there are many similar passages.

Note that he said 'hypostatic' here to silence those who consider that knowledge in itself is illumination and as a result sow confusion in the minds of many people – and first of all in their own. They do this by falsely interpreting all that one has been able to say about light, as if it related to knowledge. Nevertheless, I know that knowledge is also called 'light' because it comes from the light, which grants us such knowledge, as stated before.

⇥ 3.8 ⇤

This is why no one has ever called the knowledge coming from the senses 'light,'[39] even if the knowledge it sometimes gives is certain. Only knowledge that comes from the reasoning nous is given this name. In fact, we do not see any being gifted with reasoning activity[40] who lacks a noetic light. The angels are like an immaterial and incorporeal fire – what is that if not a noetic light? The nous that sees itself, sees as if by light – so again, what is that light, if not the noetic light?

God himself, who surpasses all noetic light and transcends essence upon essence, is called 'fire' by the holy theologians. He possesses this mysterious and invisible character in himself, like a faint image of what fire is among sensory things, whenever there is no matter to receive the divine appearance. But when it takes hold of suitable matter that is undisguised, for example, any purified noetic nature not bearing a veil of evil, then it appears as a noetic light in the way we have shown. We will show this again in reference to the saints, who submit to and contemplate the radiance of God.

⇥ 3.9 ⇤

Just as fire, if it is hidden by opaque material, may give heat without light, so the nous likewise may get knowledge but not light, as long as it is covered by the veil of evil passions. Nous is not only contemplated[41] by nous as a light, the last light seen in this way, but at the same time it is contemplation itself, like an eye in the inmost centre of the psyche. The nous is not only seen as a light when viewed in contemplation, and is so the fulfilment of seeing, it is also contemplation itself since the nous was created in order for the psyche to see.[42]

In fact, it is said that *the nous is the eye of the psyche*. Just as the eye of the senses cannot become active unless it is illumined by an exterior light, so the nous cannot act as an instrument of spiritual perception,[43] nor activate itself, unless the divine light illumines it. Just as the eye, when active, itself becomes light, confuses itself with the light, and first sees this same light flooding onto the objects which it sees, in the same way the nous, when its perception is activated, is itself entirely like light. Then it is in the light, and with the aid of the light it sees the light clearly, in a way that is not only superior to the bodily senses, but also to everything we know, and, simply, superior to all created things.

For those who have purified their hearts see God, as stated in the beatitude of the Lord, who makes no mistake.[44] *God is light*,[45] according to the most theological words of John, the son of thunder. He makes His home in them, and shows Himself to those who love Him and are loved by Him, according to the promise that He gave them.[46] He shows Himself to the purified nous as in a mirror, while all the while He Himself remains invisible. This is how an image appears in a mirror, it appears in reflection while the object remains invisible in itself. It is almost impossible to see at the same time both the image reflected in the mirror and the object that the mirror reflects.

This is how God now appears to those who have been purified in love, but one day, it is said, He will appear to them 'face to face.'[47] Those who do not believe that God appears as a light beyond light, because they have no experience of divine things and do not see them, and those who believe that reason alone can contemplate the divine, are like blind people who only receive the warmth of the sun and do not believe those who also see its rays. And if these blind people undertake to give lessons to those who see, saying to them that the sun, the most luminous of the objects of the senses, is not a light, then those who possess receptive eyes can only laugh. Those of whom you speak are in rather the same situation in relation to the *Sun of righteousness*,[48] which is above the cosmos.[49] Not only those who truly possess noetic vision, but even those who have confidence in these visionaries will bemoan the fate of such people.

Whereas God, who transcends all things, who is incomprehensible and indescribable, nevertheless consents, in a surfeit of goodness towards us, to become accessible to our nous and so become invisibly visible in his indivisible power beyond being. But those of whom you speak remain without love in regard to this purely spiritual love seen within. Moreover, they do not wish to follow the saints who, in their love towards men, lead them with words towards that light. Instead, they bring themselves to the edge of the abyss and drag down with them those they persuade to accompany them, and according to Gregory the Theologian, *they will see as fire, He who they did not recognise as light*,[50] and in whom they had no faith. But this fire is full of darkness, it is the same as the darkness which threatens us; it is that which is *prepared for the devil and his angels*, in the words of the Lord.[51] This darkness is not simply sensory, since it was made for evil angels who are deprived of sense. It is not just ignorance, for those who today allow themselves to be convinced by the heirs of this darkness will then be no more able to ignore God than they can now. They will know him even better, for it is said that: *All flesh confesses that Jesus Christ is the Lord, to the glory of God the Father*.[52] Amen.

Therefore, this light is not, properly speaking, sensory, nor is it knowledge, since the darkness that opposes it is not ignorance. So this light, although it is not knowledge, nevertheless brings with it the mystical and hidden knowledge of the mysteries of God, His pledge to us. So this pledge,[53] visible even now[54] to those who have purified their hearts, is not simply the same as knowledge, but brings with it corresponding knowledge and is itself an intelligible and noetic light, or rather it is spiritual – spiritually[55] present, and spiritually visible. It effectively transcends all knowledge and all virtue, and it alone will bring to Christians the perfection[56] accessible to them here below. This does not come from imitation, nor from reasoning[57] activity. It is the effect of revelation, and the grace of the Spirit.

⊁ 3.11 ⊱

Here is what the great Macarius, that most eloquent exponent, has to tell us, as confirmed by the testimony of Symeon: *The divine apostle Paul has shown each psyche the perfect mystery of Christianity in a most precise and luminous way. This mystery is a ray of heavenly light, produced in a revelation by the power of the Spirit, and in such a way that people might not believe that the illumination of the Spirit is simply the product of conceptual knowledge, and so that there is no risk that, through ignorance or carelessness, they might make a mistake about the perfect mystery of grace. This is why he first put forward, as a proof recognised by all, the example of the glory of the Spirit shining around the face of Moses. In effect, he is saying if what is transient is glorious, then what endures is even more glorious.*[58] *He spoke of it as a transient thing because the glory shone round the mortal body of Moses. But he showed that this immortal glory of the Spirit, which appeared in a revelation, and today shines on the immortal face*[59] *of the interior man, shines permanently for those who are worthy of it.*

He is thus saying that all of us, which is to say all those who are born of the Spirit through perfect faith and all who contemplate the glory of the Lord with unveiled face, are transfigured into the same image, from glory to glory, by the Spirit of the Lord.[60] *The unveiled face is that of the psyche since, he said, the veil is lifted when one is converted*[61] *to the Lord, for the Lord is the Spirit. He has clearly shown by this that a veil of darkness has covered the psyche, a veil that has been able to penetrate into the bosom of humanity by Adam's transgression. But today, through the illumination of the Spirit, this veil has been removed from the psyches of those who truly believe and are worthy. This is the reason for the coming of Christ.*[62]

⊁ 3.12 ⊱

Do you now see how the sensory illuminations that occurred under the old covenant prefigured the illumination of the Spirit that occurs in the psyches of those who in truth and practice believe in Christ? As if those who speak of sensory and symbolic appearances could be led by this to faith and to the realisation of Christ! Whereas, such people seek by any means to evoke unbelief in others who believe, and even, if possible, in those who have received grace in a visible way and thanks to that possess indestructible knowledge.

They have the audacity and the folly to teach their new ideas to those whom God, through His mysterious manifestations and energies, has initiated into the mysteries. They do not allow themselves even to be moved by the great Paul when he says: *But he that is spiritual judgeth all things, yet he himself is judged of no man. For who hath known the mind of the Lord, that he may instruct him? But we have the mind of Christ.*[63] Does this say that the things of the Spirit are made worthy of faith by reasoning? So whoever has faith in his own reasoning and the problems which it poses, who believes he can discover all truth by distinctions, syllogisms and analysis, can clearly neither know the things of the spiritual man, nor believe in them. He is a natural man,[64] and *the natural man*, said Paul, *does not receive the things of the Spirit*,[65] nor could he do so. So how could someone who is without knowledge and without faith make these things known and worthy of faith to other men by means of reason alone?

This means that if someone who lacks hesychia and noetic watchfulness,[66] and who has no experience of the things which occur spiritually and mysteriously, then teaches about watchfulness, he is conforming himself to his own reasoning. In seeking to show in words the Good that transcends all words, such a one has clearly fallen into the final folly. He has been made *foolish in his wisdom*.[67] In a senseless way, he has set his mind to use natural knowledge to observe the supernatural. He uses natural reason and carnal philosophy to examine and show *the deep things of God*[68] which can only be known through the Spirit and the gifts of the Spirit, and which can only be known to those who are spiritual and possess the nous of Christ.[69] In his folly he will even succeed in being God's enemy — what misfortune! — by misrepresenting the action and grace of the good Spirit, as did Beliar in opposing himself *to those who have received the spirit which is of God that they might know the things that are freely given to us of God*.[70] He will inherit misfortune for the harm he causes to those who listen to him, what the prophet calls the *misfortune due to him who gives his brother the dregs of the wine to drink*.[71]

⇥ 3.13 ⇤

Those who can judge everything, that is to say, the spiritual men, for according to the Apostle, *the spiritual man judges all things*,[72] should bring under their authority those who cannot judge, so that this judgement may permit them to know themselves with certainty. But to the contrary, to their own loss and that of their disciples, these people try to judge and correct spiritual men who are judged by nobody. *The spiritual man*, says the Apostle, *is judged by nobody.*[73] For they say that no one who does not possess a true opinion about created things may have a share in perfection and holiness. They then say that it is not possible to acquire this except by the methods of distinction, syllogism and analysis. Anybody who wishes to enjoy perfection and holiness must necessarily receive the teaching of worldly education and learn their methods of distinction, syllogism and analysis. This is the conclusion to which they wish to lead us!

By this aim, they seek to make active once again the wisdom that has been abolished once and for all time. Yet if they would come in all humility to those who can judge all things, in wishing to learn the truth, they would hear for themselves that their own doctrine comes from Hellenic thought and that it is the same as the heresy of the Stoics and the Pythagoreans, who claim that experimental knowledge from the study of the sciences is the aim of contemplation.

As for us, we believe that the true doctrine is not what is known through words and arguments, but through what is demonstrated in people's works and lives. That is not only the truth, but the only certain and immutable truth. Every word, it is said, argues with another word. But what word can argue with life?[74] We would even state that it is impossible to know yourself by the methods of distinction, syllogism and analysis; to know yourself one must free the nous from pride and evil by laborious repentance[75] and active asceticism. One who has not worked his nous by these means will not even know his own poverty in the domain of knowledge. So this practical way is the beginning of self-knowledge.

⤜ 3.14 ⤛

A judicious man will not condemn ignorance in general, and we do not believe that all knowledge should be regarded as good, so why would we consider knowledge as the goal that determines all our activity? *Truth,* says the great Basil, *has two forms. There is one that it is absolutely necessary to possess and to communicate to others, as it contributes to our salvation. Regarding the earth and the sea, the sky, and all that is in them, even if we do not know the truth about these things, this is nothing that will prevent us acquiring the promised beatitude.*[76] The goal before us is God's promise of good things to come – adoption, deification, revelation, the possession and enjoyment of heavenly treasures.

As to the knowledge that comes from worldly education, we know that it shares the fate of the present age. For if the language of the senses were able to establish reality in the age to come, the wise men of this age would become heirs to the kingdom of heaven. But according the true philosopher, Maximos: *If it is the purity of the psyche which sees, then those sages will be far from the knowledge of God.* What need do we have of knowledge which does not bring us closer to God? How could we possibly acquire perfection and holiness without it?

⇥ 3.15 ⇤

I will set aside the other opinions of these people who are mistaken to the point of giving a false interpretation of the Scriptures of the Spirit. Through this they have turned themselves against spiritual works and spiritual men. I will only add what relates to the subject of the present treatise. They say, in effect, that since God is invisible and incomprehensible, and *no man hath seen God at any time; the only begotten Son, which is in the bosom of the Father, he hath declared him.*[77] Following which, they reason 'how then are they not obviously deluded, they who claim to see God as a noetic light in themselves?' Any one of these men whom they attack can oppose them with the Logos, the only Son of God, who said: *The pure in heart will see God,*[78] and: *He that loves me, my Father will love him, and we will come and make our abode with him.*[79] But then they will reply that their contemplation is knowledge, without noticing that they are contradicting themselves.

In fact, the divine is not only invisible but also incomprehensible. So those who teach that because God is invisible, then the noetic vision of God in the light is the fruit of a wandering imagination and daemonic activity, should also reject all knowledge described in similar language because God is also incomprehensible.

We prefer not to reply to them about knowledge, for they are in agreement with us even if they do not understand what they say. In fact, there is knowledge about God and His doctrines, a divine contemplation which we call theology. On the one hand, the use and activity of the natural powers of the psyche and body certainly influence the images in our thoughts.[80] But this is not the same as the perfect beauty of the noble state which comes to us from above. It is not the supernatural union with the most resplendent light, which is the unique source of sure theology, the effect of which is to organise the inner powers of psyche and body, and to make them move in conformity with nature. In rejecting this, they have rejected all virtue and all truth.

What this means is that no truly mysterious and exalting contemplation belongs in any way to the domain of the knowledge that they describe. Contemplation of God by such means cannot be true because God is invisible, as we have learned when we have been with those who engage in real contemplation. But we will put the following question to these people: do you think that the Holy Spirit does not see what concerns God? *For it is He who searches out the deep things of God.*[81]

If someone pretended to see the pure light without the help of the Holy Spirit, you would be right to confront him, and say to him 'how could one see the invisible?' If a man rejects the spirit of the world, which the fathers call *the noetic darkness that oppresses unpurified hearts*; if he rejects that, purifies himself of all his self-will, if he moves away from any human tradition which even slightly weakens his enthusiasm for accomplishing his task, even though this tradition seems good; if he properly gathers the powers of his psyche together, as the great Basil advises, if he maintains sobriety in the care of his thoughts;[82] if he then lives meditating in his nous on what is true to nature and what pleases God, and if, above all, he truly accords his nature with what pleases God and accords his nous with the words of God, then he may transcend himself and *receive the Spirit that comes from God*, and which *knows the things of God just as the spirit of man knows what is within a man.*[83] If he receives this Spirit, according to the preaching of the great Paul, *in order to know the things which God has given him mystically by His grace, that which eye has not seen, which ear has not heard, and which has never arisen in the heart of man,*[84] then how would this man not see the invisible light with the Spirit? And how, even if it were the object of his vision, would this light not remain invisible, inaudible, and incomprehensible in itself?

Those who look will *see what eye has not seen, ear has not heard, and which has never arisen in the heart of man.* In fact such men receive spiritual eyes and *have the mind of Christ.*[85] Thus they can see the Invisible and can noetic ally think[86] of the Incomprehensible, for it is not invisible to them, but only to those who think and see only with their natural and created eyes and thoughts. As for those to whom God has adapted Himself as a faculty which directs[87] them, in this case how would He not communicate the contemplation of His grace to them in a way that they can perceive?

So when the psalmist, in *The Song Of Songs*, sings the praises of the spiritual power in their eyes, how could he not be applying theological language? *See that you are beautiful*, he says to Him, *you who are close to me; your eyes are like the eyes of doves.*[88] And they, when they perceive the beauty of the noetic Betrothed, praise Him abundantly in the same terms. The initiates know what this dove is in the eyes of the bride, since she is clearly seeing for the first time the beauty of God, her Betrothed. The psalmist describes this abundant beauty in detail for those who listen in faith. Just as when radiance in the eyes acts as light when it is united to the radiance of the sun and so sees sensory things, in the same way the nous, having become *one Spirit with the Lord,*[89] sees spiritual things clearly.

Yet here again, the Master remains invisible in a different way, a way truly superior to those who make him invisible by their earthbound thoughts, those who set out to contradict spiritual men. Nobody has ever seen the fullness of this beauty, which is why, according to Gregory of Nyssa, *no eye has seen it, not even one that is always watching.*[90] In fact, the eye does not see the fullness as it really is except to the measure that it is made receptive by the power of the divine Spirit. Beside the incomprehensibility, what is most divine and extraordinary is that, if they understand it, they understand it in an incomprehensible way. In effect, those who see do not know what allows them to see, to hear, and to be initiated whether into a knowledge of the future, or to experience things eternal, for the Spirit by which they see it is incomprehensible.

As the great Dionysius said: *The union of someone who has been divinised to the light which comes from above occurs when all noetic activity ceases.*[91] This union is not the product of a cause, nor is it just a relationship, for these are both results of activity in the nous; the union occurs as a result of interior separation, but it is not itself a separation.[92] For if it was simply separation, it would depend on us, and that is like the doctrine of the Messalians, who *go up to the hidden mysteries of God whenever they wish,*[93] as Saint Isaac said about them. So contemplation is not simply separation or negation, it is a union and a divinisation which occurs, mystically and inexpressibly by the grace of God, after we have separated ourselves from all that has come from below which imprints[94] itself on the nous. In fact, it happens after the cessation of all noetic activity. This is more than mere separation, and the inner separation is no more than the sign of that cessation. This is why every believer should consider God as separate from all His creatures, for the cessation of all noetic activity and the resulting union with the light from on high is an objective state, and part of the accomplishment of divinisation. It happens only to those who have purified their hearts and received grace.

And what may I say of this union, when the brief vision itself appears only to chosen disciples, washed clean of all perception in sense or nous? They are admitted to true vision because they have ceased to see, and they are clothed with supernatural senses because they submit without knowing. But we will show further on, with the help of God, that they have indeed seen this vision, and that, properly speaking, the faculty of such vision is neither of the senses nor of the nous.

⇥ 3.18 ⇤

Do you see now that in place of the nous, eyes, and ears, they acquire the incomprehensible Spirit? It is through Him that they see, hear and understand. For if all their noetic activity has come to rest, how could the angels and men like angels see God except by the power of the Spirit? This is why their vision is not sensory – they do not receive it by the senses. Neither is it an act of noetic perception, since they do not find it in thoughts, nor in the knowledge[95] that comes from them. They only discover it after all noetic activity ceases. So it is not the product of either imagination[96] or discursive reason,[97] neither is it an opinion,[98] nor a conclusion reached by syllogistic argument. In separating from the activity of the psyche, we find the peak of pure prayer – which is also purity of heart – and the nous does not acquire this simply by raising itself up by means of negation.

According to the teaching of the fathers, every divine command and every sacred law has as its end purity of heart. Every mode and aspect of prayer is crowned by pure prayer. Every thought[99] which strives from below towards Him who is transcendent and separate from the world comes to a halt once it has gone beyond all created things. Yet it is false to say that beyond the accomplishment of the divine commandments there is nothing but purity of heart. There are other things, many other things. There is the pledge of things promised in this age. There are also the blessings of the age to come, visible and accessible through this purity of heart. Then, beyond prayer, there is the vision that cannot be spoken of, the ecstasy in the vision, and the hidden mysteries.

Similarly, beyond abstraction from created things, or rather after the cessation – which happens within us not only in words, but in reality – there remains an unknowing which is more than knowledge.[100] There is a cloud, but it is more than radiance, and, as the great Dionysius says, it is in this radiant darkness[101] that divine things are given to the saints.

Thus the most perfect contemplation of God and divine things is not simply interior abstraction. Beyond this abstraction there is a participation in things divine, which is more a gift and a possession than a process of abstraction. These possessions and gifts are indescribable. If one says anything about them, one must use images and analogies, not because these things are seen only as images and analogies, but because one cannot show what has been seen in any other way. When we talk about things that are indescribable we must describe them in an imaginative way. Yet those who do not lend an attentive ear to it consider that this knowledge which surpasses all wisdom is simply foolishness. They trample the noetic pearls underfoot with their criticisms.[102] As far as is possible with words, they also strive to destroy those who have shown them these pearls.

⇥ 3.19 ⇤

As I have said, it is because of their love of men that the saints say as much as they possibly can about things that cannot be described. They reject the error of those who in their ignorance imagine that beyond abstraction from created things there remains only total inaction, when this inaction actually transcends all activity. But, I repeat, these things remain impossible to describe by their very nature. This is why the great Dionysius says that after abstraction from created things, there is no word, but *an absence of words*.[103] He also says: *The more we are raised upwards, so we become speechless and unknowing*.[104] But despite this inexpressible characteristic, negation alone is not enough to enable the nous to attain things that are beyond the nous.

Ascent by negation is in fact merely a noetic understanding of things that appear to be different from God. It is used as an image to represent inexpressible contemplation as well as the fulfilment[105] of the nous in that contemplation; it is not in itself that fulfilment. But those who, like the angels, have been united to that light sing of this using the image of total abstraction. A mystical union with the light beyond essence teaches them that this light transcends all things. Moreover, those judged worthy to receive the mystery, who have a faithful and prudent ear around these initiates, can also sing of the divine and incomprehensible light[106] that comes when we are abstracted from all things. But they cannot unite themselves to it and see it unless they have purified themselves by taking care to fulfill the commandments, and by consecrating their nous to pure and immaterial prayer, thus receiving the supernatural power of divine contemplation.

⇥ 3.20 ⇤

What then shall we call this power that is neither sensory nor noetic activity? How else except by using the expression of Solomon, who was wiser than all who went before him and said that it is *a sensation that is both noetic and divine*. By combining those two adjectives, he urges his audience to consider it neither as solely a sensation nor as simply a noetic activity, for neither is the activity of the nous sensory, nor is that of the senses noetic. The noetic sense is thus different from both. Following the great Dionysius, we should perhaps call it 'union', and not 'knowledge'. *We should realise*, he says, *that the human nous has the capacity to think, through which it looks on intelligible things, and a unity which transcends the nature of the nous, through which it is joined to things beyond itself.*[107] Furthermore: *The noetic powers, as well as the senses are no longer needed when the psyche becomes divinised, and they concentrate sightlessly and through an unknowing union on the rays of 'unapproachable light'.*[108] St Maximos, so rich in things divine, says of this union: *In beholding the light of the hidden glory which cannot be put into words, the saints too, like the celestial powers, become capable of receiving the blessed purity.*

⇥ 3.21 ⇤

I do not think that these great men have in mind the ascent by the negative way! For the latter lies within the powers of anyone who wants it, but it does not transform the psyche to give it an angelic dignity. It frees the thoughts in relation to other created things, but it cannot, by itself, effect union with transcendent things. Purity of the passionate part of the psyche, dispassion, effectively liberates the nous from all things. It is then united through prayer to the grace of the Spirit. This enables it to enjoy the divine radiance, so that the nous acquires an angelic and godlike form. This is why the fathers, since the time of Dionysius the Great, called this state *spiritual sensation*, a phrase that accords most with that mystical and hidden contemplation and describes it best. At such times man, in effect, truly sees neither by the nous, nor by the body, but by the Spirit. Then he surely knows that he sees supernaturally a light that is beyond light. Yet at that moment he does not know which instrument allows him to see this light, nor can he discover the nature of that instrument, for he cannot follow the traces of the Spirit.

This is what Paul said when he had heard the inexpressible words and had seen invisible things: *Whether in the body, I cannot tell; or whether out of the body, I cannot tell: God knoweth.*[109] In other words, he did not know whether he saw through his nous or through his body. He did not see by sense perception, but his vision was as clear as that which permits the senses to perceive sensory things, and even clearer. He saw from beyond himself, and was ravished by the indescribable sweetness of his vision, outside of all objective thought as well as outside of himself. Under the influence of this ecstasy, he even forgot prayer to God. It is this of which St Isaac speaks, confirming the great and divine Gregory: *Prayer is the purification of the nous, which is brought forth solely by the light of the Holy Trinity in the midst of astonishment.*[110, 111] And again: *Purity of nous is what allows the light of the Holy Trinity to shine at the moment of prayer. The nous then transcends prayer, and this state should not properly be called prayer, although it is a fruit of the pure prayer sent by the Holy Spirit. Then the nous no longer prays any definite prayer, it finds itself in ecstasy amidst incomprehensible realities. This is the unknowing that is higher than knowledge.*[112]

Paul was returned to wholeness and his nous stepped back[113] from every created thing when he was ravished in that most joyful reality, which he beheld as a light, a light of revelation, although it did not reveal sensible bodies. It was a light with no limit either in depth, or in height, or to either side. He saw absolutely no limit to his vision, or to the light that shone on him, as if it were a sun infinitely brighter and greater than the universe. He held himself at the centre of it, having become all eye, such was his vision.

❯❯ 3.22 ❮❮

This is why the great Macarius says that this light is infinite and beyond the heavens. Another saint, one of the most perfect, saw the whole universe contained in a single ray of this noetic sun – even though he himself did not see the full nature and the measure of that light, seeing it only to the measure that he was able to receive it. In this contemplation, in his union with this light beyond the nous, he did not learn its nature, but he did learn that it really exists, is supernatural, beyond all essence, and different from all created things. He also learned that its being is absolute and unique, and that it mysteriously gathers all created things in itself.

This vision of the Infinite cannot permanently belong to any individual, nor to all men together. He who does not see this light will understand that it is he himself who lacks the capacity to see because he is not perfectly adapted to the Spirit by complete purification, it is not the Object of vision that falls short. When the vision comes down to him the seer knows with certainty that it is the light, even if he only sees it faintly. He knows it surely by the passionless joy that wells up in him, by the calm that he feels in his nous and by the fire of divine love that begins to burn in him.

In proportion to his practice of what is agreeable to God, in his rejection of everything else, in his attentiveness to prayer, and to the degree of elevation of his psyche towards God, so he experiences an ever more luminous contemplation. He then understands that his vision is infinite because it is the Infinite, and because he cannot see the end of its radiance. Moreover, he sees even more how feeble is his own capacity to receive the light.

⇥ 3.23 ⇤

But such a man does not consider that the vision of which he has been made worthy is simply the nature of God. Just as the embodied psyche communicates its life to the living body, and we call this life 'psyche,' all-the-while knowing that the psyche which is in us, and which communicates life to us, is distinct from that life. So God, who dwells in the God-bearing psyche, communicates light to it. However, the union of almighty God with those who are worthy of it transcends that light. God, while remaining entirely in Himself, dwells entirely in us by His power that transcends the essential. He does not communicate His nature to us, but His own glory and splendour.

This light is thus divine, and the saints rightly call it 'divinity' because it is the source of deification. So it is not only 'divinity' but 'deification-itself,' and the rule of God.[114] It appears as distinction and multiplicity in the one God, but it is no less He who is the Divine Principle, more-than-God and more-than-Principle. This is the One in the one Divinity. This is why it is the Divine Principle, more-than-God and more-than-Principle, since God is the Existence of this Divinity, as the doctors of the Church have taught, following the great Areopagite Dionysius, who called the deifying gift that proceeds from God 'Divinity.' So when Gaius asked Dionysius how God could be beyond Thearchy, he replied in his letter: *If you regard the substance of the gift which deifies us as 'Divinity', and this gift is the source of deification, then He who transcends every source, including the Divinity spoken of here, also surpasses the source of Divinity.*[115]

So the fathers say that the divine grace of the light that is beyond the senses is God. Yet God in his nature is not identical with this grace, because He is able not only to illumine and deify the nous, but can bring out of non-being every noetic essence.

⇥ 3.24 ⇤

Do you now recognise how those who see the light and nevertheless regard it as invisible are more expert than those masters of worldly wisdom who do not see it? Those who are elevated to the degree of divine contemplation know that they see a light with their noetic sense. They know that this light is God who, by his grace, makes luminous those who participate in the mysterious union. And if you ask those who see the light how they see the Invisible, they will answer you, *not in the words which man's wisdom teaches, but which the Holy Spirit teaches.*[116] In effect, they lack nothing, they have no need of human wisdom, since they possess the teaching of the Spirit. As the Apostle relates, their glory is in this: *That in simplicity and godly sincerity, not with fleshly wisdom, but by the grace of God, we have had our conversation in the world.*[117] They will also say 'things divine, O man, are not in the least limited by our own knowledge. On the contrary, many things of which we are ignorant have their origin in God'. And thus, following the Apostle, it is by *comparing the spiritual to the spiritual* in this way that we establish that the grace of the New Covenant is in agreement with the Old.

The Apostle called this demonstration from the Old Covenant 'comparison,' for after having established the new things in this way, we can also show that the gifts of grace are superior to those of the law. If one asks them how one can see the invisible light, those who live and see by the Spirit will reply thus: 'How did Elijah, the prophet of God, see the light? The cloak in which he wrapped his face[118] showed that he was not seeing in a sensory way. Moreover, the surname by which all knew him[119] clearly announces and testifies that he really had seen God, even though his sensory eyes were hidden by his cloak. Everybody called him *Theoptes* and even *Theoptikotatos*, the greatest seer of God.'

⇥ 3.25 ⇤

And if you question them again, asking: 'Why do you say that prayer resounds mystically in your innards, and what sets your heart in motion?' They will point to the earthquake Elias felt which preceded the noetic manifestation of God.[120] They will also refer to the sounding of the stomach described in Isaiah.[121] And if you then ask them why prayer produces warmth in us, they will speak of the fire which the same Elias named as a sign of God before His appearance, a sign that then becomes like a light breeze when close to being clothed by the divine radiance, which is named the Invisible by he who contemplates it.

They will speak again of Elias, who appeared and really was like a fire when he physically ascended in a chariot of fire.[122] They will also speak of the other prophet whose innards were burned as if by fire; the words of God had become fire in him.[123] And if you wish to enquire further about what happens mysteriously within them, they will tell you about things very similar to those we have spoken of already, things equally spiritual. They will say always and to everyone: *Have you not heard, that a man has eaten the bread of angels?*[124] *Did you not hear the Lord say that he will give the Holy Spirit to those who ask Him night and day?*[125]

What is the bread of angels? Is it not the divine light beyond the heavens? According to the great Dionysius, the nous unites to this, directly or by transmission,[126] in a way that transcends the nous. God gave a promise of this illumination to men by sending manna from above for forty years. Christ fulfilled this promise by sending the illumination of the Spirit to those who earnestly believe in Him, and who make their faith manifest in their works, by offering them his luminous body as nourishment. This last is a pledge of the mysterious communion with Jesus in the world to come. So there is no astonishment in the fact that these events of the Old Covenant prefigured other graces of Christ. Therefore, do you see now that these symbolic illuminations are the outer manifestations of noetic illumination, and of mysteries other than knowledge?

⊁ 3.26 ⊀

Since those who reject the divine light of grace say, as you tell us, that the light which appeared on Tabor was a sensory light, we will ask them whether they regard as God the light which shone on the chosen disciples at Tabor? Because if they do not regard it as God, Peter will convince them of their mistake. According to Mark, he kept vigil on the mountain and saw the glory of Christ,[127] and in the second of his epistles Peter himself writes that he was eyewitness of His majesty when he was with Him on the holy mountain.[128] The interpretation of the Gospel preaching which is given quite clearly by the one with the golden tongue,[129] will definitely silence them, for he said: *The Lord appeared resplendent, His body retaining its shape, in the radiance of divinity.* Their lips will certainly be sealed by Dionysius the Great, who clearly calls the event *theophany,* and *the vision of God.* In addition, Gregory, surnamed the Theologian, says that *the Divinity manifested to the disciples on the mountain was a light,*[130] and there are many others who have said the same. In conclusion, Symeon, who celebrated in his beautiful prose the lives of nearly all the saints, wrote that the

Theologian loved by Christ *saw the very Divinity of the Word unveiled*[131] on the mountain.

But if these people, in accordance with the truth and the witnesses of truth, called this manifested light 'Divine light,' and also, the 'light of God,' they will necessarily agree that the most perfect vision of God is like a light. This is why Moses too saw it in that way, as did almost all the prophets, particularly those to whom He appeared while they were awake and not during their sleep. But even so, all the sacred visions of the prophets had a symbolic character and those who contradict us simply want it to be otherwise.

Yet the divine revelation given to the apostles on Tabor was not a symbolic light that appeared then disappeared. In fact, it bears the quality of the re-appearance of Christ which is yet to come. This same light will eternally illumine those who become worthy of it in the age without end, as the divine Dionysius says. Basil the Great speaks of it as the prelude to the second coming, and the Lord in the Gospels calls it *the Kingdom of God*.[132]

⋊ 3.27 ⋉

Why then do they oppose what the saints say about it, those who see God mysteriously as a light, when that vision is indeed like a light, both today and in the age to come? Is it because these saints do not say that this light is a sensory light, but call it 'noetic,' as Solomon said of the Holy Spirit?[133] Yet these are the very people our opponents malign, saying the divine vision of God they see in prayer is simply sensory light, while on the other hand they oppose any sensory reality in the divine gifts of grace! How then, forgetting themselves, can they heap scorn on those who say that the divine light is not sensory? Do you see their inconsistency and their inconstancy? They seem eager to criticise, but not to see the good!

So how then would these infallible exponents of old and new manifestations of the light[134] respond, if it happened that an animal without reason was then present on the mountain? Would it have perceived this radiance that is more luminous than the sun? I do not think so. It is not written that the herds felt the Glory of The Lord that illumined the shepherds at the time of Christ's birth.[135] So how could this light be sensory if the present and open eyes of the unreasoning animals – which see sensory things in the normal way – do not see it when it illumines them?

So if it is the eyes of human senses that saw it, they could only see it in as much as they are different from eyes that lack reason. In what other way would they be different? In one way only – it is the nous that sees with human eyes. It is not a matter of a sensory faculty, or beings without reason would also have been able to see it. Was it a noetic faculty perceiving the light through the senses? No, it was not a faculty of this kind, otherwise everyone, especially those in the countryside around, would have seen a radiance brighter than the sun. So if it was not this faculty which permitted the apostles to see the light, it was not, properly speaking, a light of the senses. Furthermore, nothing known through the senses is eternal, but the light of the Divinity, often called *the glory of God*, has neither beginning nor end. So this light can in no way be a sensory light.

⇥ 3.28 ⇤

If the light is not sensory, although the apostles were judged worthy of perceiving it with their eyes, then it is perceived through a means other than the senses. That is why the radiance of Jesus' face was indescribable, unapproachable, and timeless – because it acted through an inexpressible reality. This is why they say that this radiance was not, properly speaking, accessible to the senses. It is the same as that light which is the place of saints hereafter, when they go to receive their allotted place in heaven. There is a light there of which this radiance is no more than a foretaste, a light here below which is accorded to the saints like a pledge. But if that is called 'light,' and sometimes appears in a strange way to become accessible to the senses, it is nevertheless part of a reality that transcends the nous itself, and the names that are given to it are extended from their ordinary meanings. How, then, could it properly be called sensory?

Otherwise, when we pray for the deceased, why do we cry continually as we call on the thearchic Goodness to *keep their psyches in a place of light*? What need have these psyches of a sensory light, and why would they be afflicted by the darkness that was the opposite of this light, if it was simply a sensory darkness? Do you see that none of these things properly belong to the domain of the senses? We also showed earlier on, when we mentioned the dark fire prepared for the race of daemons, that this is also not simply a matter of ignorance or knowledge.

It was therefore not necessary to make statements about the indescribable and luminous appearance of Jesus on Tabor that depend on the lower forms of reasoning, that is, on human reasoning and unstable thoughts. But it was necessary to be obedient to the voice of the fathers and wait for the exact knowledge that comes from experience in purity of heart. This last knowledge actually accomplishes the union with this light; it mystically tells those who find it that this light cannot be compared to any being, as it transcends all created things. For how can we regard as sensory something that transcends all created things? How could the radiance of God be as that of a created being? So this light is certainly not sensory.

⇥ 3.29 ⇤

The great Macarius says: *When the psyche, like the prodigal son, returns to God, his Master and his Father, in fear, love, and shame, God receives it without thinking of its transgressions and clothes it in a robe of glory, a robe of the light of Christ.*[136] Is there another glory and another light of Christ beyond that seen by Peter when, fully awake, *he was with Him on the holy mountain*?[137] How could it become a garment for the psyche if it belongs to the domain of the senses? The same theologian said elsewhere that: *This light is beyond heaven.* Could something sensory be 'beyond heaven?'

Elsewhere, Macarius says, *the Lord made the composition of human nature that was assumed by Him sit on the right hand of the divine majesty in the heavens,*[138] in a fullness of glory, visible, not on his face alone as with Moses, but on his whole body. If nobody perceives this light, does it shine in vain? If the light is sensory, then the answer is yes. However, is it not actually the food of the spirits, of angels, and of the just? This is why, when we pray for the dead, we ask Christ to place their souls where they are watched over by the light of His face. How could these psyches be joyful, and moreover, how could they live in the middle of a light which shone in a sensory way? The great Basil says on his part that, when the Master appears in the flesh, the pure in heart will *see eternally this power whose radiance comes from the beloved Body.* How could a light which is seen only in the purity of heart be seen by the senses? According to Cosmas, the divine musician, *Christ on the mountain appeared as infinite light.* How could a sensory light be infinite?

⇥ 3.30 ⇤

Stephen, who was the first after Christ to bear witness to Christ: *Turning his eyes upwards, sees the heavens open and the glory of God, and Christ standing on the right hand of God.*[139] Is it then possible to reach up to realities beyond the heavens by means of our senses? Yet this man saw such realities while remaining here on earth. What is even more marvellous was that he not only saw Christ, but also his Father. How could he have seen that the Son was on his right, if he had not also seen the Father? The invisible allows itself to be seen by those whose hearts are purified, but by a mysterious power, in a manner which is neither sensible, nor noetic, nor apophatic, for the sublime majesty and the glory of the Father cannot be in any way accessible to the senses.

On the other hand, the position on the right was symbolic, but the vision was not. Although the position itself was only a symbol standing for Him Who is fixed and immutable, like the absolutely unchangeable permanence of the divine nature, yet Stephen saw it in a mysterious way. For the position to the right was not a trick by the Only Begotten, intended to show a different reality, but by being always to the right of the Father, He clearly wanted to show His own glory to someone who was still in the flesh but had surrendered his very psyche for that glory.

One can neither see nor conceive by negation, yet Stephen saw the glory of God. And if this was a noetic vision, or if it was the result of deduction or analogy, then that would mean that we too should be able to see as he saw. We too are able to represent the God become man by analogy – showing Him standing or seated in heaven on the right of the divine Majesty. Then why was this vision not already, or even always, in the nous of the disciple of the Evangelist? Why did he grasp it only at that exact moment? *Behold*, he said, *I see the heavens opened and the Son of Man standing on the right hand of God.*[140] What need had he to turn his eyes to heaven, and for heaven to open, if this vision had been no more than knowledge obtained noetically? Yet in what way did the First Martyr have this vision if he saw it neither noetically, nor with the senses, nor by negation, nor if he conceived these divine things by deduction or by analogy? I will dare to tell you – spiritually! This is what I have said about those who see the pure light through revelation, as so many fathers have said before me.

The divine Luke also teaches this, in the verse already quoted at the beginning of this chapter, saying of Stephen: *He, full of faith and the Holy Spirit, turning his eyes to heaven, saw the glory of God.* And you too, if you are full of faith and the Holy Spirit, will be able to contemplate spiritually things that are invisible to the nous. But if, on the other hand, you remain devoid of faith, you will not even believe those who bear witness to what they have seen.[141] But if you had even a small measure of faith, you would listen piously to those who would tell you from their own experience about things that are indescribable. You would not lower these mysteries to the level of sensory or noetic things, even if such terms were applied to them. You would not fight against the truth as if it were an error, nor would you reject the ineffable grace of God that has been given to us.

➤ 3.31 ◄

In fact, the fathers call this contemplation 'especially true,' for prayer energises the heart with spiritual warmth, and delight, and the joyful tears of grace. It is of course the noetic sense that is responsible for grasping all this. I say 'sense' because the perception involved is manifest and clear, free from delusion[142] and imagination. Furthermore, in a certain way the body also participates in the grace that acts through the nous. The body harmonises with this grace, and it too becomes sensitive to the hidden mystery occurring in the psyche. Grace then communicates a perception of what is being produced at that moment through the senses of anyone who looks from the outside on those who possess this grace. This is also what made the face of Moses appear to shine, for the interior radiance of his nous spread over his body; he shone so strongly that the brilliance of the light prevented those who saw him with their senses from fixing their eyes on him.[143]

This is how the face of Stephen appeared like the face of an angel.[144] From within himself his nous came into a new state of being, whether actively or passively, becoming angel-like and angel-pure, re-born into the knowledge of angels, and became one through an indescribable participation with the light which transcends all things. This is also how Mary of Egypt, or rather Mary of Heaven, rose bodily into the air when praying, perceptibly and actually changing her position. For as her nous rose, her body also rose and, leaving the earth, was seen as a flying body.[145]

➤ 3.32 ◄

When the psyche is inspired as if aroused by the ardent beloved, the only desirable one, the heart arises and spiritually leaps, and marked by grace for communion, it is hence urged on towards that Body in the clouds which announces the coming of the Lord.[146] And so when, in unceasing prayer, the noetic fire appears and the noetic torch is lit, and when the nous awakens its desire through the heavenly fire of spiritual contemplation, then, in a mysterious way, the body too becomes light and warm. To those who see it, according to the writer who described the spiritual ladder,[147] it appears to come from a furnace visible to the senses. For myself, I believe that the sweat of Christ as He prayed[148] was also a sign of heat felt by the senses, and that this can only be communicated to the body in prolonged supplication to God. What will those people reply to that, those who claim that the origin of the heat produced by prayer is daemonic? Will they teach us to avoid fervent, energetic and continuous prayer, lest the body receive heat proportional to the struggles of the psyche? Is this what they wish to prevent? Then they are teaching that prayer neither leads a man to God, nor to the imitation of God, and does not transform him to make him any better!

We know for ourselves that by voluntarily accepting the pain of asceticism we rid ourselves of the pleasures that, alas, we had formerly preferred, once we had broken the commandment. Then, during prayer, we taste with our noetic sense a divine joy unmixed with pain. The prophet who had experienced this joy which – O miracle! – had transformed his body itself to make it accessible to the dispassionate and divine love, proclaimed before God: *Your words are sweet to my palate, sweeter than honey to my mouth;*[149] and also: *My soul shall be satisfied as with marrow and fatness; and my mouth shall praise thee with joyful lips.*[150] Through this, the possibilities of ascent that are laid out in the heart participate in the 'godlike happiness' and angelic 'pleasure,' by the *visitation of divine enlightenment*, as Dionysius the Great called it.

⋊ 3.33 ⋉

This divinely purifying sorrow manifests not only in the psyches of those who enter the spiritual struggle, it also passes into their bodies and into the physical senses. The tears of sorrow poured out by those who feel this pain because of their sins are the obvious proof of this. Why then do we not receive the signs of divine joy according to the Spirit just as piously when they are manifested by the faltering senses of the body? Is this not why the Lord says: *Blessed are they that mourn, for they shall be comforted,*[151] because they will receive the joy that is the fruit of the Spirit? The body also participates in this consolation in many different ways. Those who have experienced this know it. On the other hand, even those who see them from the outside observe the good character of such people, their sweet tears and their conversation full of grace to those who come to see them. As it is said in the Song of Songs: *The honey of bees flows from your mouth, O my spouse.*[152]

In fact, it is not only the psyche that receives the promise of good things to come, but also the body, which runs the race of the Gospel with it. Those who do not admit this also deny that the body lives in the age to come. And if it is true that one day the body will participate in these indescribable good things, even now it can participate in them according to its nature when God gives grace to the nous. For this reason we say that these gifts are received by the senses, but we add *by the noetic senses*, because these transcend the natural senses, since it is pre-eminently the nous that receives them. This is because our nous ascends as far as possible towards the first nous and participates in it divinely, transforming itself and so transforming the body that is attached to it and making it more divine. In this way it shows and prefigures the absorption of the flesh by the Spirit in the age to come. It is not the eyes of the body but the eyes of the psyche that receive the power of the Spirit that allows them to see these things. We therefore call this power 'noetic,'[153] even though it is above the nous.[154]

⇥ 3.34 ⇤

At the same time, we will warn those who listen to us against thinking that these mysterious spiritual activities are material or corporeal. But some people are truly the victims of this opinion. With their impure and sacrilegious ears, with their thoughts that neither know, nor believe, nor follow the words of the fathers, they have received the teaching of the holy with very little holiness! They have trampled it under foot and set themselves against those who explained it to them.

They have not believed the great Macarius, perhaps they do not even know that he said this: *The spiritual soul of those without trial remains untouched, but for those with apprehension of holiness and faith, who have been tested and tried, comes communion with the Holy Spirit from whom alone they receive the heavenly treasure of Spirit and are made known and come into a new state of being. The profane can in no way contain this power within their nous.*[155] His words on this subject are sincere, listen to them so that faith may reach you and you may be worthy to receive these treasures. It is then that the true experience of the eyes of your psyche will show you what good things and what mysteries Christian psyches can receive in communion here below.

But when you hear talk of the 'eyes of the psyche,' which can actually experience the heavenly treasures, do not confuse these with 'reason.' In fact, these 'eyes' exercise their faculty just as well on the things of the senses as on things noetic. Think of this in the same way that you would think of a city you had not yet seen – you cannot experience it simply by thinking of it. So it is with things that concern God and things Divine; you do not experience them simply by thinking or talking about them. If you do not possess gold in a tangible way, if you do not hold it visibly in your two hands, if you do not see it with your own eyes, then you do not grasp it, you do not see it and you do not possess it, even if the thought of gold passes through your head ten thousand times. The same is also true of thinking ten thousand times of divine treasures.

Without confirming the divine things by experience, and without seeing them with the noetic eyes that transcend reason, you see nothing, you have nothing, you do not truly possess any of the divine things. I have spoken of 'noetic eyes' because it is through these that the power of the Spirit acts, permitting them to see these things. Yet this holy vision of the divine and more than luminous light transcends the noetic eyes themselves.

⪥ 3.35 ⪦

This is why the Lord did not call all his disciples to the spiritual vision that appeared on Tabor, which was mysterious and invisible to the faculties of sense, but only chosen disciples. The great Areopagite, Dionysius, says that in the age to come we will be enlightened: *By the visible theophany of Christ, as were the Disciples at the Transfiguration, and will participate in noetic illumination with a passionless and immaterial nous and in a union transcending the nous in a more divine imitation of the supra-celestial Minds.*[156]

Even then, we will not come to conceive that the light shining from the beloved Body is a sensory radiance, perceived by the senses without the power of a reasoning psyche. Indeed, only this last power can receive the power of the Spirit, which in its turn can contemplate the light of grace. The radiance which cannot be perceived by these means cannot be perceived at all. The saint has shown this himself to those who have a nous. In the age to come, he says, we will be illumined by this light, in a time when there is no need either of light, nor of air, nor of anything belonging to the present life.

The God-inspired scriptures tell us that, according to the Apostle, *then God will be all in all.*[157] Then we will have no need for sensory light. For if God is everything for us, then the light also will be divine. How could it then be perceptible by sense in the true meaning of the term? The fact that he added *while becoming ever more divine like the angels,* and that we can speak of it in three ways,[158] shows that angels also receive this light.

If it were sensory, how could this be? How could a sensible light not be visible through the air? We would then see the light more or less distinctly, not as a measure of each individual's virtue and the purity resulting from that virtue, but as a measure of the purity of the air! *The just will shine like the sun.*[159] So each of them would appear brighter or darker not in proportion to their good actions, but merely depending on the purity of the air around them! What is more, in this case the good things of the age to come would be accessible to the eyes of the senses, now and forever. Everyone would see those good things which not only has *eye not seen and ear not heard,* but which also *have not entered into the heart*[160] of the man who tries to penetrate incomprehensible things by verbal reasoning. If it is sensory, how could this light be invisible to sinners? Or, according to these people, would there be a barrier formed of shadows and cones, of conjunctions resulting in eclipses, and of cycles of light in various forms? Will we need the vain activity of astronomers in a life of ages without end?

>| 3.36 |<

But how will the bodily senses grasp a light that is not truly sensible? By the power of the all-powerful Spirit, the power by which the chosen apostles themselves saw it on Tabor, when it blazed out not only from the flesh which carries the Son within it, but also from the cloud which carries within it the Father of Christ. It will be different in the age to come. Then, according to the Apostle, the body itself will be 'spiritual' and no longer 'natural'. *It is sown as a natural body, he said, and it is resurrected as a spiritual body.*[161] It is precisely because it will be spiritual and will see in a spiritual way that it will perceive the divine radiance.

Now we can see that, in truth, we have a noetic psyche, which exists in its own right within dense and mortal flesh which clothes it and drags it down. So the psyche becomes entirely like the body and open to illusion, which is why the intelligence of our noetic sense is hidden. In the same way, in the most blessed life of the age to come, it will be the body which will be as if hidden for those *sons of the resurrection,*[162] those worthy of transformation to the oneness of angels, in accordance with the gospel of Christ. With this triumph of the nous, the body will become so subtle that it will no longer appear to be material and it will no longer limit noetic activity. In this way, they will enjoy the divine light in their body and their senses.

>| 3.37 |<

And why have I only spoken of the relationship which will be established then between the body and the noetic nature?[163] Saint Maximos said: *The psyche becomes God by participation in divine grace after it has itself ceased all noetic and sensory activity, as well as having ceased from all the natural activities of the body; for the body is divinised at the same time as the psyche, through its own corresponding participation in the process of deification. Thus God alone is made manifest through the psyche and the body, because their natural properties are overcome by the superabundance of God's glory.*[164]

So, as I said at the beginning, God is invisible to creatures, but is not invisible to Himself. But then – O miracle! – it is God who will see, not only through the psyche within us, but also through our body. This is why we will then see the divine and inaccessible light distinctly, even with our own bodily organs. This was the pledge and the prelude of God's munificence that awaits us in the future. Christ showed it mysteriously to the apostles on Tabor. How then can we say that the radiance of the Divinity, which is beyond all words and all vision, is in the domain of the senses? Do you now understand that, in the proper sense of the term, the light that illumined the apostles on Tabor was not a sensory light?

⇥ 3.38 ⇤

Nevertheless, the divine light that exists beyond all sense perception was in fact also seen by the eyes of the senses. Those who contradict the spiritual men recognise this for themselves, and in this are in agreement with us. But if the divine light is apparent to bodily eyes, could it not appear to noetic eyes as well? Could the psyche be an evil thing, incapable of uniting itself to the Good and becoming aware of it? No heretic has ever presumed to say this! Would it be a good thing if the body were superior to the psyche? How, in fact, would the psyche not be inferior to the body if the body could participate in the light of God and the psyche could not? Since it is by the mediation of the psyche that the body sees the light of God, and not the other way round, how could this material and mortal body be more akin to and more devoted to God than is the psyche?

But since the Transfiguration of the Lord on Tabor was a prelude of the visible manifestation of God in the glory yet to come, then, if the apostles had been judged worthy to contemplate it with the eyes of their bodies, why should those whose hearts have been purified today not see the prelude and pledge of this appearance with spiritual eyes? But the Son of God, in His incomparable love for men, not only unites His divine hypostasis with our nature by assuming a psyche-bearing body animated by a nous-bearing psyche, in order to appear on earth and live among men.[165] He also unites by an overwhelming miracle with the human hypostases themselves, mingling Himself with each one of His faithful in their communion with His holy body. He then becomes one body with us, making of us a temple for the whole Divinity. For in the very Body of Christ *dwells all the fullness of the Godhead.*[166]

Why would He not then illuminate those worthy of communion with the divine radiance of His body, which is in us, enlightening our psyches as He illumined even the bodies of the disciples on Tabor? However, since at that time His body, the source of the light of grace, was not yet united to our bodies, He illumined externally those who approached in reverence and this illumination was transmitted to the psyche through the medium of the sensory eyes. But now that His body is mingled in us and exists within us, it truly illumines the psyche from within.

⇥ 3.39 ⇤

It is written that in the age to come we will we see the Invisible *face to face*.[167] Yet those who have purified the heart may receive therein a foretaste of this promise now, by means of the nous, which forms an invisible sense. For the nous is of an immaterial nature and is made known by light, begotten from the original and sublime Light in which all things participate and which transcends all things.

By turning entirely toward the true Light in ceaseless prayer, the nous is purified and ascends toward God. Without turning back, the nous is then deemed worthy and divinely transformed, becoming like an angel, and is illumined with the angels by the divine splendour of the first light. This appears by participation in which the archetype is the cause, revealing itself as a hidden and irresistible beauty, resplendent in unapproachable radiance. David, the divine musician, noetically sensing that radiance in himself, rejoiced in it and shared with the faithful that great and mysterious gift, *the glory of our God is upon us*.[168] If we did not feel and see in ourselves the radiance of God and if we too sought it only through distinctions, reasoning and analysis, instead of believing the fathers in all simplicity of heart, then how could we tolerate it when someone says that somebody else possesses the radiance of God?

So John has done well to show us in his Revelation: *Nobody can know what is written on the white stone which the victor receives from God, except him who receives it*.[169] It is not only that it would be absolutely impossible for a man who does not possess the stone to know this, he will not even know of its existence, at least until he listens with faith to those who have seen it. He will consider that true contemplation is blindness, not because it transcends sense and knowledge like a holy cloud, but because according to him it absolutely does not exist. And if, in his inexperience and lack of faith, he is wicked enough to cause slander, if he is full of empty thoughts and a shameless despiser of the most venerable fathers, he will not only announce that this thing does not exist, but he will even give false teaching about the divine radiance on account his daemonic imaginings. And as you say, brother, today some people have come to this!

And here is another pretext they invoke: that God is invisible, while the devil simulates an *angel of light*.[170] But they do not understand that truth existed before all simulations. This means that if the devil, simulating what truly exists, simulates an angel of light, this is because there truly exists an angel of light, a good angel. As the angel of light, what light is it that he reveals? Is it not the light of God, of whom he is an angel? God is the light and the angel of God is the angel of the light. It is not said, in fact, that he simulates the 'angel that is light', but the 'angel of light'. If the wicked angel simulates only one kind of knowledge and virtue, we could understand by this that the illumination which comes to us from God only brings us knowledge and virtue. But since the evil angel also brings an imaginary light that is different from both virtue and knowledge, then there is truly a noetic light that is true and divine, and which is different from both virtue and knowledge. The imaginary light is the Evil one himself, a shadow who imitates the light.

Whereas the true light which illumines angels and those men like unto angels, is God Himself who is truly a mysterious light, and who manifests as light and transforms to light those of pure heart. So we call Him Light, not only because He overcomes the darkness of ignorance, but also, according to Saint Maximos[171] and Gregory the Theologian,[172] because he illumines psyches. And you will understand clearly from Saint Nilus that this illumination is not only knowledge or virtue, but that it transcends all human virtue and all human knowledge. *The nous which is brought into itself,* he says, *no longer contemplates anything sensory, nor any form of thought, but only the unveiled nous and the divine radiance. From these flow peace and joy.*

Do you see this contemplation, which goes beyond all works, all manner of being, and beyond every thought? Did you hear the words of the early father who said that he saw his own nous *clothed in a celestial colour,*[173] illumined by the divine radiance? When he shows you the way that leads you to this blessed experience, and this vision, let yourself be convinced again by his teaching. *When attention seeks prayer it finds it. For if anything follows the train of attention, it is prayer, and so it must be cultivated.*[174] Those who have truly prayed, applying their nous to divine prayer, are illumined by the radiance of God. You might also consult the divine Maximos, who said: *He who has rendered his heart clean not only knows the meaning of things that are inferior to God, but he may also look on God himself.*[175]

⇥ 3.41 ⇤

Where are they, those who teach of that worldly wisdom which has been made foolish, and which not only obtains the knowledge of created things for us, but also lifts us up towards God? It is said: *When God has come to be present in the heart, He judges it good to write his own message there with the Spirit, as was done with the tablets of Moses.*[176] Where are those who think that God cannot be received within our hearts, when Paul, in front of others, said that the law of grace will be received not on tables of stone, but on tables of flesh, which is to say, written on our hearts?[177]

Similarly, the great Macarius said: *The heart directs and governs all other organs of the body. When grace endows the heart, it rules over all the members and all the thoughts. For there, in the heart, the nous abides as well as all the thoughts of the psyche and all its hopes. It is there that grace inscribes the laws of the Spirit.*[178] So let us listen again to Maximos, who in purity illumined us with knowledge and with more than knowledge: *The clean heart is one that has presented to God a nous completely empty of all forms, so that it is ready to be imprinted only by the signs of God, by which means it becomes visible.*[179] Where then are those who maintain that God can be known only through the knowledge of created things, and who refuse to know and accept the evidence which results from union? And this, which God said through one of the God-bearing fathers: *Do not enrol in the school of a man or a book, but that of My rays and My radiance within you.* How could a nous that is clean of all forms,[180] marked only by the imprint of divine signs, fail to be superior to knowledge that comes from created beings?

⇥ 3.42 ⇤

The imprinting of the nous by the divine and ineffable signs of the Spirit is very different from the apophatic theology that raises the reason[181] towards God. Theology is also far removed from the vision of God in the light; it is as different from intimate conversation with God as knowledge is different from possession. To say something about God is not equivalent to meeting God! To say something we need words, words we can articulate, and we also need skill. Unless we merely want to possess knowledge, neither using it ourselves nor communicating it to others, then we also need to provide reasons from which exact demonstrations can be made and a variety of examples gathered from the forms of the world. Nearly all of this is gathered by sight or hearing, and is drawn more or less from this world, so that the wise ones of this age can also use it without needing to purify their life and their psyche.

However, we cannot possess God within us unless we are purified by virtue to the point where we empty ourselves. We cannot associate with God in purity – and immerse ourselves in light without mixture to the limit of the possibilities of human nature – unless we rid ourselves of passions, and, turning our back on sensations and all that is sensory, ascend above thoughts and reasoning and the knowledge they procure, to abandon ourselves entirely to the immaterial and noetic activity of prayer. It is by finding the unknowing which surpasses all knowledge that we can be filled with the resplendent beauty of the Spirit, and in this we can invisibly contemplate the rewards of the nature of the immortal cosmos.

Do you understand, then, in what an abyss that much-vaunted intellectual philosophy is lost? Its basis is sensation, and its end consists of a knowledge of the different aspects of sensation, knowledge which can be found without inner purity, and which does not in itself purify anyone of passion? On the contrary, the origin of spiritual contemplation is the Good, and this is made firm by purity of life. It is also a true and authentic knowledge of created things and of reality, but it does not come from study. It comes from purity and it is the only thing that can distinguish what is truly good and useful from what is not.

The end toward which spiritual contemplation leads is the promise of the age to come, the unknowing which surpasses all knowledge, the knowledge which surpasses all thought, the secret communion in the hidden and inexpressible vision, the divine contemplation and mystical taste of eternal light.

⤜ 3.43 ⤛

If you hear and understand what I say to you, then you will know that this is truly the light of the age to come. It is the very light that illumined the disciples at the Transfiguration of Christ, and today it illumines the nous that has been purified by virtue and prayer. Dionysius the Areopagite clearly stated that in the age to come the bodies of the saints are both adorned and enlightened by the light of Christ which appeared on Tabor.[182] As Macarius the Great says: *When the psyche is united to the light of the heavenly image it is then initiated into its very substance, into the knowledge of the mysteries, while on the great day of the Resurrection, the body will also be illumined by the same heavenly image of glory.*[183]

Note that he said *in its substance* so that nobody will think that this illumination comes from knowledge and concepts. To put it differently, the substance of the spiritual man is composed of three parts; the grace of the heavenly Spirit, the reasoning psyche, and the terrestrial body. Further, Macarius says: *The deiform image of the Spirit that is now as if imprinted within us, will then give to the body itself an external deiform and heavenly character.* Furthermore: *God, reconciled with humanity, restores the psyche that has received the true faith in the joy of the lights of heaven while it is still in the body. He then illumines the noetic sense anew by the divine light of grace. Later, he will also clothe the body in glory.* He also says: *Only someone who has received them through experience is aware, through the eyes of his psyche, with what good things and what mysteries Christian psyches can commune with here below. But at the time of the resurrection the body itself can receive these good things, and see them and possess them when it becomes Spirit itself.*

Is it not clear that this is the same divine light that the apostles saw on Tabor? That this is the same light that purified psyches contemplate in our own time, and which has the same form of existence as the good things in the age to come. This is why the great Basil said that the light shining on Tabor at the time of the Transfiguration was a prelude to the glory of Christ at the time of the second coming. He says this clearly elsewhere: *The divine power appears like a divine light seen through a pane of glass, illumining those who have purified the eyes of their heart, that is to say, through the flesh which the Lord had borrowed from us.* Is this not the same light which shone on Tabor with such intensity that, obedient to His will, it allowed even the eyes of the body to perceive it, since it was visible in the hearts of all who were purified? Like a sun, it shone from the adored Body, filling them with awe and enveloping their hearts with light. *May we too find ourselves with them, contemplating the glory of the Lord with unveiled faces, as if in a mirror.* It would indeed be beautiful to invoke this saying of the great one and join together in prayer and in trust.

>‹ 3.44 ›‹

That great Light was contemplated by the pure at the Transfiguration, when it approached them in their earthly bodies and appeared to them in the flesh. But how does anyone see it today, and how is it possible to conceive it? If you wish to know, go and learn from those who see, as I too have learned from them. As David said, *I believed, that is why I have spoken.*[184] We should add what the Apostle said: *We too believe, this is why we speak.*[185]

He who has detached himself from material possessions, from human glory, and from carnal pleasure, in order to embrace life according to the Gospel;

one who is confirmed in this renunciation, submitting to those who come into their measure and stature according to Christ;[186] one who thereby sees the dispassionate, sacred and divine love flare up vividly within him – such is one who desires God above all nature, and seeks union with Him that transcends the very cosmos. Entirely possessed by that desire,[187] he finds it necessary to carefully observe the activities of the body[188] and the powers of the psyche[189] in the hope that he might find in them a way to unite himself to God. He then learns, either by himself or from experienced men, that some of these are altogether irrational, while there are other actions which, even when they contain an element of reason, cannot defend themselves well against sensations.

In as much as opinions and thoughts arise, since they come from the activity of reason, one will not be free from the centre of sensations, which is to say, from the imagination. However, one who has detached himself has the wisdom to understand that the spiritual psyche is the means by which he may attain his aim. For the Apostle also said: *The natural man does not receive the things of the Spirit.*[190] He searches thus for a life that goes beyond all this, a life which is truly noetic and not mixed with things from here below, and he listens to the words of Nilus, so wise in things divine: *Even if the nous should rise above the contemplation of corporeal nature, still it does not as yet see the perfect place of God. For it might well be engaged in the contemplation of intelligible things and share in their multiplicity.*[191] Furthermore: *Consideration of real things impress a certain form on the nous and draw one far away from God.*[192]

⇥ 3.45 ⇤

But we learn from the great Dionysius, as well as the celebrated Maximos, that our nous possesses on the one hand a power of understanding that is able to see intelligible[193] things, and on the other hand a power of union which transcends the nature of the nous, and through which it is joined to the things beyond itself.[194] The nous seeks that which is highest of what is in us, the unique, perfect, unified essence that is altogether inseparable from that which belongs to us. It is this that defines and unifies the windings of the nous, as being the form of all forms,[195] through which it possesses the certainty of rational knowledge, and which progresses, like a creature that creeps, by dividing and contracting.

In effect, the nous descends into these forms of activity, and through them, into the multiplicity of life, communicating its activity to every other faculty. Nevertheless, it has another capacity that is higher than this which the nous may access, and even be active in this sphere alone, once it separates itself from the everyday aspects of life which are unstable, ever-changing and earthbound. This is like a knight[196] who possesses a capacity which is different and higher than that which he uses for riding; so that not only when he is on the ground, but also when he is on horseback or in his chariot, he can maintain this higher activity within himself, on condition that he does not entirely lose himself in the attention needed for riding. Likewise, the nous may also enjoy a higher and more sublime activity if it is not wholly or always turned towards the world below. It is true that this is much more difficult than for the knight, for by nature the nous is linked to the body, and so entangled in the knowledge of physical forms, and in all the diversity of life here below, from which it is difficult to detach. Therefore, when the nous gives itself to its proper activity, which consists in the returning to and watching over itself, it may then transcend itself, and so be united to God.

⇥ 3.46 ⇤

This is why someone who wishes passionately to live with God flees the life that is subject to judgement. He chooses the monastic life, and is a stranger to marriage. He wishes to live without trouble or care in the sanctuary of *hesychia*, far from all intercourse with the outside world. As far as is possible, he frees his psyche from every material link and joins his nous in unceasing prayer to God. In this way he concentrates himself entirely within and finds a new and indescribable way of ascending to heaven through what we might call the intangible darkness of interior silence.

With indescribable joy, he carefully joins his nous in a silence which is absolutely simple, complete, and full of sweetness, flying beyond all creatures. Going out of himself like this and giving himself completely to God, he sees the glory of God and contemplates the divine light, which is not simply sensory but forms the holy and beloved vision enjoyed by those whose psyche and nous are without blemish. When the noetic sense is used for union with what is beyond it, the nous cannot see without this divine light, just as no bodily eye can see without the light of the senses.

⇥ 3.47 ⇤

In this way, our nous goes out of itself and unites with God, at the same time transcending itself. God also goes out of Himself and unites Himself with our nous in an act of condescension.[197] *He who is above everything and transcends all things, in a superabundance of loving care goes out of Himself, yet remains within Himself, as if drawn by our love and by our desire.*[198] In this very union, which transcends the nous, He unites Himself to us. Moreover, it is not only with us that God unites by condescending grace, but also with the heavenly angels. Again we learned this from Saint Macarius: *In His infinite kindness, the Great-One-beyond-being made himself small so that he could mingle with His noetic creatures, by which I mean with the psyches of the saints and the angels, so that through His divinity they too can participate in the immortal life.*[199] How would He not go this far in His condescension, He who humbled Himself unto the flesh, unto the flesh of death[200] – as far as death on the cross[201] – in order to lift the veil of darkness drawn over the psyche after the fall, and thus communicate His light?

⇥ 3.48 ⇤

Tremble, then, you men without faith who lead others into faithlessness, you blind who wish to lead the blind;[202] you who move so very far from God, dragging others with you; those of you who teach that God is not light, because you yourselves do not see the light. Tremble, you who not only turn your own eyes away from the light to return to darkness, but call the light 'darkness,' so making the great condescension of God become vain by this, at least as far as you are concerned! You would not be in this state if you had believed the words of the fathers, for those who do believe give evidence of a great reverence, not only for the supernatural grace, but also for graces that are open to question.

In this respect, Saint Mark says: *There is a grace which the child does not know, but which one should neither deny, since it may be true, nor accept, as it may lead to delusion.*[203] There exists, you see, a grace that is true but which is different from dogmatic truth; for what can be questionable in dogmatic truth? So there is an active and manifest grace that is beyond knowledge. Because of this, it is not good to assume that grace which has not yet been put to the test is therefore illusion. This is why the divine Nilus also counsels us to ask God to clarify phenomena of this kind. *At that moment,* he said, *pray with fervour for God Himself to enlighten you, as soon as possible, on whether a vision comes from Him, and if it does not come from Him, that He will drive the delusion far from you.*[204]

Certainly, the fathers have never hesitated to explain to us what are the signs of delusion, and what are the signs of truth. A delusion, in fact, even if it imitates the face of goodness, even if it clothes itself in colourful appearances, will not cause a good action. It will not lead us to hate the world, nor to despise the glory of men, nor to desire heavenly things, nor to repress harmful thoughts. It will not obtain for us spiritual rest, joy, peace or humility. It will not bring pleasures and passions to an end, nor put the psyche in a good disposition. All these virtues are produced by grace, while delusions have the opposite result. There are also those who, according to their great experience, have defined the particular characteristics of noetic vision, which can be recognised by the effects it produces. *By these effects,* it is said, *you will know if the noetic light that shone in your psyche comes from God or Satan; so you will not consider He who has destroyed the illusion as a deceiver, nor will you take illusion for truth.*[205]

⇥ 3.49 ⇤

In the present age, even the light that is free from illusion does not give us infallibility. *He who says that it does,* according to one of the fathers, *is in the party of the wolves.* How far they wander from the truth, those who use the excuse of human weakness to say that men who have received grace are mistaken. They do not hear the author of *The Ladder,* who says to us: *No human being, but only an angel, can avoid the mistakes that come from sin.*[206] Furthermore, *certain people discover their humility through their weaknesses, and thanks to their faults they are reconciled to the Mother of grace.*

As men, it is not angelic dispassion that we seek, but human dispassion. According to the same saint: *You will know unmistakably that it is within you when you feel an indescribable abundance of light, and an inexpressible desire for prayer.* Again: *Only the psyche which is liberated from every bad predisposition can contemplate the divine light. But many are they who possess a knowledge of the divine doctrines while they still have predispositions.* And again: *Those whose psyches are weak recognise the watch that the Lord keeps over them by other signs, while the perfect recognise it by the presence of the Spirit.* Furthermore: *Among those who are at the elementary stage, the growth of humility gives certainty that they are progressing according to God's will; for those who are midway, it is the ending of inner conflict; among the perfect, it shows in the increase and great abundance of divine light.*[207]

⇥ 3.50 ⇤

Therefore, if this noetic light does not provide knowledge, as the fathers said, but is itself knowledge, and since a great abundance of this light is proof of perfection which is pleasing to God, the life of Solomon would be more perfect and more pleasing to God than those of all the saints since the beginning of the ages, to say nothing of the Greeks we admire for the abundance of their wisdom. Yet this light also illumines certain novices, although less distinctly. It also leads to increased humility in the perfect, although this appears differently than with beginners. It is well to say that: *To the perfect, the smallest things are never trivial, while to novices, even great things are never quite perfect.* In bestowing His grace, God clearly brings to light His love of man. According to the esteemed Diadochos: *At the beginning we usually feel strongly that the psyche is illumined by its own light through grace, while in the middle of the struggle, grace generally acts within the psyche, for the most part without our recognising it.*[208] As one who truly spoke in the Spirit, Nilus, said: *The Holy Spirit takes compassion on our weakness and comes to visit us even though we are impure. If He should find our nous praying to Him out of love for the truth, He then descends upon it and dispels all the legions of thoughts and reflections that besiege it.*[209]

And Saint Macarius said: *God is good, in His Love for men, He satisfies the petitions of those who pray to Him. The divine grace sometimes comes to dwell in those who exhaust themselves in prayer, even if they have not manifested equal zeal towards the other virtues. Prayer is given to such a person in proportion to grace, in joy according to what he has asked from God, even if he lacks all the other virtues. This is not to say, however, that he should disregard these other virtues, but that, by perseverance and practice in this struggle, he strives in his heart to become obliging and obedient to God, thus seeking to acquire all the virtues. Thus, indeed, the grace of prayer granted by the Spirit will go on to bear fruit, bringing with it true humility, a real love, and the full array of virtues that he asked for at the beginning of his struggle.*[210]

→| 3.51 |←

Do you see the importance of calling on the Father? He rebuilds what is yet to be built, but does not dig up the foundations on the pretext that the walls are not yet rebuilt; nor does He knock down the walls because the roof has not been put on. He knows, in fact he understands by experience, that the kingdom of heaven is sown like a grain of mustard in us. It is the smallest of all seeds, but then it becomes so big, and so far surpasses all the powers of the psyche, that it becomes a pleasant nesting place for the birds of the sky.[211] But these people of whom you speak come to judge because they lack judgement, in their inexperience, they find themselves lacking in what could have been useful to their brothers. Impudently taking to themselves the judgement which belongs to God, they say that one person rather than another is worthy of grace, choosing any basis they like for this judgement.

But it is for God alone to designate those who are worthy of His own grace. If He Himself has welcomed a man, says the Apostle: *Who are you, you who judge the servant of another?*[212] As for us, let us then go back to the point where we began, and, adding a few more words, end this treatise, which is beginning to become over long.

→| 3.52 |←

Someone who does not believe in the great mystery of new grace, who is blind to the hope of deification, cannot disdain the pleasures of flesh, money, riches, or human glory. If he does so for a brief moment, it is immediately superseded by pride at having attained perfection, so that he falls back into the category of the impure. Someone who desires this hope, even someone who has accomplished all the good actions, seeks for a perfection that is more than perfect, and even infinite. He does not think about what he has already acquired and so he progresses in humility. He sometimes thinks of the superiority of the saints who preceded him, and at other times of the *great abundance* of divine love towards men. In sorrow he weeps and cries out, like Isaiah: *Woe to me! I am impure, I have unclean lips, for my eyes have seen the Lord Sabaoth.*[213] But this sorrow brings progress in purification, and the Lord of grace adds consolation and illumination. This is why John Climacus, who teaches from experience, says to us: *The depth of sorrow has seen consolation and purity of heart has received illumination.*[214] So it is the purified heart which receives this illumination, although even an impure heart can take in what one can say or know on the subject of God.

It is therefore evident that this illumination surpasses all words and all knowledge, whether we call it 'knowledge,' or 'noesis,' because it is the Spirit that conveys it to the nous. *It acts*, it is said, *through another form of noesis, a spiritual form that cannot be contained, even by faithful hearts, unless they have been purified by works.* This is why it is said: *Blessed are the pure in heart, for they shall see God.*[215] For God produces this vision and is Himself its object. How would they be blessed, if this vision were knowledge of a kind that the impure might possess? The one who was illumined and who gave a definition of illumination has therefore spoken well. *Illumination is not a kind of knowledge, but a hidden energy, which we see without seeing*, because the vision is not sensory, and *which we recognise without knowing,*[216] since it is known, but not by means of thought.

I could add other testimonies, but I fear even these have been offered in vain. For, according to the same saint, he who wants to describe in words the perception and action of divine illumination to those who have not experienced it, is like someone who tries to use words to describe the sweetness of honey to those who have never tasted it.[217] It is to you, however, that our words are addressed, so that you may know with certainty what is true, and so that you will know that we too agree with the words of the fathers.

The end
toward which spiritual
contemplation leads is the promise
of the age to come, the unknowing which
surpasses all knowledge, the knowledge which
surpasses all thought, the secret communion
in the hidden and inexpressible vision,
the divine contemplation
and mystical taste
of eternal
light.

COMMENTARY ON THE TRIADS

Robin Amis

COMMENTARY ON THE TRIADS

PART ONE: SPIRITUAL KNOWLEDGE

Two Kinds of Knowledge and Wisdom

Part One of the First Triad is concerned primarily with the nature of spiritual knowledge and with how this differs substantially from other forms of knowledge. Paradoxically, the kind of knowledge described is a true mystery in the classical meaning of the term, a kind of truth that, although essentially Christian, is almost entirely unknown within the churches today.

However, this ancient Christian concept of knowledge is embedded in the mindset of early Christianity. It existed in a world that believed and observed that as our state of consciousness can change, so it can bring enormous benefits not only to the changed individual, but also to the society in which one lives. Secondly, we can say that this change was intimately linked as both cause and result of a special kind of knowledge that comes from outside the sensory world, and whose presence is a characteristic of a state of consciousness which was subtly different from what is now generally known by that term. If it is put into practical use in life, this knowledge, first defined by St Paul, changes our awareness of the world, and to change the way we know the world is the same as changing the world as we experience it.

It is the existence of this kind of knowledge – its authenticity and its terms, as rigorous as those of science although quite different from the latter – which explains the power of religion during the first centuries of the church, as well as the many centuries in which it maintained its authority over the mediaeval mind. The author of the Triads touches on several factors that are important in approaching this question, focusing on the existence of two different kinds of 'wisdom'. The Greek word is *sophia*, a word of great significance in the Eastern church. The primary church in Byzantium was Agia Sophia (Holy

Wisdom) in Constantinople and the Cathedral in the centre of Thessalonika, where Palamas was Archbishop when it was the second city of the Eastern Roman Empire, has the same name. There are two forms of wisdom, says Saint Gregory, one of which attains what he describes as the aim of human life, the other 'misses the mark'.

The hesychast tradition to which Gregory belonged at one time used paradox in a very Zen-like way. As Karen Armstrong notes (in *A History of God*), Orthodoxy is rooted in mystery and paradox, rather than legalistic do's and don'ts. Palamas himself in this First Part of his work has produced a paradoxical text. It is also a text of great intellectual precision, for Palamas was trained in the philosophy of Aristotle in his youth. But paradoxically, in the Triads he uses that intellectual precision to make people aware of the dangers in the normal uses of intellect. We often regard intellect as a state of identification, as the part of the mind with which we are identified. Intellect when the mind is in this condition functions in a certain way. When we break identification, then intellect functions in a different way. It retains what it has learned, but whenever it remains free of identification it functions in integration with both the heart and the motor centre, and in relation to nous as the command centre. It is when it is in this condition that the results differ quite remarkably from those normal to western individuals. The difference in our state of mind is what we mean by a different consciousness.

This key aspect of the early wisdom teaching is virtually unknown today in the churches of the contemporary West, who now often think in a way formed not by this spiritual consciousness, but by a humanistic form of reasoning that is essentially non-Christian in its origins and style. The concept of two different kinds of knowledge is not only of practical importance, but also contains the seeds of a possible reconciliation between scientific knowledge and genuine religious knowledge. In simple terms, Palamas taught that to find salvation we have to recognise that the answers to everyday and even technical questions require one kind of knowledge, and the answers to spiritual questions require another. Palamas was not so much against all knowledge other than theological, as he was convinced of the importance of distinguishing the different methods of getting knowledge, the worldly from the spiritual, the sensory from that which is given by God. From the fact – agreed by both sides of the debate – that we cannot know God directly, the answers given by the Early Fathers differed very greatly from those given by the scholastics as represented by Barlaam. The Barlaamites asserted that we can learn about Him by studying the things He has created, which is the general view upheld by theists and western forms of Christianity.

In speaking from the tradition of the Fathers, Palamas speaks from a different perspective. He says that the rationalist answer is misleading, because in fact *we cannot describe the Good in words*. The knowledge of God, like the knowledge of the Good, is given through grace, and not in words. We will find later in the book that we can learn about God only from God Himself, by grace of the Holy Spirit. All answers that come from sensory experience in some way actually leave us uncertain, so that people who follow that path will not find the *logoi*, or divine words, in the divine Nous, which means that they will not have a correct idea of the divine words in their psyche.

This position implies that to get to God we need to recognise that we have an 'image of God' that already exists within our psyche. We might also say that there needs to be agreement between our thoughts of God and our memories of experiences confirming the existence of the divine. This is why, if we think we can discover the image of God through ordinary ways of thinking, we delude ourselves. It is beyond the range of our minds to correctly conceptualise God, so if we are to have a correct understanding of God, this must come from God Himself. When this knowledge about God and about life in God takes root in our awareness, it begins to change us. What this means is that to obtain the wisdom of God we must choose the knowledge that comes from God, and not that which comes from the world. In particular, we must choose the appropriate means to access the divine wisdom The power of reason is a created faculty and as such is suitable for enquiry into the created or sensible world; the divine wisdom is uncreated and thus inaccessible to rational enquiry, it is a wisdom revealed by grace. Palamas stands in the tradition of the Fathers, Saints and Apostles, by sharing the knowledge of how we might prepare ourselves to receive the divine wisdom, by following the process of *katharsis, theoria* and *theosis*: purification, illumination and divinisation.

The tradition taught by Palamas is, among other things, a tradition of knowledge which comes from St Paul's wisdom of God and which can be followed back to its source. This tradition is 'embodied' in seekers who have gone before us, is found in their words and even more so in their actions, and is recognisable by the way these people are subtly changed.

Palamas summarises the two sorts of wisdom as follows: *The knowledge that expects to find the image of God in worldly wisdom is false knowledge. The psyche does not become in any way like Truth itself when it obtains this worldly wisdom. As this knowledge cannot lead it to truth, the boasting of those who flatter themselves that they have learned the truth through it is futile. Such people should listen to Paul when he calls the worldly wisdom 'carnal' and speaks of it as 'the knowledge which puffs up' and as a 'nous of flesh'? How could the wisdom of the flesh provide the image of the divine to the psyche? 'Consider,' he says, 'that among those who have been called, not many are wise according to the flesh, nor are many of them mighty, nor are many of them well-born.' Noble birth does not make the psyche noble, nor does physical strength make it strong; nor does the wisdom of the flesh add any wisdom to our thinking.*

Indeed, the beginning of wisdom is to become wise enough to discern and then prefer what is practical, heavenly, and spiritual – that which comes from God, leads to God, and make as God those who acquire it – from what is useless, earthly and base.

The saints as masters of universal knowledge

Put simply, in the past there were certain people who could answer questions from a different kind of understanding. With sufficient intensity in study and practice we will actually begin to perceive differently. At this moment we begin not merely to think but to know that there are two entirely different kinds of knowledge.

One person who understood this difference and could speak from this different kind of understanding was Palamas. There have been many others in other times and other places. Further evidence for this difference in understanding comes from the early Christians who, almost two thousand years ago, described the two kinds of knowledge by the Greek words *esoterike* and *exoterike*. Exoteric knowledge is built up by study of external and observable appearances and manifestation and becomes ever more complex. As it does so, it forms divisions between one subject and another, a process that lead to specialisation. Saint Basil the Great, first of the famous Cappadocian Fathers, clearly distinguished *esoterike* or inner philosophy from the outer or *exoterike* form. Esoteric teachings are not necessarily secret, although they have often become hidden in eras when their importance was generally not understood. Their essential function was to teach people about the inner or psychological elements of their lives in order to help them obtain control over themselves and their actions.

For a very precise glimpse of the kind of theory of knowledge that might have come if the inner tradition had remained unhidden we can turn to Gregory of Nyssa, brother of St Basil the Great, whose works repeatedly touch on material more often restricted to the oral tradition. St Gregory of Nyssa, in his *Life of Moses*, wrote: *The perfection of everything that can be measured by the senses is marked off by certain definite boundaries . . . The person who looks at a cubit or at the number ten knows that its perfection consists in the fact that it has both a beginning and an end. But in the case of virtue we have learned from the Apostle that its one limit of perfection is the fact that it has no limit.*

Like virtue, inner knowledge is without limit and it is also unifying knowledge. As such, it could answer those great and vital questions of humanity. Indeed, for such questions this different kind of knowledge is not simply useful, it is necessary. Yet, even in the time of Palamas, what we just described as 'worldly knowledge' had re-emerged to challenge this inner knowledge as known through experience by the hescyhasts. From the way Palamas described such worldly knowledge we can see how closely it came in its intellectual forms to our modern way of thinking.

Palamas describes this worldly knowledge through the reported assertions of Barlaam, as follows: *We not only concern ourselves with the mysteries of nature, we measure the celestial cycles, and study the opposed motions of the stars, their conjunctions, phases, and ascendants, and consider what they mean, and we take great pride in all this. Since the inner principles of these phenomena are found in the original and creative nous of the divine, and the images of these principles exist in our psyche, we try our hardest to understand them and to overcome our ignorance about them by methods such as distinction, syllogistic reasoning and analysis. We do this because, in this life and after it, we wish to be conformed to the likeness of the Creator.* (Part One, First Question)

Thus early Christian knowledge differed from modern knowledge in its main conclusions about life. Modern thought generally supports the idea that the world 'happens' according to certain laws whose origin is unknown and has no purpose. By contrast, the early Christians believed that, since the world is created, it has a cause and a purpose. That purpose is theosis, or union with the divine, by which we become perfected. This contrasts with the ordinary view that we are bound by our nature to be imperfect. The moral implications of this difference between the two points of view is enormous, and this difference is the primary reason why the inner interpretation of Christianity is so very important in a general sense, not only for those who follow the hesychast way. In this sense, the way we think of life determines how we live, and the whole of our world rests on our resolution of the choice between these two views of reality, the religious and the scientific.

With a belief in the absolute reality of science comes all the 'baggage' of that view – belief in the emptiness, the aimlessness of things, in the paramount nature of our pettiest wishes, in the primacy of ambition over compassion and of productivity over beauty. The alternative, to rediscover the inner understanding of Christianity that was the civilising force that formed our modern world, is to restore meaning, purpose and compassion to the place in our world they have long been losing, for it was the gradual departure from that view of Christianity which was responsible for the decay of our civilisation.

1.3 A forgotten form of wisdom

There is a kind of wisdom that is only discovered by searching deep within our psyche, where it is associated with forgotten memories of those briefly glimpsed experiences of inner light which Palamas calls divine illumination. In most people today, these memories are almost entirely hidden by delusions and what the early church called passions. To bring them back to the surface, we must struggle with these obstacles.

We have within us the images of reasons which are also in the Creative Nous. So what is it that, since the beginning, has disabled these images? These 'images of reasons', (from the image of the Logos in which we are made) are obscured by the fact that we ignore them, either to the point where we become unaware of them, or to the point where they conflict with the way we have been taught to think and act. As Palamas puts it, this original image within has been devalued: *Because of sin, and also our ignorance and disregard of the commandments* and because *the passionate part of the psyche, aroused to do evil, has corrupted them, disrupting the vision of the psyche and leading it astray from the original beauty.* Man is made in the image and likeness of God (Genesis 1.27), that is, he has within him the image of God, but he must attain to the likeness of God. Although he contains the image, as he is, he is not yet a likeness of God.

Under normal conditions today we are generally motivated or 'driven' by the outside world, acting and re-acting according to external influences. This situation must be reversed if we are to attain to the likeness of God – we must open and become receptive to the inner influence of our spiritual nature. The remedy lies in obeying the law that tells us to be on our guard against sin. Sin is what creates these obstacles in the first place. According to Palamas: *If we want to keep our divine image and our knowledge of the truth intact, we must therefore abstain from sin, we must know the law and commandments by the practise of them, and we must persevere in all the virtues, and return towards God through prayer and true contemplation.*

His point is that in order to become like God, we must again become aware of the divine image within us. Christ – *the image of God in the world* – showed us how. As Christ is the icon or image of God, then the image of God within us is also Christ within us. We will only become a true likeness of the image by obeying the divine commandment: *Thou shalt love the Lord thy God with all thy heart, and with all thy soul, and with all thy mind, and with all thy strength. This is the first commandment. And the second is like, namely this, Thou shalt love thy neighbour as thyself.* (Mark 12:30-31)

A philosophy shaped by the senses will not achieve this. To keep the divine image and our memory of the truth alive in us, we must put into practice the law and the commandments, particularly the 'new commandment' of the gospel quoted above; we must therefore *persevere in all the virtues and return to God in prayer and contemplation.* Otherwise, says Palamas: *Without purity one would not be any less mad, nor any the wiser, even by studying natural philosophy from Adam to the end. Yet even if you were to know this natural philosophy, if you purify and strip away the bad habits and imperfect doctrines from your psyche, you will gain the wisdom of God, which has overcome the world. Then you will enter joyfully into eternity with 'God, the only wise one'.*

1.4 Remembrance of God

According to the hesychasts, one of the main practices that help one to attain to the likeness of God is *mneme Theou* – the practice of remembrance of God – which, to be exact, is the effort to remember the special memories of timelessness, of infinite light, of infinite joy. We forget them most of the time because we have been educated by a society which ignores them and has forgotten the inner tradition which is not only the outer form of these memories but, in some sense, the 'lost inner structure' of our civilisation.

It is only when we remember this 'different reality' that is normally hidden in our memory, a remembrance which comes from God and leads us back to God, that we can come into Christ within ourselves, and only then that we can begin what we might call 'the long walk to salvation'. Palamas comments here that the new rationalistic thought of his time – like those who today think of scientific knowledge as being the only truth – regarded the Christian way of life as derisory. *Certain people ridicule the aim recommended to Christians, on the basis that the inexpressibly good things we have been promised for the age to come are too modest a goal! Instead, they seek to introduce speculative science, which is all they know, into the church of those who practice the wisdom of Christ. They say that those who do not possess scientific knowledge are ignorant and imperfect beings; that everyone must give themselves entirely to Hellenic studies and disregard the teachings of the gospels.*

In fact, *to enter joyfully into eternity* will only become even partially possible for us when we have eliminated many of our wrong habits and false beliefs and remembered who we are. The tradition of the Fathers that Palamas represented would say that the method of rationalism is inadequate precisely in the sense that it can never lead to our spiritual salvation. The application of the rationalist method alone actually prevents our entering into the 'perfection' of Paul, who said *whoever is in Christ is perfect.*

When Palamas says that purity brings salvation, he did not mean that worldly ignorance must be eliminated, but specifically referred to ignorance about God and the divine dogmas. *If you conform to the rules prescribed by our theologians, and make your whole way of life better, you will become filled with the wisdom of God, and in this way you will become an image and likeness of God in reality. Then you will have attained perfection simply by obeying the gospel commandments. Saint Dionysius, who wrote The Ecclesiastical Hierarchy, clearly defined this conformity to the doctrine of this Hierarchy when he said: 'Divine Scripture teaches us that we will only obtain the likeness of and union with God through the most loving observance of the holy commandments and by the doing of sacred acts'.*

Palamas then goes on to say that if holiness were produced by knowledge, men of knowledge would all be saints, and adds: *If a person really could rediscover and perceive the divine image within, transform his character for the better and rid his soul of the shadows of ignorance simply through worldly education, then the wise ones of the Greeks would have been more closely conformed to God. They would have seen God better than did the fathers who came before the Law, and the prophets who were under the Law, of which most were called to this honour while they lived a simple life! Did not John, the highest peak of the prophets, spend all his life from earliest infancy in the desert? Is he not the person whom all those who abandon the world wholeheartedly follow as their model?*

1.5 Ways to salvation

The ways to salvation were first mapped out for us by knowledge coming from God, knowledge that was revealed by the prophets, in the Gospel, and has been renewed by the saints in the centuries since that time. This knowledge is eternally true, and its meaning can still be discovered within us to this day, though not by our usual ways of thinking. It was because of this fact that Christ did not teach science, but sacrifice, and so inner tradition teaches a quite different kind of knowledge. This different knowledge comes not only from that long-lost memory but also from the method of the hesychasts, who can lead us to it and reawaken it within us.

Palamas poses this question: *Why then did 'He who is before all ages', who appeared after him, and 'came into the world to bear witness to the truth', to 'renew the image' and to make it rise again to the Archetype, why did He not effect this return by worldly methods?* He tells us that we are taught to achieve this union in Christ by loving the Gospel commandment so much that we put it fully into practice in our lives. In giving us this practical knowledge of what to do, then in this way we will become open to 'a higher knowledge' experienced within us through the action of the Holy Spirit. This higher knowledge is certainly different from ordinary knowledge – it is experiential, gained through our experience of spiritual life; it does not corrupt or cause conflict or uncertainty, and so strengthens faith; such knowledge is not only intellectual, but also has emotional and spiritual content; and it leads to union with the divine.

It is through this union, says Palamas, that we will become a true image and likeness of God. This is certainly possible, even to people who have no worldly knowledge. However, before we can gain this 'knowledge from within' we have to know that it exists, how it is to be found and how we are to be made able to obtain it. This initial stage in seeking the higher kind of knowledge comes from what St Paul calls the wisdom of God, but it is not the full thing. It is taught by human beings who have the inner knowledge gained from experience, by those who have purified themselves and who have attained to the 'likeness of God', whom we call saints. It forms the inner core of Christian doctrine, which then leads us in time to direct knowing.

Was it because ordinary knowledge does not lead to salvation that instead of teaching us to study the sciences, Christ taught that we should: *Sell all that you possess, give to the poor, take up the cross, and make every effort to follow me?* By losing all that is ours in this way, we remember and rediscover what is really ours. In this is the key to all Christian spirituality, monastic and non-monastic – the need to break with the past. Our past conditions our present through our attachments to ideas, thoughts and feelings, as well as things, which form our idea of who we are and it is this which obscures the idea and reality of God. Christ, the embodiment of the *wisdom of God*, says that we should dispose of all the possessions that bind us. It is because of these that we react to worldly sensations and worldly knowledge. When we have freed ourselves from the pull of these things, we should put all our efforts into following the inner tradition, that which comes from the incarnate *wisdom of God.*

Preparation for communion

All spirituality up to this point is nothing but *preparation for communion.* This preparation may consist in prayer, worship, self-control and study – it represents a threshold in the Christian inner life. However, it is by breaking with the effects of the past in us, our self-conditioning, that we can open to the Holy Spirit and it is by this that it becomes possible for the Christian life to bear fruit in us.

It is because worldly wisdom does not lead to God that Christ came in the flesh to show us the way out. It was for this that he died on the cross – died to the flesh and then lived to be our God. In the words of St Athanasius: *God became man, that we might become god.*

All study, all prayer, all liturgy before this moment, all spiritual life leads only to this point, and leads inexorably to this point if we apply ourselves to it in patience. Although communion itself represents this point, without preparation for communion, without a real valuation of our Lord, communion is not fully fruitful. In the terms of the psychological method, this break with the past is a break with the patterns of habits laid down in us, which we habitually repeat year after year with very little change, and up to this point the path is little other than this struggle against habits. The break is sometimes made by mastering our internal reactions to external events and the opinions of others, and by giving up those ideas and feelings which we treat as 'possessions.' It can also be seen as a break with our habits, of thought, feeling and behaviour. This is no easier than giving up external possessions! And it seems that it cannot be done all-at-once, as when entering monasticism, it can only be done progressively. It is a process that involves intentional suffering, for letting go of what we are attached to is often painful.

Palamas speaks about the fact that Christ's crucifixion has led so many people to salvation by saying that it shows the foolishness of ordinary knowledge, for such knowledge has never led to salvation. We need to understand that he is not talking here of an idea, but of an experience we can recognise. For modern seekers of salvation it is important to understand this idea of the foolishness of ordinary thought, and to understand it well enough to recognise when we are faced by statements that are foolish in this sense. So the answer was not in words, but in demonstration. *For the Word of God came in the flesh. The light arose from 'He Who was made for us wisdom coming from God', for He was 'the light which gives light to every man who comes into the world.'*

And that ancient light was in some way new in the world; a memory became accessible, became a recurrent experience, became a present reality. It was only since the coming of Christ, according to the chief of the Apostles, that: *This day has dawned, and the morning star has risen in our hearts.* It is hard to be clear about the exact meaning of this, but it is perhaps best understood by saying that since the time of Christ, that same light which was experienced by the prophets of the Old Testament is now made accessible to all of us through the heart. This explains the concern of the Early Fathers, and of more recent teachers of the 'prayer of the heart', who all recommend placing the nous in the heart. To do this, we need some kind of help. Palamas describes this by saying that people need: *A special wick that will light their way out of the philosophies and knowledge of the world. This is what will lead them to the knowledge of God.* The wick, as the means of keeping the light burning, is the remembrance that Christ redeems us from the error of worldly knowledge and lights the way for us to attain our 'likeness of God.'

A way of psychological renunciation

If we are not going to become monks and nuns, or hermits, then how are we to read this instruction that we should: *Sell all that you possess, give to the poor, take up the cross, and make every effort to follow me?* There is an inner meaning to this that is a key element in the Christian teaching and its importance to non-monastics.

In the life we live now, we may not be able to 'die to life' in the ordinary monastic sense but to surely follow the teaching of our Lord, we must break the hold of the world over us in some way. This way is implied in the term 'individuality' – we must become true individuals.

The perennial approach to living a spiritual life is that we should 'die to the world', not only inwardly but outwardly, an approach that was satisfied by entry into a monastic life that provided the conditions to prevent us closing in around our own in-grown selfishness. However, few of us are able to embrace this choice. Nevertheless, there is an alternative, it is even suggested by 'monos', the Greek word for monk. In its original meaning we can understand that monos is a 'true individual', a man or woman who has a mind of their own, a properly formed and mature mind, one not formed by outside influences. This kind of mind was described by St Gregory of Nyssa in the following passage: *A good many men do not draw their conclusions from the very nature of reality, but merely consider how other men have lived before them; and so they fall completely short of an accurate judgement about reality, and take as their criterion of what is good, irrational custom instead of the watchful nous. Hence they force their way into political office and power, they make a good deal of merely external show since they are unaware of the fact that this will come to an end after this life. For custom is no sure guarantee of the future, for very often it leads us to join the goats and not the flock of sheep.* (Gregory of Nyssa, *From Glory to Glory*, p. 161)

To achieve this, it is not a matter of simply changing our external lives. Internally, each man or woman must be a true individual, each of us with a mind of our own. It is not the outside of the cup that must be made clean, says the gospel, but the inside. In addition to a spiritual awakening, we become an individual when our psyche has been inwardly transformed:

1. The true individual's thinking is based on experience gained in the effort to live spiritually.

2. The true individual's feelings have been purified of 'false emotions' – what were called the passions in the early church, and the negative emotions as they are called by more recent teaching (which are not the passions as such, but relate to them).

3. The true individual's actions are conscious and are not conditioned by past experience, they are not merely habitual.

As I understand it, this is the proper inner result of the preparation to which the early stages of monasticism are dedicated. But although inner change can be reinforced from the outside, if we can open our 'inner eye' and by its action renounce our habits of life and thought, there is also an alternative at this point in the path. The same change can be achieved inwardly while we remain almost unchanged in our outer circumstances, so that the change is almost invisible to those around us. This, the possibility of an inner or purely psychological renunciation, is the alternative to monasticism when that solution is impossible to us, as it so often is in these times. Modern man has many weaknesses, but he does have one possibility that was once open to very few men and women and now is open to larger numbers – the possibility of using self-knowledge to open ourselves further to the grace of God. This is what has been called the psychological method.

Practice of the 'Psychological Method'

Self-observation shows us what we must renounce. But self-observation is not simply a direct intentional act, it also has to be approached indirectly.

In working on ourselves to put into practice the inner renunciation of the psychological method we must discover by observation what it is that we must renounce. It is easy for me to say that I must renounce myself, must renounce my ego, but this is not only difficult to do, it is even difficult to be sure what my ego is, and how I can distinguish it from other 'parts' of me that I need to keep. Here are a few of the elements of ego that we can begin to observe: what I think I am; what I think I have; what I think I am entitled to; what I think I need, etc. But ego exists mainly because we are confused about our own nature, and this in turn is because when we enter this path we do not know ourselves. And this must be taken literally – we are not sure what it is in within us that is our true self!

Thus the psychological method offers an answer to the question of what we should renounce. It tells us that we must separate ourselves from the influence of the outside world, and it is when we do so that we shall discover and begin to form our 'true individuality'. We renounce our false self in order to find true individuality. Otherwise, in the words of Palamas, we shall: *Grow old in vain, sitting beside a smoking lamp, being told to cease purifying ourselves in stillness by the control of thoughts, and to abandon the unceasing prayer which lifts us up to God.*

1.6 The fall of the psyche

The fall of man is in one sense a fall into delusion. Every human psyche seems to undergo this fall, because when we are still young, outside influences become too strong. Few people learn to rise above them again and become true individuals. The Fathers of the church understood the fall, as described in the first chapters of Genesis, as a precise description of the imperfect state of the inner life. Palamas tells us that *we were driven out of the place of delights,* the earthly paradise, and this happened when we formed a desire for the taste of the fruit of the Tree of Knowledge.

This is the inner fruit, whose pursuit is *curiosity*! So Palamas adds: *Because we did not want to cultivate and watch over it according to the commandment, we gave ourselves up to the evil advisor, who got in there by deception and seduced us with the beauty of the knowledge of good and evil.*

When we assimilated or 'assented to' this fruit of the Tree of Knowledge we fell into a world in which our psyche was dominated by delusion. This inner version of the path of Christian renunciation has been called a psychological method. It forms the basis of certain Orthodox methods of psychotherapy. What is it that 'falls'? What we call the nous. To overcome the fall, the nous has to be freed from these delusions. Until it is freed, it will not function correctly. But many people, wishing to avoid this difficult necessity, choose to follow alternatives suggested by the pleasure-seeking dualistic mind, and instead chase after the knowledge of good and evil, the knowledge which exists in antinomies, that is, knowledge in which it appears that everything has pairs of opposites.

Rather than work on ourselves, by 'watching over our hearts' to overcome our delusions, we make value-judgements instead. One result of this is that too many of our conclusions are biased in our own favour.

1.7 Purification of the heart

We enter the School of God and begin the purification of our heart when we acquire the beginnings of the divine knowledge and so come to realise the terror of the situation. At this point our growth becomes driven by the fear of God: *'The fear of the Lord is the beginning of knowledge', it is this which brings to birth unceasing prayer to God in compunction and in fulfilment of the gospel commandments. Once reconciliation with God is re-established through prayer and fulfilment of the commandments, then fear becomes love.* It is then that: *The sorrows of prayer, transformed into joy, lead to the appearance of the flower of illumination. Then, like a perfume from this flower, knowledge of the mysteries of God is given to those who can retain it. This is education in true knowledge. One who is devoted to the love of vain philosophy, engrossed in its figures and its theories, never sees even the beginning of this, which is the fear of God.*

How can this enter the psyche? Even if it could, how would it be able to live in a psyche that is surrounded, bewitched, and enclosed by varied and conflicting arguments, at least until it says goodbye to all these things and gives itself entirely to the School of God, at last giving itself wholly to His love by following the commandment. This is why it is good that the fear of God is the beginning of wisdom and divine contemplation. This fear cannot dwell in the psyche with any other feeling, it clears them all out. Then it polishes the psyche by prayer, making it like a tablet ready to be imprinted by the gifts of the Spirit.

Although the fear of God is a gift of grace, it is our effort in prayer and renunciation that prepares us for receiving divine gifts. The first way in which people normally escape the fear of God is through forgetting themselves in physical self-indulgence, the attractions of the flesh. This happens when our animal nature makes certain aspects of this dualistic knowledge attractive to us, and binds us to it by the strength of that attraction. Rarely does this situation leave someone enough energy or time to purify their psyche. The second escape route is the search for distraction, the way in which we allow the mind to find distractions that fill our time, so that we forget the fear of God or the need to work on ourselves.

1.8 Education in true knowledge

Many of us are unaware that there is an inner form to religion that goes beyond the outer practice and is more than studying the words of others. This inner form requires personal effort. In this respect Palamas quotes the commentary of St Basil the Great on this passage from Exodus: *You are idle, you are idle, that is why you say, 'Let us go and sacrifice to the Lord'. This is a good way to take it easy, let us use it to pass the time! Indeed, the worst form of leisure is that of the Athenians, who forever passed their time in the discussion of novelties, a pastime, which some people imitate today and in doing so, spend their lives in pleasing the wicked spirits.*

Breaking our habits, particularly those of either of the two escape routes, attraction and distraction, begins to free us from our bondage to the external world. But there are very many of these bonds to be broken. The modern tendency, perhaps little known in Palamas's time, is to seek outlets to dispose of excess energy by expressing it. This is a false solution, since the expression of habitual tendencies always strengthens their hold over us. In the following passage Saint Basil lamented that he had passed the greater part of his life studying external knowledge. *As for me, I have devoted a long time to vanity and wasted nearly all my youth on the fruitless effort I gave myself in learning the sciences of a wisdom made foolish by God. But one day, as if emerging from a deep sleep, I realised the uselessness of the wisdom of the princes of this world, which came to nothing. I wept for a long time for my pitiful life, and prayed to be given instruction on what to do.*

The difficulty of the psychological method is that because the most important changes have to be made in our hearts and in our habits, and because they depend on our carrying out inner exercises, which occur silently and without movement; they cannot be learned simply by acting as other people act. This means that before we learn to carry out these exercises, we have to learn about them, that is to say that before practical work comes instruction, or theoretical study, and that will be followed by a long period when we learn to put that theory into practice. For this reason, the psychological method begins by studying the special kind of knowledge associated with Saint Paul's 'wisdom of God', and success on this way depends on our learning to put that knowledge into practice.

1.9 A true way

Since the time of Christ there has been a true Way that can be obtained by grace. It uses the divine knowledge that cannot be obtained from 'easy' external sources. Its ultimate source is within us, where it is found or formed when we strive to follow the divine commandments.

Palamas quotes the apostle James: *If any of you lacks wisdom, he should ask God, who gives to all, and it will be given to him.* Palamas also says that knowledge of this teaching is first given to us by people who have previously experienced it through their own attempts to follow the teaching, but that we will only understand it properly by discovering it within ourselves in the same way. This is why Palamas tells us that St Paul says it is not those who hear the law who shall be saved, but those who accomplish it.

Do you not see, says Palamas, *that knowledge alone achieves nothing? And why speak only of knowledge of what we should do, or of knowledge of the visible world or of the invisible? No, even a knowledge of God, Who created all this, will not achieve anything on its own.* So it is not what we think or know which will bring us to salvation, but how we live. According to St John Chrysostom: *What will we gain from the divine doctrine if we do not live a life that pleases God, the way of life which Our Lord came to cultivate on earth?*

Ordinary knowledge is without love, so it breeds pride and achieves nothing. In the words of St Paul, *knowledge puffs up, but love builds up.* And the *sensual man* (a person ruled by their passions) *does not receive the gifts of the Spirit.* This is perhaps because such a person only trusts worldly knowledge. The problem with worldly knowledge is that it is only applicable to the material and personal level of life. As Palamas, following St John, puts it, this knowledge is: *Daemonic, earthly and sensual. Therefore it does not receive the gifts of the Spirit, because it is written: 'The natural man does not receive the gifts of the Spirit.' This other wisdom regards such gifts of the Spirit as foolishness, as delusions or false judgement. It seeks to completely suppress the greater part of them, carries on an open struggle to render them in the sense of their own subjectivity and, insofar as they are able, to introduce false doctrine. It even skilfully shapes certain of these gifts to use them for its own ends, as sorcerers do with foods sweet to the taste.*

1.10 Different aims for different kinds of knowledge

Worldly knowledge is different from spiritual knowledge, it comes from the outside world, and when it provides power to achieve something, that something is in the outside world. Spiritual knowledge comes from within us, and provides power to achieve something in the spiritual world: the power to attain salvation.

Palamas describes how worldly knowledge opposes spiritual knowledge and also misleads by adopting the same terms. Those who teach this worldly knowledge – the knowledge which originates from outside us – often use the words of inner tradition to advise people to 'know yourself' or 'attend to yourself'. This happened in the time of Palamas, and it is a common feature of 'New Age' ideas today. Yet, as Palamas says, what the rationalists of his day meant by 'self-knowledge' is quite different from the meaning given it by those who have been taught by the spiritual wisdom. For example: *They teach the transmigration of the psyche, saying that you cannot know yourself and so be faithful to the teaching unless you know the body to which you were previously attached, the place where you dwelt, what you did there, and what you heard there. They say that one learns these things through obedience to the evil spirit, who deceptively whispers such things to us in secret! This, then, is where they with their 'Know yourself' lead those who cannot clearly perceive the deception and so think that they speak just as our fathers spoke!*

All human beings possess a faculty for which we have already used the classical Greek name of nous. But correct information, if not correctly understood by the nous, is spiritually dead; it can only be understood by the inmost heart of those who are spiritually mature. Such an individual contains a nous that is so different from what is normal today that it can be regarded as a different kind of nous, a nous of purity, clarity, subtlety and transparency, which the Fathers described as *the nous of Christ.*

1.11 Worldly knowledge is no help on the way to salvation

The next short chapter is again entirely about the fact that worldly knowledge is of no value in the pursuit of salvation, a theme Palamas repeats throughout the book. As he puts it, for those on the spiritual quest knowledge of worldly matters is useful only to teach us what to ignore! In this chapter he tells us that: *When we hear these Hellenists saying pious words, we do not think that they venerate God. We do not number them among our teachers, because we know they have stolen these words of ours. This is why one of them said about Plato: 'Who is Plato, if not Moses speaking in Greek?' So we know that if they have something beneficial, they have obtained it from us without fully understanding it. On examination, we also understand that they give it a different meaning. And if one of the fathers says the same thing as one of these worldly men, the similarity is only in the words. The meanings are quite different.*

Palamas then says that those who follow the path that he represents may possess *the nous of Christ*, and that those who follow the path of worldly wisdom *express human reasoning*. In the words of the Lord, as given by the prophet Isaiah: *As far as the heavens are far from the earth, so far is my thought from yours.* In summary, James is quoted: *Every good and perfect gift is from on high, coming down from the Father of lights.*

1.12 The foolishness of the world

So it is that when Palamas was writing, over six hundred years ago, he described how a rational or scientific education is 'made foolish' simply in the sense that it is unable to bring people to God. It does not answer every question!

It should be clear by now that what Palamas meant was that the emphasis on rational forms of thinking and education that were taking shape in his time were unable to bring people to God. Wherever and whenever the shift to Rationalism occurred, the churches began to change. This change occurred as they lost their experiential grasp on their faith and the process continues to this day. Modern methods which educate people simply for economic reasons, to make them 'better workers,' more able to work in the new technologies, take everyday thought further and further from the world-view taught by Christ. And in the words of Palamas, all that sets itself against the Light 'becomes darkness'.

As for me, I would also say that noetic things are not weakened by one another, and I would add that all beautiful things see their own beauty strengthened by the appearance of the higher Beauty. How could this not be so, now that very Power, the Source of Beauty, has appeared? We will not say that the 'second lights,' by which I mean those natures that are above this world, have been made useless by the first Light Who illuminates them. Nor will we say that our reason and our intelligence, although very much lower than those lights, but lights nevertheless, have become darkness on the appearance of the divine light, since this has come 'to light every man who comes into the world.' But whoever opposes this Light, be they angel or man, becomes darkness, because he separates from it by his own free will and so finds himself abandoned by the Light.

1.13 Old and New Testaments

One purpose of the Old Testament was to provide advance information of the New. Once that grace appeared on earth in the form of Christ's incarnation, that original purpose no longer applied; now the Old Testament symbolically confirms the New.

Palamas tells us that it was by opposing what Saint Paul called the wisdom of God – by trying to put forward an external answer to the question of how people might obtain what the church called salvation – that what he called the wisdom of the world became folly. *It was necessary that this wisdom was there, not to be made foolish, but to be accomplished according to the ancient Law. Paul wrote about this: 'Do we thus abolish the Law? Never! On the contrary, we confirm the Law.' The Lord invites us to look closely at this, for it contains eternal life. He also said: 'If you had believed Moses, you would have believed in me.' Do you see the extraordinary agreement of the Law with grace? For this reason, when the true light appeared, the Law became still better, because its hidden beauty was revealed.*

Palamas adds that the influence of Hellenistic rationalism turns *the scriptures of the Spirit against the Spirit, against spiritual works, and against spiritual men.* Palamas continues this argument into the next section, which begins by saying: *The foolish philosophy of the worldly wise neither comprehends nor reveals the wisdom of God. How could it be otherwise, when 'the world did not know God by it?'*

1.14 The supernatural peace in us is given by Christ alone

The tradition which has reached us from the Holy Fathers is wiser than that which is founded on rational argument. It is demonstrated by works, instead of being proven by words. By putting its ideas into practice we learn the meaning of the doctrine. By observing the results of this, we confirm its validity. These are the 'scientific criteria' of the interior science of the early church. Because they are only accessible to individuals, and not to collective demonstration, they tend to be undervalued in our times.

The supernatural Peace in us is granted by Christ alone, says Palamas, telling us that the knowledge that leads to that peace is knowledge from God, which, as we have already seen, is different from the knowledge that comes from the world. In this regard, St Paul said: *Knowing God, they did not glorify Him as God.* Palamas goes on to say: *If they have come to conceive of God, they have done so in a way that is not appropriate to God. They have not worshipped Him as the Creator of all things, as the Almighty, as the one whose vision extends over all, or as the unique Being, without beginning and uncreated.* Palamas sums up: *All those who have not only received these traditions but have also reaped their fruits by experience really know in themselves that 'the foolishness of God is wiser than men'.* So only practical experience reveals the differences between the two kinds of knowledge. This is the 'first proof' that the worldly wisdom is misleading.

This First Part is thus concerned with distinguishing the different methods of getting knowledge, the worldly from the spiritual, the sensory from that which is given by God. This is referenced later, in Part Three, when Palamas quotes Saint Basil the Great: *Truth has two forms. There is one that it is absolutely necessary to possess and to communicate to others, as it contributes to our salvation. Regarding the earth and the sea, the sky, and all that is in them, even if we do not know the truth about these things, this is nothing that will prevent us from acquiring the promised beatitude.* (Triad 3.14) Palamas also sets out the goal of spiritual knowledge in terms of receiving the gifts of God: *The aim before us is God's promise of good things to come: adoption, deification, revelation, the possession and enjoyment of heavenly treasures. As to the knowledge that comes from exterior education, we know that it shares the fate of the present age. For if the words of the senses were able to establish the reality of the age to come, the wise men of this age would become heirs to the kingdom of heaven. But according to the true philosopher Maximos: 'If it is the purity of the soul which sees, then those wise ones are far from the knowledge of God.' What need have we of knowledge that does not bring us closer to God? How could we possibly acquire perfection and holiness without it?* (Triad 3.14)

1.15 The origins of folly

Reason which turns against the Spirit does not come from the 'wisdom of God,' says Palamas: *The power of that 'reason rendered foolish and non-existent' wages war against those who accept these traditions in simplicity of heart and so it mistakes the words of the Spirit, as in the example of men who neglect them and so have set creation against the Creator. It turns against the mysterious activities of the Spirit, which acts better than reason in those who live according to the Spirit, and attacks the Spirit by attacking such men.* At this point Palamas speaks about such people being inspired by daemons, instead of by God. This term clearly links with classical Greek thought, in which 'daemons' refers to 'spirits', so that translations which render the word 'daemons' by the modern English 'demons' are in a sense misleading. To be clear, this passage is careful to identify the sources of inspiration and is not a criticism of inspiration as such.

1.16 The wisdom of God not given to fools

The wisdom of God does not take root in a psyche that is cunning and/or is influenced from outside. The two things are incompatible. Palamas quotes Solomon: *A holy and disciplined spirit will flee from deceit, and will rise and depart from foolish thoughts.* He then continues: *What we say now is not said about philosophy in general, but only about the philosophy of such people. If in fact, according to Paul, we cannot at the same time 'drink the cup of the Lord and the cup of the daemons,' how could someone possess the wisdom of God and still be inspired by daemons? That is not possible, absolutely not! And if, as Paul said elsewhere that 'in the wisdom of God, the world did not know God' then be careful! It is not the wisdom of these unwise sages that he has named 'the wisdom of God', but the wisdom that the Creator breathed into creatures.*

1.17 The two wisdoms conflict and lead to different results

The criterion of true wisdom is that it enables ascension to God. The true philosopher is the person who possesses the wisdom of God, through which he may ascend to God. The philosopher who is not true has *a false imitation of true wisdom.* Such wisdom, says Palamas, is: *The negation of all wisdom. And how could we name the negation of wisdom the 'wisdom of God?' Besides, the daemonic nous is a good thing inasmuch as it is nous, but becomes bad whenever it is misused. While it is better than us at knowing the measurements of the world, the orbits, conjunctions, and definitions of moving bodies, it is a nous without nous, full of darkness, since it does not use its knowledge in a way that pleases God.*

In the same way, the Hellenic wisdom thinks it can base itself on the wisdom of God found in created things ... But it does not see that everything always has an origin! It therefore turns aside from the veneration of the true God. According to Dionysius the Great, it 'makes unholy use of godly things to attack God,' and so becomes a foolish and senseless wisdom. How could this be the wisdom of God?

This is why Paul shows us that wisdom has two forms. He says: 'In the wisdom of God, the world has not known God through wisdom.' Do you not see that he spoke on the one hand of wisdom which is of God, and on the other, simply of wisdom, which causes ignorance of God? This last is what the Greeks discovered. It is different from that of God, and is demonstrated by the double use of the word 'wisdom'. What does this sage of God say further on? 'We teach the wisdom of God.' Palamas again quotes St Paul, to demonstrate that this doctrine and the general run of Hellenistic thought excludes any agreement. *'We speak wisdom among them that are perfect; yet not the wisdom of this world, nor of the princes of this age, that come to naught'. This is a wisdom 'which none of the princes of this world have known'. This latter wisdom is found in us in Christ Jesus, 'who has been made by God for our wisdom'.*

1.18 Seeking with the senses makes us blind in the soul

Those who seek God with their senses misunderstand the nature of spiritual reality, although they may handle practical truths very well. This misunderstanding often makes them unconscious in their hearts. *By examining the nature of the objects of sense perception, these people have arrived at a certain concept of God, but not at an understanding truly worthy of Him and appropriate to His blessed nature. For their 'foolish heart was darkened' by the hideous intrigues of wicked daemons who passed on their teachings to them. Indeed, if a correct concept of God had appeared in the thought of these philosophers, how would they have believed it when the daemons presented their polytheistic teaching?* This relates to the Gospel teaching: *A good tree is not able to bear bad fruits, nor a bad tree to bear good fruits.* (Matthew 7:18, Luke 6:43)

Palamas sums up the ways in which the Christian view differs from that of the Hellenists by saying: *Paul sometimes speaks of this wisdom as 'human wisdom', as when he says, 'My preaching does not rest on the persuasive words of human wisdom'. And again, 'We do not speak in words which teach human wisdom'. But he also thinks it right to call those who have acquired this wisdom 'wise men according to the flesh' or 'wise men become fools', 'the disputants of this age' and their wisdom is qualified by him in similar terms: it is 'wisdom become folly', the 'wisdom which has been done away', 'empty deceit', the 'wisdom of this age,' and it belongs to the 'princes of this age, who are coming to an end'.*

1.19 The feeding of the psyche

The body needs to be fed from the outside world, but the psyche needs to be fed from the spiritual world through the nous. When the nous and psyche feed on the outside world, this means that they obtain their satisfactions from outside, which will trap them in the material and transient world. *For myself, I listen to the father who says, 'Woe to the body which does not get food from outside itself, and woe to the psyche which does not receive grace from above itself.' For the body will perish once it has been turned into a lifeless being and the psyche will be caught up with daemonic life and daemonic thoughts when it turns away from what is proper to it.*

It is the aim and use of philosophy that makes it wise or foolish, not philosophy itself. *But if someone says that philosophy, in the sense that it is natural, is a gift from God, then they speak the truth, without contradicting us. However, this does not lighten the accusation that weighs on those who misuse philosophy and lower it to an aim that is against its nature. For they make their own condemnation even heavier when they use God's gift in a way that is not pleasing to God. Even the nous of daemons was created by God, and so it naturally has understanding, but we do not hold that its activity comes from God, even if the possibility of action comes from Him. Therefore one can properly call that kind of reasoning unreasonable.*

Palamas notes that nothing is evil in itself; evil comes when something is turned aside from its real purpose. *Hellenic wisdom is 'daemonic' because it arouses quarrels and contains almost every kind of false teaching, and because it is alienated from its appropriate aim, that is, from the knowledge of God. At the same time we recognise that, even in this state, it may participate in the good in a remote and indistinct manner. We should remember that nothing evil is evil because it exists, but only when it deviates from the activity appropriate to it, and so from the aim belonging to that activity.*

1.20 Discernment leads to understanding

We have to learn to 'divide' things correctly, not only distinguishing between things, but also distinguishing between right and wrong purposes for which they may be used. Correctly dividing in this way, exercising discrimination, gives understanding. This idea of 'dividing' occurs frequently in early Christian thought. Christ in the gospel asks: *Who appointed me judge or a divider over you?* (Luke 12:14) The liturgy of St John Chrysostom prays for all bishops *who rightly divide the word of truth.* To explain this concept, Palamas uses an analogy which he refers to several times in the first volume of the Triads, that of the use of snake venom as an antidote for snakebite. In this instance he notes how what is used to cure may also be used to harm in order to illustrate the need for discrimination, the need to *divide correctly.*

There is great therapeutic value in substances obtained from the flesh of serpents, so doctors consider that the antidote drawn from them has no equal. Yet when poison is prepared with deceitful purpose, the sweetest food is used to hide its deadly nature. Likewise, there is some benefit to be had even from the words of the worldly wise, the same as there is in a mixture of honey and hemlock. But those who seek to separate the honey from the mixture must take care that they do not drink the deadly residue by mistake. If you examine the problem, you will see that most of the harmful heresies originate in this way. This is what happened with those who make an icon of knowledge, the 'iconognosts', who claim that man receives the image of God as knowledge, and that it is this knowledge that conforms the psyche to God. But, as it was said to Cain: 'If you make your offering correctly, without dividing correctly ...' Very few are able to divide well and one may only divide well when the sense of the psyche is trained to discern good from evil.

The practice of discernment

If we divide correctly, then we will understand, and only when we understand will *hope in God liberate us from all care*, says Palamas. Dividing depends on discernment – *diakrisis* in Greek. Saint Anthony the Great, regarded as the founder of Christian monasticism, said this about this process of distinguishing between that which feeds the heart and that which simply links us to external life: *The nous then starts to discriminate between the body and the psyche, as it begins to learn from the Spirit how to purify both by repentance. And, taught by the Spirit, the nous becomes our guide to the labours of body and psyche, showing us how to purify them.* (First Letter of St Anthony the Great)

We should try to understand what this means in terms of inner experience. What happens is that with certain inner practices the light in the inner mind or nous grows brighter. If this happens to you, you will find that as it does so you begin to become directly aware of the difference between, on the one side, the body and all its activities, and on the other, the activities of the psyche – thoughts, feelings, sensations and active impulses. Then, as this watching continues, you will begin to get intimations about how to act, in body and mind, in such a way as to purify the busy modern psyche.

Saint Anthony continued: *The nous separates us from all the fruits of our animal life which have been mingled with all the members of the body since the first transgression, and brings back each of the members of the body to its original condition, having nothing in it from the spirit of Satan.* The process continues just as Saint Anthony describes when we begin to be aware of activities –

desires and memories of desires – that originate not from the psyche itself but from our body. It is only now, 'with new eyes', that we begin to see that over the years these desires have become compulsions (the spirit of Satan), which is to say that we have become slaves to these desires so that they reduce us to something far less than our full human potential. This awareness, in its purifying action, slowly separates out this silent inner eye, the nous, from all the activity around it, so that for increasing periods it looks on all this activity while remaining unmoved. After long periods of this separation of the nous, the compulsions of the body begin to fall away, and the once-fallen psyche becomes once again a simple reflector of realities.

The serpent analogy carries the idea that the distinctions by which we must divide things are between those that prolong life and those which bring death, and that this distinction applies not only to physical substances but also to knowledge. However: *If you make your offering correctly, without dividing correctly* ... So then Palamas adds: *But why do we need to run these dangers in vain, when it is possible to contemplate the wisdom of God in his creatures not only without danger, but with profit?*

There is a knowledge that kills, and a knowledge that gives life. For those who divide correctly there is hope, and the hope introduced by St Paul unlocks the door to spiritual understanding so that in this state the psyche is led naturally to understand all created things. This creates in the psyche a love that leads it towards its Maker, and then *it finds treasures which cannot be expressed in words*. Then, using prayer as a key, it penetrates with this into mysteries of which St Paul said: *Eye has not seen, ear has not heard, and which have not entered into the heart of man.* St Paul teaches that these mysteries are revealed by the Spirit alone to those who are prepared.

1.21 To divide is to recognise

Correct division will enable us to eliminate all wrong assumptions about ourselves and the world in which we live. The analogy of using the serpent's poison as a medicine has certain implications, which Palamas now develops. *Do you see which is the shortest way that now leads us with least danger and most profit to these supernatural and heavenly treasures?* To find God through worldly science, we first have to remove all wrong assumptions: *If you begin with worldly wisdom, it is first necessary to kill the serpent after overcoming the pride that comes to you from this wisdom. How difficult this is! No wonder it is said that 'the arrogance of philosophy has nothing in common with humility'. After you have overcome this, you must separate and throw away the head and tail, for these extremities are evil in the highest degree. By the head, I mean manifestly wrong opinions concerning things noetic, divine, and primordial. By the tail, I mean illusions about created things. As to what lies between, that is, discourses on nature, you must separate out the harmful ideas from these by using the abilities of critical analysis and observation belonging to your psyche, just as pharmacists purify the flesh of serpents with fire and water. However, to do all this, and make good use of what has been properly set aside, much effort and much judgment will be required!*

So he distinguishes the two kinds of knowledge according to their origin, by what means and from which source they are obtained. The first kind of knowledge, obtained from worldly education, is natural to us and available to almost everyone. But this kind of knowledge must be obtained by effort and exercise, it is not a gift of grace. *Nevertheless,* says Palamas, *if you put to good use that part of the secular wisdom which has been clearly separated from the rest, no harm can result, for now by its nature it will have become an instrument for good. Even so, it cannot in the strict sense be called a gift of God and a spiritual thing, for it is derived from the order of nature. It is not sent from on high. This is why Paul, who is wise concerning all things divine, calls it 'carnal', saying: 'Consider that among us who have been chosen, there are not many of us who are wise according to the flesh.' Who could make better use of this wisdom than those whom Paul calls 'externally wise'? But even though they have this wisdom in their nous, he calls them 'wise according to the flesh'.*

In the effort to overcome pride, we must then eliminate in ourselves wrong opinions about our own minds, as well as our illusions about created things.

1.22 Only the inner wisdom purifies the psyche

In conclusion to Part One Palamas states that it is not knowledge of the exterior sciences that brings salvation, purifies the cognitive faculty of the psyche and makes it a likeness of the divine Archetype. These are instead the fruits that are gained when the sacred wisdom transforms the psyche. He then uses the analogy of marriage. Just as the pleasure of sex is a result of our nature, and not a gift of grace, so worldly wisdom is the result of effort, it is not a gift from God. *In lawful marriage, the pleasure whose aim is procreation cannot truly be called a gift of God, because it is physical and given us by nature, not by grace, even though that nature has been created by God. In the same way, the knowledge derived from exterior education, even if it is used well, is a gift of nature and not of grace; it is given by God to everyone without exception. It is part of our nature, and we can develop it by practice. This last point, that nobody acquires it without effort and practice, is evident proof that it is a natural and not a spiritual gift.*

But, he reiterates, there is another wisdom that is a gift from God and it is this which makes human beings godlike. *It is our sacred wisdom that is properly called a gift of God, it is not a gift of nature. Even simple fishermen who receive this wisdom from on high become, as Gregory the Theologian says, 'sons of Thunder', whose word encompasses the very bounds of the universe.* Palamas concludes: *If a man who turns toward the prescriptions of the law to seek purification gets no help from Christ, even though the Law has clearly been given by God, then neither will learning the worldly sciences help. Then will it not also be true that Christ will be of no help to someone who turns to the rejected philosophy of the worldly men to gain purification for his psyche? It is Paul, the spokesman of Christ, who tells us this and bears witness to it.*

PART TWO: SPIRITUAL PRACTICE

Spiritual Disciplines of the Early Church

The second part of Book One focuses on the nature and practice of watchfulness, the second of the three main stages of the Christian spiritual path (self-control, watchfulness and love) each of which might be regarded as separate disciplines. It lays the foundation of a technically exact description of the ancient Christian spiritual discipline and gives the reasons for a system of practices that for long before the time of Palamas had also included the traditional Prayer of the Heart. This is still taught today in more or less the same form, mainly by monastics of the Orthodox Church, and was once described to me by the Abbot of one of their communities as 'the principal export of Mount Athos'. These exercises, which include physical posture as well as 'noetic prayer' or prayer of the heart, can be looked at in one sense as the equivalent in the inner dimension of everyday work in the outside world.

They form what at first sight is a direct equivalent of those Indian Yogas that lead to God Realisation, but in fact this method is very different from any of the Indian methods now widely taught in the West. In most forms of Yoga, the primary effort is one of individual discipline – for instance the Raja Yoga of Patanjali begins by sorting out external life, then progresses to dealing with the body, then the mind, a process in which the effort of the pupil appears to be the major element. On the other hand, the ancient Christian disciplines often emphasise that the effort begins from the nous, then to the heart as a kind of dialogue in which the Spirit calls to the heart of the individual, and to which heart has to waken and respond.

The process in each case is apparently similar, but the aim and means are different. It appears that all Christian methods are centred on the heart. This part of the Book One describes how, by directing the nous back into the heart, the God-seeker must progressively take up the reins of the psyche, and it is this process that appears so much like the disciplines used in Yoga. The process even passes through similar phases, leading eventually to the awakening of a form of what is known in the Western churches as infused contemplation, in which the action of the nous and the connection with the Spirit feeds the heart, informs it, and takes command of it in order to complete the individual's transformation, so that we can say with David: *The shadows are no longer dark, thanks to you, and night for me will be as clear as day now that you have taken possession of my reins.* (Psalm 139:12)

Taking control of attention

In all practical methods of spirituality, attention is a key aspect. One of the key accusations against the hesychasts who Palamas sought to defend in these Triads was about whether those who seek God should keep their attention outside or inside their bodies. For those who follow this tradition, the answer to this question is quite definite: they must as far as possible keep it *inside* the body, but this is not so simple and it is difficult even to understand its full experiential implication. So this second, and shortest, of the three sections of Book One is mainly concerned with the most important of the Christian methods of using attention in the spiritual life. What this boils down to is a quite surprisingly sophisticated 'psychology of attention' which certainly seems in many ways new to modern thought and which is likely, when fully understood, to have novel therapeutic applications.

The essence of this 'psychology of attention', as we will discover later, is that when attention is held within the body, the activity of the psyche is reduced, the wasteful use of energy normal to the psyche is controlled, and the state of the psyche and of the nous within it is improved.

If someone is not convinced by the saints, he now asks, *how would they not also reject the God of the saints?* He reminds us that it was that Jesus who said to the Apostles, as they in turn said to the saints who followed them, that *he who rejects you rejects me.* That is, such a person rejects truth itself. And how, he asks, should those who reject the truth reach agreement with those who seek the truth? Palamas then summarises, through the words of his questioner, what the rationalists had been saying against the belief of the hesychasts – that the attention of the nous should be held in the body. *These people say, in effect, that we are wrong when we wish to confine our nous within our body. Instead, they say, we must at all costs shift it out of our body. They severely criticise some of our people and write against them, under the pretext that our people encourage beginners to look into themselves and to introduce their nous into themselves by means of breathing practices. They say that the nous is not separate from the psyche, so how can we bring into ourselves something that is not separate from us but is part of our psyche? Then they add that these friends of ours speak of introducing divine grace into themselves through the nostrils.*

So Palamas attempts in this part of the book to answer the question that follows the previous statement, which is: *Why do we try so hard to bring our nous into ourselves? Why do we not think that it is wrong to confine it in our body?* His answer to this question contains several different key facts about the Christian's relationship to the body: the body can be transformed and made spiritual, and that then it becomes a suitable and even necessary vehicle for the spirit and for spiritual life; this transformation of the body occurs as a part of true contemplative prayer, and the transformed body is a proper support for that prayer; the transformation of the body depends on bringing the attention of the nous into our bodies and thus into the psyche; self-control is the means by which the attention of the nous is brought into the body – control that is first exercised over the body, then over the thoughts and feelings, finally leading to love.

2.1 The body as the temple of the Spirit

The first practical key Palamas introduces is that it is appropriate for the human nous to live within the body. What he means by this is that the focus of our attention must be withheld from the outside world and as far as possible held back from external activity. This state is very difficult to attain even briefly, but when attained, is quite remarkable in its effects.

Palamas begins this answer to the question by quoting several passages from the Gospel. Our bodies are: *The temple of the Holy Spirit which is in us*, and again: *Ye are the temple of God.* He adds that God Himself says: *I will dwell in them, and I will walk in them, and I will be their God.* Palamas gives several reasons why the nous should be withdrawn into the physical body. To understand these reasons we need to change the way in which we think about our bodies. The body is not 'myself', not 'I', but a vehicle or 'temple'. The purpose of our bodies is to be the 'temple of the spirit', the vehicle of the divine.

If we think of the body in this way, it is no longer something that ties us to the earth. Palamas argues elsewhere: *When He was on earth, Christ dwelt in a human body, which is to say that God Himself lived in this 'house of flesh'. So the body is not evil in its nature.* However, it can behave in either way, good or evil, depending on 'who' inhabits it – depending on our attitude to it. If this is so, he poses the question: *Why should anybody who, in possessing a nous, think it improper to bring their nous into a body whose very nature it is to be the dwelling place of God? How then would God have caused the nous to inhabit the body in the first place? Was He also wrong? The truth is, brother, that these words apply more properly to those heretics who claim that the body is an evil thing made by the Wicked One.*

Palamas's thinking is in line with St Paul, who argues that psychologically it is how we think about the body which is important. It is this which determines whether our relation to the body is unnatural or debased, natural and depending on the psyche, or supra-natural and spiritual.

Three levels of relating to the body

1. **Unnatural:** Our thoughts and feelings concerning the body are unnatural when they come from outside us and out of the dead past, as Palamas has expressed in the paragraph where he quotes St Paul about the 'body of death.' *It is those who speak the language of here below who will fall, those who say falsely that the words and life of heaven are just like those on earth. For if the Apostle, too, calls the body 'death,' – in fact, he said: 'Who will deliver me from this body of death?' – it is because material and corporeal thought really takes its form from the body. Accordingly, to contrast it with spiritual and divine thinking, he rightly calls it 'body', and not simply body, but 'body of death'. A little earlier he had shown more clearly that he does not accuse the flesh itself, but that sinful desire which overcame it later because of the fall. 'I am sold to sin' he says; but he who is sold is not a slave by nature. And again: 'I know that what is good does not dwell in me, that is, not in my flesh'. He does not say, do you see, that it is the flesh which is evil, but what dwells in it. What is evil is not the fact that the nous lives in our body, but an evil power, 'the law which is in our members, which struggles against the law of my nous'.*

The practical inner sense of this is that when our thoughts about the body come from the outside world, they can very easily evoke in us imaginings about our body and its pleasures. These imaginings can lead to us subordinating our lives to biological law and it is through such imaginings that we are then 'sold to sin.' As I understand it, this is important because it means that we do not do what God created us to do and, among other things, this means we will not achieve salvation.

2. Natural: Our attitude to the body is natural when it is no longer shaped by external influences or internally subject to such imaginings that go beyond the normal physical needs of the body. We can learn to distinguish clearly these two influences, but at first it is not easy to do so.

3. Supra-natural: The body transcends its ordinary nature when, having returned to our natural state, we respond fully through our nous to the divine presence. The practices of hesychasm lead precisely to this transformation. *This is why those who joined to God with their life cry out to God, with David: 'My soul thirsteth for thee, my flesh longeth for thee,' and 'my heart and my flesh rejoice in the living God.' And with Isaiah: 'My bowels shall sound like a harp for Moab, and thou hast renewed my inward parts as a bronze wall,' and also, 'We have conceived, O Lord, because of thy fear, and have been in pain, and have brought forth the breath of thy salvation.'*

2.2 Bringing attention into our inner life

The method is to establish the authority of the nous within our body, and then within our psyche, in order to obtain control over all actions which originate with us. According to Palamas, we are to establish this authority over the powers of the psyche in the threefold form of self-control, purification and watchfulness.

To overcome this 'law of sin', (that law *which is in our members, which struggles against the law of my mind,* as St Paul calls it) *we expel it from the body, and in its place we introduce supervision by the nous.* That is, we must bring our attention into our body in order to establish authority over what occurs within it and what comes from it. *By this authority we bring each power of the psyche, and every member of the body which will respond to it, under the rule of the nous.*

What is meant by the term 'law' in this translation? This meaning is not the same as the idea of a scientific law, nor the modern English sense of statute or rule. This use of the word is actually older than that, it is taken from St Paul, in Chapter 7 of Romans: *We know that the Law is spiritual, but that I am of the flesh, being sold to sin. For I do not know what I am doing, and I do not do what I wish; but I do what I hate to do. Now if I do what I do not want, I agree with the Law, that it is good. So now it is no longer I who do it, but sin that dwells within me.* (Romans 7:14-18) The Greek word for law is *nomos.* The law of the spirit is one authority, the law of sin is another, and *no man can serve two masters.* When we are obedient to one law we disobey the other.

Self-control

The monastics purify their bodies by self-control that prevents uncontrolled reactions to externals. So Palamas could write: *For the senses, we determine the object and the limits of their actions. This work of the law is called 'self-control.'* Those working with the psychological method cannot always turn their attention away from the world, so they must not only notice these reactions occurring within themselves, but also guard their responses to them by guarding their thoughts, a process which has to be learned over time.

Purification

We transform our will and our desires by the purification of the emotions, returning each of them to its basic state, which is love, so that: *For the passionate part of the psyche we achieve the best state of being, which bears the name 'love'.* The psychological method provides a number of powerful means for this process, not the least being the prayer of the heart, the transformation of emotion, and the purification of sexuality. We should add that this idea of purification is not the same as elimination of sexuality, although it takes this form for true monastics.

Watchfulness

We purify our nous by alternating attentive work and attentive prayer. Much of the effort in the early stages of prayer is to bring our thoughts back to prayer as a task. For those working with the psychological method in particular, the same process can be brought into any attentive work. *We also improve the rational part by eliminating all that prevents the thoughts from turning towards God. That part of the law we name 'watchfulness'.* Palamas now tells us: *So one who has purified his body by self-control, one who by divine love has made his wilfulness and his desires a means of virtue, one who presents to God a nous purified by prayer, that one receives and sees in himself the grace promised to those whose hearts are pure. He can then say with Paul, 'for God, who commanded the light to shine out of darkness, hath shined in our hearts, to give the light of the knowledge of the glory of God in the face of Jesus Christ'.* But then he says: *We have this treasure in earthen vessels. Consequently, in order to know the glory of the Holy Spirit, we carry the light of the Father, in the person of Jesus Christ, in earthen vessels, that is to say, in our bodies. So will we lack nobility of nous if we too keep our own nous within the body? Who could argue with this, save a man who is spiritually asleep and whose nous is without divine grace?*

2.3 The eye of the psyche or eye of the heart

The psyche is one says Palamas. It uses the body as its vehicle and it has many powers. One of these powers is the nous. The nous is known as the *eye of the heart* or the *eye of the psyche*, often translated the eye of the soul. Our nous is normally dispersed in its response to sensations. To practise watchfulness, we first have to gather and unify the nous in the heart, the primary organ of the psyche and which is also the seat of the thoughts.

Palamas tells us that he knows 'by exact experience' that: *Our reason is not inside us, as if in a container, because it is incorporeal, nor is it outside us, because it is part of us; it is in the heart, as if in its organ. We do not learn this from a man, but from the very Creator of man, who taught that 'it is not what enters, but what comes out of the mouth, that defiles a man', and He also said: 'For it is from the heart that evil thoughts come.'*

The heart, says Palamas: *Is the seat of reason, and the primary organ of the power of nous.* Consequently: *As long as we seek to monitor and rectify our reason by strict watchfulness, how else would we watch it, if we do not gather our nous back within – scattered without as it is by the senses? How could we monitor our reason, if we did not bring it back to the interior of this same heart that is the seat of our thoughts?* This 'inmost heart' is: *The governing organ and the throne of grace.* Palamas quotes Macarius in this respect. *For the heart governs and reigns over the whole bodily organism, and when grace possesses the ranges of the heart, it reigns over all the members and the thoughts. For there, in the heart, is the nous, and all the faculties of the soul.*

The attention of the nous must be drawn back into this control centre. To prepare for this, it is absolutely necessary to change the situation of the nous in the following way: by overcoming dispersion, to gather it into a unity after it has been dispersed; by withdrawing attention from the activity of the senses, bringing the nous into and holding it within the body; by withdrawing the attention into the deepest part of ourselves, *where we find the nous and all the thoughts of the psyche, that is to say, in the heart*; and to maintain attention in total stillness so that the nous is entirely withdrawn into itself. It is when the nous is withdrawn into itself that it ceases to act in the other parts of the psyche. Instead, it falls still.

Palamas concludes: *Do you see now how very necessary it is for those who decide to maintain watchful stillness to turn back their nous and confine it to the body, within the deepest part of the body, which we call the 'heart?'*

Let us look at these points in more detail, describing it as well as I am able as an investigator with limited experience of the points discussed.

1.   To gather the nous into a unity after it has been dispersed. We can develop a sense of this by constant practice ... a sense of simply looking at the things that are in front of us in simplicity and clarity.

2.   To bring the nous into and hold it within the body. As we develop more inner stillness, we become able to withdraw our attention back into the body, still with the eyes open. As we do so we become aware of the body, of the face around the eyes etc., and we find ourselves no longer 'engaging' with the world outside in the usual way, no longer reacting to things around us. The surface activity of the psyche begins to fall away, building greater stillness. At a place like Mount Athos, where monks still practise the ancient stillness of hesychia in their pursuit of salvation, one can at first feel slighted by the behaviour of some monk who declines to notice you as he walks past you, eyes turned down to the path in front of him. In time one comes to realise that this is nothing personal; it is exactly the opposite, they are being as impersonal as they can in practicing this withholding of attention, and we are doing nothing more than testing their intention. In doing so we are fulfilling one of the normal roles of humans in the world, in the way that everything in the world tests our intention to turn away from the world.

3.   To withdraw the nous into the deepest part of the psyche, *in the inmost heart*. We withdraw the attention from the everyday activities of the psyche, from thoughts, from physical feelings, from imaginings and sensations, inner and outer.

4.   To bring the nous to total stillness, entirely withdrawn into itself. In time, at this point, we enter a state of emotional stillness. Eventually the world of change falls away and one simply is – but at the time one does not register or think about that fact and its novel absence of sensation. It is in that deep darkness we first meet the uncreated light of illumination.

2.4 We must look into our hearts for the Holy Spirit

We must search for the action of the Holy Spirit in our hearts. If we discover the Holy Spirit inside us, He will begin to pray in our hearts. This is the peak of prayer and the true aim of our actions in our prayer life.

Now Palamas asks: *If, as the Psalmist says, 'the king's daughter is all-glorious within,' why do we search for her outside? And if, as the Apostle says, 'God gave His*

Spirit to cry in our hearts, Abba, Father,' how is it that we too do not pray with the Spirit in our hearts? And if the Kingdom of Heaven is within us, then whoever focuses his nous outside of himself, how could he not also find himself outside the Kingdom of Heaven?' For the true heart, says Solomon, seeks understanding.

Palamas then says that Solomon calls the understanding, which all the Fathers seek to attain, *noetic and divine*, adding: *A spiritual nous is inevitably wrapped in spiritual understanding. Whether it is in us or not, we must never stop seeking this understanding.* The heart that is awake enough to function correctly continually looks within itself to seek an inward perception. That inward perception is 'noetic' and its 'organ of sensation' is the nous. Since that perception is in us yet not inside us it is a mistake to search for it in the outside world – it must first be found within us. Ultimately, noetic perception is then brought to life by the Holy Spirit.

Do you see that if we desire to combat sin and acquire virtue, to find the reward of the struggle for virtue, which is noetic understanding, we must bring the nous back into the body, and into itself? The opposite, to look for noetic visions by making the nous 'go out', not only into sense perceptions, but out of the body itself – that is the greatest of the Hellenic errors, the root and source of all corrupt doctrine ... Such doctrines breed stupidity. As for us, we not only return the nous to our body and into the heart, but also within itself. To bring our nous back into the body, and then into itself is not something that can be done all at once, but must learned progressively, through patient practice.

2.5 Two different kinds of attention have quite different results

Instead of acting just as the eyes of the senses act, always restless, outward looking, incapable of seeing themselves, the nous can function in two quite different ways, characterised by different kinds of attention. Normally, it turns outward and is lost in the activities of the world, but when it turns inward it rises to God *as if on an infallible road.*

People who do not practice spirituality, says Palamas, do not understand certain things about it. Without experience, as we would put it today, they do not see for example that: *The essence of the nous is one thing, its activity another.* Nor do they see that: *The nous is not like the eye, which sees other visible objects but cannot see itself.*

St Dionysius calls the two kinds of attention, 'linear' and 'circular.' Linear attention attends to the outside world, and to the repetitive processes of our thoughts, etc. *The nous operates in one way in its function of exterior observation, this is what the great Dionysius calls the movement of the nous 'along a straight line'.*

Circular attention is the return of the attention of the nous first into the body and finally full circle to its point of origin in the nous. The process is such that, when it ceases to be dispersed, it comes back to itself, then it acts from itself, and then it becomes aware of itself. Palamas describes circular attention in this way: *It has another way in which it comes back to itself, then acts from itself when it becomes aware of itself. This movement the same Father calls 'circular.' This is the most excellent and appropriate activity by which the nous comes to transcend itself and become united to God.* The result of this is that it becomes able to perceive things above its own nature. It is because of this that it is able to ascend towards God, and it is through this that man obtains the possibility of uniting to God. Palamas quotes St Basil: *The nous, when it is not dispersed without, returns to itself, and thereby ascends to the contemplation of God.* According to Dionysius when this process is established, *it is no longer subject to error.*

Man's task, therefore, is to overcome the dispersion of his psyche by establishing this circular attention. *The result of this*, says Palamas *is progress towards God 'as if on an infallible road'.*

2.6 To guard against our animal nature we must be centred

We must be on our guard against the animal side of our nature, against what might be called 'primate pack behaviour' as well as certain ways in which we allow imagination to get the body to act in ways we like or wish but which are actually against our basic aims in life – particularly against our spiritual aims.

But biological life has things it wants us to do before we turn aside from it and go to God. So it wishes us to abandon this ascent to God and live according to our delusions, for these will lead to our fulfilling its biological tasks. (We will discover later that it is this biological life that lies behind the 'law of sin' mentioned earlier.) Nonetheless, Palamas insists that the body in and of itself is not evil, but needs to be brought under the control of the spiritual. St John Climacus says: *The hesychast is someone who strives to confine the bodiless in his body.* So how can we live like Christ if we do not enclose the nous, which is the seat of our awareness, inside our bodies? *For naturally, if the hesychast does not keep the inner life within the bounds of the body, if he makes a division on account of its natural form, if the outer and distinct is not properly aligned towards the essence of nous, then as long as this natural form has life, the image of life appropriate to the union of its parts is not complete.*

2.7 Spiritual methods for beginners

The practice of attending to the breath can be helpful for those starting on the path of stillness and is simply used to bring the attention into the body.

Spiritual life begins when we decide to become a true individual (the Greek word *monos* had the original meaning of alone, unique and is now used for 'monk'). To attain this, it is absolutely necessary to recall and keep the nous within the body. For this reason, because it is so difficult at the beginning, techniques such as attending to the flow of the breath into the body are sometimes taught to beginners in order to help them bring their attention into the body. Although this technique is intended for novices, in certain modern forms of pseudo-traditional practice, this 'training exercise' is now wrongly taught as the final goal.

The point of regulating the breath is so that: *In this way they will be able to hold their nous steady by watching their breath until, by the grace of God they might progress, having withdrawn the nous from what is around it, having purified it, and in doing so might truly become capable of returning it to a unified recollection.* This gathering-in of the nous from what is around it, into a unified re-collection may also in this context be described as 'single-pointed concentration'.

But the real goal is to free the attention of the nous from being distracted by attending to anything – including the breath. *At the same time, we can say that this control of the breath is a spontaneous result of the attentiveness of the nous. The in and out movement of the breath becomes peaceful during intense reflection, especially in those who practice stillness in body and in thought.*

Breath-control is thus achieved not by holding attention on the breath, but when attention is centred in the nous. In this state of single-pointed concentration, or 'one-pointed remembering', in a condition of inner stillness, the breath spontaneously becomes peaceful. Activities in the psyche and the body fall back to a peaceful minimum. The reality is a tough discipline. As Palamas describes it: *In effect, people like this practise a spiritual sabbath, insofar as they cease all personal activity. They strip from the awareness of the psyche all changeability, all imaginings, all sense perceptions, and, in general, all voluntary activity of the body. Even involuntary acts, like breathing, are restrained as far as possible.*

2.8 The threshold of spontaneous growth

When conditions are right, development of the psyche continues naturally, so that it is possible to reach a threshold from which spiritual growth occurs spontaneously. We need to struggle to reach this point, which is when 'circular attention' is established in us. This is not as difficult as it sounds. Palamas says of this intensive effort that the real growth occurs spontaneously in those who are fully prepared.

For those who have made progress in hesychasm, all this occurs without painful effort, and without the need to think about it, for the complete entry of the psyche within itself necessarily and spontaneously produces it. But with beginners, none of these things happen without a struggle. Patience is a fruit of love 'for love bears all' and we have been taught that we can attain to love when we whole-heartedly apply ourselves to our aim with steady patience. But why say any more about this? Those who have experience can only laugh when they are contradicted by the inexperienced. Their teacher is not words, but work and the experience that comes from their own efforts. It is this last which bears useful fruit, and it is this which renders barren the comments of the critics. Thus the man who seeks to turn his nous back into itself needs to send it, not in a straight line, but into the infallible circular motion.

Palamas then suggests a special posture, which has three purposes. Firstly, fixing the attention helps prevent the eyes wandering to the surroundings. Secondly, we can learn how to create an 'associative link' between a specific posture and a particular form of internal activity, and use this as a means of 're-minding' ourselves to maintain attention. *How will he not gain great profit in this if, instead of letting his eye roam hither and thither, he should fix it on his breast or navel as a point of concentration? In this way, letting his posture take the outward form of a circle, he will not only collect himself, but will shape himself to the interior movement of the nous that he seeks to have his nous follow.* Thirdly, it is easier for some people to keep their attention on the heart in this position, thus providing a way of fulfilling the instruction for the Jesus prayer to 'keep the nous in the heart'. *By taking this posture with his body, he will return the power of the nous, which otherwise drains out through the sight, back into the interior of the heart.*

Guarding the nous and heart against their normal reactions to outside events prevents waste of energy, which can then go into spiritual growth. In modern terms, spiritual growth depends on our building up certain energies and transforming them. This is greatly assisted by preventing unnecessary waste.

The problem is that, as a result of habits formed particularly when we are young, as well as other factors, we automatically respond to outside events. To paraphrase Macarius, the inner man automatically adapts to exterior forms. It is to compensate for this 'unnatural' condition that such spiritual practices are necessary. The energy saved is then concentrated in the interior of the 'inmost heart'. It seems as if this energy in time overcomes the energy of the 'law of sin' that acts in the area of the solar plexus.

If the power of the animal intelligence is situated at the centre of the belly, where the law of sin exercises its rule and is given pasture, then, armed with prayer, why should we not direct at exactly the same place 'the law of the nous, which opposes' this power? Then the evil spirit who has been driven away by the 'font of regeneration' will not return to install himself there with seven other spirits even more evil than itself, and so making 'the latter state worse than the first'?

It has been said that spiritual growth requires an increase in energy and that this depends on two things: increasing the flow of energy through our system, and minimising waste of energy. On the one hand, withdrawal of the attention into the nous is experienced as an increase in the flow of energy, rising up in time into the heart. On the other hand, the cessation of wasteful activity that results when we bring the attention back into the nous greatly reduces the loss of energy within us that is the normal result of excess activity of body and psyche.

For anybody who shares these goals, and not only for monastics, all of this becomes easy only after we have withdrawn attention from many irrelevant thoughts, some of them going back to our early life, and many feelings with a similar history, and other pre-occupations. However, this amounts to a massive change in our habits, and habits have enormous inertia. This is not easy for beginners, especially in our times when people are more and more brought up in a secular society which encourages, and where people expect, swift gratification and the avoidance of difficulties. In summary, learning to bring attentive prayer repeatedly to the exact point at which this energy is concentrated will prevent the re-assertion of the destructive passions, negative emotions and thoughts that usually rule in that location.

2.9 Nous and the power of attention

This part of the hesychast teaching is all about attention. Attention is the activity of the nous that opens up the inner life. The kind of attention necessary is further explained where Moses says that we must give attention to ourselves as a unity (Deuteronomy 15:9). This can only be done by the purified nous, when it is set to guard the psyche and the body against the action of the passions that normally rule them.

How, exactly, are we meant to exercise this attention, to 'attend to ourselves'? Palamas gives the following answer: *With the nous, evidently, for we cannot be attentive to ourselves as a whole with any other power. But if you keep this guard over your psyche and body, it will easily deliver you from the evil passions of both body and psyche. So attend to yourself, take a grip on yourself, be aware of yourself, or rather mount guard, take command, master yourself! This is how you will make the unruly flesh submit to the Spirit, so that 'there will never again be a deceitful word in your heart'.*

When the power of the world becomes active in opposing your control, do not react or respond to it in any way. Then the forces that attack you from the lower parts of your nature cannot touch you, and the Spirit will rule your life. By turning your attention to God in this way, even your flesh will be transformed, and all desire will be turned to God. Palamas says: *'if the spirit of him who rules,' that is, of the evil spirits and harmful passions, 'rises within you,' as Scripture says, 'do not leave your place.'* In other words, says Palamas, in a statement which gives us the measure of this remarkable man: *Do not cease watching over any part of your psyche or any member of your body.* That is to say, stay firm in your vigilance against those forces which tend to dominate the psyche and body. Do this and the negative emotions, harmful passions and intrusive thoughts will not prevail. Then you will be as your Lord wishes, and can face Him with confidence – a most important factor in this path on which the obstacle to divine help is found in our own fear of being 'found out'. With this change, then, we can open our hearts with confidence to Him *who tries the hearts and the reins from above.* He will not need to test you, because you will have examined yourself. Paul teaches us this when he writes: *For if we would judge ourselves, we should not be judged.*

It is then that the divine light can reach us. Palamas quotes David in this context. *You will then have the blessed experience of David, and will say to God 'The shadows are no longer dark thanks to you, and night for me will be as clear as day, for you have taken possession of my reins'.* David says, in effect: *Not only have you made all the desires of my psyche your own, but if there is a spark of desire in my body it has returned to its source, it is bound to you by that origin, raised and united to you.* The result is a transformation in stillness. *Those who abandon themselves to sensual and corrupting pleasures exhaust the whole desire of their psyche on the flesh, so that they become entirely 'flesh'. It is then, as the Scripture says, that the Spirit of God cannot dwell in them. But in the case of those who have elevated their nous to God and exalted their psyche through divine longing, their flesh too is transformed and elevated. Then it participates in the divine communion and becomes the dwelling and possession of God. It is no longer the seat of enmity towards God and no longer possesses any desires opposed to those of the Spirit.*

2.10 Praying with the body

This practice of bringing attention into the body forms the basis of a psychological method that is useful to those who, in Palamas's words, *do not yet know how to reject spiritual evil by spiritual means.* Here Palamas also begins to introduce the subject of the physical effects of certain spiritual exercises.

Those who practise these exercises will find it particularly helpful to create the 'associative link' of regularly combining a specific posture with a particular form of internal action. This will help strengthen attention in the early stages. Palamas also tells us that this method of 'attentive posture' is used in prayer even by the perfect. But in the West, these curved postures are not for absolute beginners, who are advised at first to use posture in a slightly different way, taking the position known as the 'posture of the sage'. This posture, if practised correctly with a straight back, automatically raises the quality of the solar plexus. Effectiveness in this is shown by an increased muscular tone adjacent to the solar plexus and a reduction of distraction due to uncontrolled feelings and activities.

The key attitude in this kind of prayer is that of the publican in the Gospel who, in his simple prayer, was too ashamed to raise his eyes to heaven. *In the Gospel, the Lord actually said, he didn't even dare to raise his eyes to heaven. Those who seek to turn their vision back into themselves in their prayer correctly imitate the publican. Some people call them 'omphalopsychics,' intentionally maligning them as if they were adversaries. Yet who among them ever said that the psyche was in the navel?*

2.11 Physical changes follow spiritual awakening

In this chapter, while again speaking ostensibly about the criticisms of the rationalists, Palamas also gives important information about the interaction of spiritual growth and certain physical states which serve as evidence of an improved psychological state. This knowledge provides a valuable and practical guide on the way.

The rationalists, explains Palamas: *Try to discredit this work of watchfulness. When they talk about watchfulness it is not to lead people to it, but away from it. They endeavour by all these means to discredit the work of watchfulness, as well as those who devote themselves to it, finding an excuse for this in the practices which are linked to it.* He goes on to say: *They slander without distinction anybody who employs physical symbols to represent, define, or study things that are noetic, divine, or spiritual.* But these criticisms have no effect on the saints. *The saints do not suffer at all as a result of this. Instead, they receive praises and crowns without number in heaven, while these people wait outside the sacred veil and can do no more than ponder the shadows of the truth.*

2.12 The masters of hesychasm teach practical solutions

Palamas now talks about the line of succession by which he and others learned these practices. This defines the tradition in terms of experience as taught by those who were themselves able to practice those methods successfully.

How can we be sure of all this? As far as Palamas is concerned, these teachings were passed down to us by the great masters of the Eastern church of long ago. The important thing was that they came from men who had succeeded in putting the teachings into practice and he constantly drew on the words of such people. Palamas says of Symeon the New Theologian: *Almost from beginning to end his life was a miracle since God glorified him by supernatural miracles. And also Saint Nicephorus, who spent long years in the desert, in hesychia and later lived in the most deserted parts of the Holy Mountain, allowing himself no respite. These two saints taught clearly the practical method to those who have chosen this way, practices which some people now oppose.* Here we have a brief glimpse of an important part of the history of this tradition. Nicephorus had not simply taught watchfulness, he had collected the teaching from the writings of the Fathers, as was done again in the middle of the eighteenth century by Paisious Velitchovski.

The question may well be asked: 'how can this tradition be true or relevant since it is so little known or respected?' However, neither fame nor the respect of the worldly can ever be a measure of truth. So although the tradition may appear fragile, the truth it carries has been durable enough to live for two millennia. The fact is that these practices have escaped popular notice, and that the numbers of those committed to the practices has waxed and waned. But this is not due to any inherent fragility, but an indication that although simple, this is not an easy truth. It makes demands on an individual that hitherto few have been willing to face. Now that the mask of civilisation is slipping again and hard realities intrude everywhere, perhaps now we will find the courage to make demands on ourselves, instead of on the world and those around us. It is a path that brings us to what we will never find written in any book – the truth about ourselves, and our divinely-promised inheritance, which is the reward.

But why speak only of the saints of the past? These men who testified a little time before us, and who are recognised as having possessed the power of the Holy Spirit, have passed these things on to us out of their own mouths. For example, that theologian called the 'True Theologian,' the most reliable of the witnesses of the real mysteries of God, was celebrated in our time. I speak of Theoleptus, the Bishop of Philadelphia, who was truly inspired by God, who illumined the whole world like a chandelier. And Athanasius, who for many years graced the patriarchal throne and whose tomb was honoured by God. And Nilus, originally from Italy, who emulated Nilus the Great; also Seliotis, and Ilias, who were in no way inferior to him. Then there were Gabriel and Athanasius, who had the gift of prophecy. Such people also lived in the time of Palamas and he was taught by some of them. He thus advises his readers: *Let yourself be convinced by the fathers, listen to their advice on how to make your nous return within you.*

These wise Fathers are not something that disappeared once and for all at the end of the Middle Ages. Even today, at the start of the third Millennium, I have met more than one such man. But today they are hard to find, because the world scarcely values them. Nevertheless, the 'living water' of their teachings still runs fresh and, as it is said, 'he who seeks shall find'.

PART THREE: SPIRITUAL ILLUMINATION

An Analysis of Interior Experience

The third part of the first Triad refers precisely to the third of the three stages of the hesychast path. It describes the way we can directly experience the action of the divine within us. To the hesychast and to those who follow the teachings of the Early Fathers of the church, it is this experience that is known as the knowledge of God. It is the product of the progressive awakening of what some modern psychologists term the new emotional consciousness. This third section is so directly related to Christian inner experience that it provides what might be called an experimental solution, a clearly defined statement of the testable elements of that doctrine. It is experimental in the sense that any Christian who develops the necessary spiritual ability can also investigate these states of consciousness and being and can then compare their own experiences against Palamas's description.

In this context it is important to note that this text was not peripheral to the teachings of the church. In a time of political troubles that included the progressive conquest of the Eastern part of the Roman Empire by the Turks, and in which social confusions spilled over into theology, the teachings of Palamas were accepted as doctrine by the Councils of the church, which gave final form to those doctrines in 1351. In referring to 'testable elements' of the doctrine we also mean that the rendering of the Greek words into consistent terms in English – with a very few necessary deviations – reveals that this part of Palamas's book provides a coherent and internally consistent terminology for the elements of the Christian mystical psychology and mystical and charismatic experience. This means that all the terms used are clearly explainable in terms of each other, just as are all the terms of the physical sciences clearly related to each other. However, while the physical sciences create their theoretical models by combining experimental observations and individually developed meta-concepts drawn from a variety of sources or simply invented, the classical Christian theoretical models taught by the Early Fathers of the church drew from a single coherent doctrine. They did so in such a way that the total representation is testable by the individual under certain conditions, and verifiable by its congruence and concordance with the experiences of the saints and Fathers of the tradition. These conditions are in fact referred to in the first two parts of this work; by putting the ideas into practice we learn the meaning of the doctrine, and by observing the results of that practice, we confirm its validity by reference to those who have already trodden the path.

These are the 'scientific criteria' of the interior science of the early church. Because these results are only accessible to individuals and not to collective demonstration, they tend to be undervalued. Those with experience easily grasp what is meant when they are described, but those without experience have difficulty. Intellectual studies play little part in this process, except inasmuch as they lead those who are habitually aware only of externals to turn their attention inward.

The nature and experience of the divine light

Remembering the light precedes actual moments of illumination, and brief illumination precedes permanent illumination. In order to make the illumination constant we need to understand its reality and its significance. *The light shineth in darkness, and the darkness comprehendeth it not.*

Modern forms of knowledge are like the intellectual forms of classical Greek philosophy from which they were developed. Those who build their knowledge on logical analysis in this way still today reach the same conclusions as they did in the time of Palamas. The saint says of such people that they believe that knowledge can only be obtained through rational enquiry, and that this is therefore the only kind of illumination possible to us. Palamas disagrees with this in a way that challenges the whole of our contemporary concept of knowledge. If we understand the sense underlying this challenge, and if we can centre our inner eye in the place from which Palamas is speaking, we will find a whole new world opening up to us. For this third part of the First Triad is about the experiences of illumination, which at some point in our life we may have already experienced a little, and which we should hope to enjoy in full as our inner life, our Christian life, comes to its fruition.

Palamas first tells us – just as they do today – that the rationalists of his time assume that the only thing that comes from the contemplative process is knowledge. He says unequivocally that this is not true. After this, he emphasises that the only knowledge that is certain can be obtained from our experience of life. It is immediately clear that either he is speaking from a different experience, or from an understanding of that experience that is very different from the way in which it is normally understood today. In fact, both of these possibilities are true. He speaks from deep experience of something which most people's lives barely touch on, but which is relatively commonplace for those he would describe as the purified – experience of illumination itself. He speaks about life in a way shaped by these illuminations and he also speaks from a life shaped by such illuminations. He speaks of an unknown, forgotten country within us and speaks of it in a way that will help us first to find it, and then to come to dwell in it.

Then he puts the shadow-side of this argument, returning to the subject of the rationalists who even then were undermining the belief on which these experiences were built, the thinkers who drove out the possibility of personal experience of God and opened modern man to a Godless future. For instance, he tells how in his time some of these rationalists joined the schools of the hesychast contemplatives only to provide misleading reports about the teachings and actions of those who lead those schools. *If anyone contradicts any of their opinions,* he tells us, *they say that this is a sign of passion, which in turn is a mark of delusion. They use many ruses, and interpret their own words in different and contradictory manners. They do not possess the firmness and simplicity of truth, but easily fall into contradiction and, ashamed at the accusation of their own conscience, seek, like Adam, to hide themselves in complication, conundrums, and ambiguities about different meanings of words.*

3.1 The need to guard against clever lies

Palamas describes here the way his opponents make lies appear as truth. *They describe vices alongside virtues, and their impious words appear to be so close to pious words that a small addition or subtraction is enough to easily transform one into the other, so that the meaning of the words is completely changed.* Palamas is describing a technique that is still regularly employed, particularly by politicians, by certain members of the churches, and by people who wish to make their teachings or themselves more impressive. Of course, the translation of words referring to inner experience into purely outer meanings has a very similar effect. *This is why nearly all false opinions wear the mask of truth. This will deceive anyone who does not notice the small additions or omissions. This is the dangerous means used by the evil daemon, so skilled in the art of deception. Telling a lie close to the truth, he invented a double ruse; the small distance is not noticed by most people, who easily take a lie for the truth or the truth for a lie when it is close to it. In both cases this completely separates us from the truth.*

At this point we need to realise that we, in third millennium, face other obstacles to proper understanding. Important teachings have not been passed on, even in translation, and the translations we do have are usually not made in the same spirit as that in which they were written. So not only do we suffer from an incomplete knowledge of our own tradition, but also that knowledge has been misrepresented through bad translation. Another obstacle to understanding is that we have lost the ability to understand symbolic language – the language of the spirit – in preference to defining everything in terms of the material. Since the teachings of the Fathers are so little known in the West today, it is easy to misunderstand their symbolic statements and parables about inner experience and assume that the outer or literal meaning is the true sense of the text. Palamas is one of several authors who clearly uses images to describe inner processes for which adequate language does not otherwise exist. Such language also has the effect of making one work harder to grasp the truth, for knowledge gained easily is also easily lost.

3.2 Purifying the heart by prayer

Underneath the layer of polemic that crops up throughout the book is the key teaching about the effect of prayer in purifying the heart. Speaking of the opponents of hesychasm, Palamas explains that they report people's words while slightly modifying what they say, as if to make it clearer, but in fact the added words change the meanings of complete sentences. Palamas then quotes particular examples of this form of misrepresentation. The first is: *Beginners in hesychasm are indeed advised to avoid too much reading. They are to give themselves to prayer in thought alone until unceasing prayer becomes the normal state of their thinking, even if they have physically moved on to another occupation. The students find the same counsel given by Saint Diadochos, Philemon the Great, Nilus, so rich in things divine, John, the author of the Ladder, as well as many fathers now living. This is not because reading is either useless or wrong. But those people added this word 'wrong,' and by doing this, they made the good advice of the fathers seem to be something that is actually harmful. This kind of small distortion is difficult to recognise, and if we don't recognise it, can be entirely misleading.* Another example he gives is: *All the saints have shown in their words and their actions that prayer drives out evil spirits and passions. All the wise men think this and teach it, but not one of them ever said that these evil spirits had become merged with our essence. By making this arbitrary addition, those who spoke to you made the whole aim of our efforts seem wrong.* The term 'evil spirits' can be hard to comprehend for the modern mind. It can perhaps best be understood by our experience of those activities, desires and states that are harmful to the psyche. However it is understood, the remedy is the same, since *prayer drives out passions.*

3.3 The noetic light and the knowledge of God

Palamas talks here about a noetic light, and about knowledge of God, and he tells us that knowledge should only be called light if it has been directly communicated to us by the divine light. He refers to St Paul in this regard, then adds that Dionysius defines the effects of this light. *The presence of the noetic light unifies those it illumines and reintegrates them in a single and true knowledge.* So when we become aware of the presence of the light of grace within us, this communicates the light of knowledge to us, which includes self-knowledge, and it is this that liberates us from the ignorance that normally fragments us.

Palamas adds that Dionysius called this light 'noetic': *While the great Macarius, clearly concerned with those who receive the light of grace in the form of knowledge, says it is 'perceptible to the nous.' He says 'you will see by its effects if the noetic light which has shone in your psyche comes from God or Satan.'* Macarius also said: *As the visible eyes see the visible sun, so it is with the eyes of their psyche that these men see the noetic light which reveals itself and will shine from their bodies at the moment of Resurrection, to make them resplendent with eternal light.*

Palamas goes on to say: *As for the light of knowledge, we may never say that it is 'noetic.' On the contrary, that light sometimes acts like a 'noetic' light. At the same time, the nous sees it as an intelligible light through its noetic sense. When it enters reasoning psyches, it liberates them from the ignorance which bound them to their state, bringing them back from diverse opinion to unified knowledge.* Palamas then quotes Dionysius: *The Good is described as the light of the nous because it illuminates the nous of every supra-celestial being with the light of the nous and because it drives from souls the ignorance and the error squatting there.*

At the beginning of this chapter he gave us an example. *God has shined in our hearts to give the light of the knowledge of the glory of God in the face of Jesus*

Christ. Thus the Transfiguration of Christ and His saints is revealed to those who experience it, both then and now, because of a light in the hearts of those who perceive it. Thus, there are two lights of which he speaks, the noetic light and the light of knowledge. The light of knowledge comes from the noetic light but is not the noetic light. The noetic light is an eternal light.

It is this inner light that reconnects us to true knowledge and by eliminating the shadows of ignorance, it reunifies or re-integrates us. This is the light the Fathers called the noetic light. Regarding this light, Palamas tells us: it appears in the psyche as soon as we truly love God; just as the sensory light is seen with eyes of the senses, the noetic light of the psyche is seen with the nous, the 'eye of the psyche'; and this is the light that shines from the body at the moment of resurrection.

Palamas then gives us the classical test by which we can verify the source of such a light – we will know by its effects whether this light comes from God or Satan. *So the knowledge which comes after ignorance has been driven out is one thing, while the noetic light which makes this knowledge appear is another.*

This light of knowledge is itself not noetic. It is on the level of our thoughts, but it sometimes appears like a noetic light. At those times the nous sees such knowledge through its noetic sense just as if it were a noetic light. When this happens, it liberates our psyches from ignorance and illusion. God is seen through the nous not in His essence, but in a marvellous revelation of His presence to the nous that has been purified of passions. At this point, we must begin to understand the nature of the passions as understood by the Early Fathers.

Passions and negative emotions

Christ taught us that those who have pure hearts will see God. For this reason, it is necessary to understand the kinds of impurities that get embedded in our hearts, and to discover ways of freeing ourselves from them. Not surprisingly, the early church was very much concerned with the main source of impurity, which it called the passions (Gr. *pathos*). The meaning of this word was in certain ways very different from what we call passion today. It did not then have its modern romantic connotation, while the implications of terms like 'passionate belief' would also have been very different. Passions were understood as states in which we are passive to forces acting within us, which are usually caused by our response and reaction to events outside of us. Passions are not moments when we are ruled by our heart in the deeper sense, but times when we are ruled by the effect of what is outside us, particularly by the natural or material world, as well as by the feelings that are the core of that subservience. Passions, according to the Fathers, are evoked by desires, imaginings and remembered feelings, by remembered pleasures which we then wish to repeat. They act on us through our imagination, through daydreaming of past events and fantasies of the future. They have the power to make us think, act and dream, according to the demands of material nature, at the cost of losing all sense of the importance of our deeper and more spiritual purpose.

Passions can act within us to make us eager to repeat some past experience that was pleasurable but often otherwise trivial. They can marshal all our resources for something which, in our right mind, we would regard as beneath our notice. And if we think we are being prevented from this imagined pleasure we can become angry, bitter, resentful, or even depressed. In this way, disappointed pleasures become one of the main sources of negative emotions. In Hamlet, Shakespeare used the term 'passion' in a similar way: *Give me that man that is not passion's slave and I will wear him in my heart's core, aye, in my heart of hearts.*

Passions and energies

There is a little-known 'law' by which the more active we become, the more we are inclined to be caught by two related problems. The more energetic we feel after prayer and more active we become, the more the debris of the past lying at the bottom of our lives is stirred up to the surface. Suddenly, we begin to remember things we want to do, places we want to go to, and so forth. Forgetting that to which we are indebted for this energy, we start making plans. All this happens in the imagination and begins by filling us with daydreams of far-away places and beautiful vistas, of being rich, or famous, or living on marvellous foods. This is also a manifestation of what the early Christians called the passions. The Gospel of Thomas reports that on regarding the world, Jesus said: *I found them all drunk, I found none of them athirst.* This refers to man's enthralment to the passions. In satisfying the desires of the world, no energy remains for the life of the spirit. Another aspect relating to the passions appears when we are overworked. In addition to the physiological problems which arise if this goes on for too long, what happens is that the passions are awoken but we are unable to satisfy them. Then we become angry or depressed. This is one of the primary causes of what we now call negative emotions and negative emotions have the effect of making the heart less sensitive. They cancel out the motivating force given us by our experiences of grace.

The first rule is that – other things being equal – an increase in activity leads to an increase in desires and expectations. The second rule is that – other things being equal – unrewarding over-activity leads to an increase in negativity. This situation, in either its positive or negative forms, presents us with a test – it is a test of our true humanity!

If we cannot resolve this, then we are not yet fully human in that we have yet to develop the ability to gather this energy and use it for our higher aims. Thus this test remains a threshold that everybody must pass before they can hope to develop enough finer energy to attain real spiritual growth. Somehow we have to get our life into the right condition without spending all our energy on the growing flood of new desires wants and distractions.

Negative emotions are a great danger in the search for salvation, because once they reach a certain intensity they begin to colour the whole of our lives. Russian philosopher P. D. Ouspensky's approach to negative emotions was based on the observation that they are in a sense an unnatural to us. At the same time, we can observe that when we are 'full of negativity' we refuse to fight against it because we find ways of justifying our negativity. We become passive to our passions. Often we claim that it is a necessary response to a particular situation.

First, Ouspensky said that we should learn to look at them with this in mind: *Negative emotions are never necessary and never justified.* This will help us see them clearly without judgement. Secondly, he said we should train ourselves never to express negative emotions, and to make this simple idea a principle in our lives: *Do not express negative emotions in any situation.* In other words, turn the other cheek! But this is not so easy. It is not repressing negative emotions, but simply not expressing them. The ideal way is to use them as a means for self-development. If you are able to observe them arising in you, urging you to react, yet not yield to this impulse, the negative energy can be transformed into a higher, or finer, form of energy.

Even if this result does not always come, it is well worthwhile attempting to make a habit of not expressing negative emotions. At the very least, by not expressing them we will begin to see them more quickly and more clearly.

3.4 Noetic vision lies beyond negation

Blessed are the pure in heart. The human nous becomes superhuman by conquering the passions and negative emotions. In this respect, Palamas said of the nous: *When it is victorious over the passions, it may transcend itself and so become angelic. The nous will then find the light, and will become worthy of a supernatural vision of God.* This is one of the key passages in the Triads. Palamas begins here to develop his thesis of the divine revelation, that we do not see God in His essence, but God nevertheless reveals His presence to those who are worthy of this knowledge through His energies. The nous *does not see the essence of God, but it sees God by a revelation which is both appropriate to and consistent with God himself.* The revelation or vision is not God but is sent by God to confirm His existence and to show us that He is aware of us, and carries with it other knowledge. It is not the product of our own intellectual activity.

This vision *does not happen through negation. One really sees it, and this seeing is superior to negation, for God is not only beyond knowledge, He is even beyond unknowing.* Palamas emphasises that this revelation: *Is also truly a mystery, the more divine and extraordinary since divine manifestations, even if they are symbolic, remain unknowable in their transcendence. In fact, they appear according to a law which is neither that of divine nature nor of human nature — being, as it were, for us and yet beyond us — so that there is no name which can properly describe them. This was well demonstrated when, in reply to Manoah's question: 'What is your name?' God replied: 'It is marvellous'. Yet this vision, being not only incomprehensible but also un-nameable, is no less marvellous for that.*

3.5 The light of theosis

When someone enters into the communion of *theosis*, they become aware of the divine light within them. Their nous is then glorified by the grace of the Word, Who gives them the divine light given Him by the Father, just as He was made glorious when He revealed it on Mount Tabor. The light that is within the nous is also beyond the heavens.

When the saints contemplate this divine light within themselves, they see it having once obtained the divinising communion of the Spirit, with the mysterious accompaniment of inspired illuminations. It is then that they see the garment of their deification by the grace of the Word, as their nous is glorified and filled with a brilliance of extraordinary beauty. In the same way, when on the mountain, the divinity of the Word glorified with divine light the body that was bound to Him. For He Himself has given 'the glory which the Father gave Him' to those who are obedient to Him, as the Evangelist says: 'He willed that they should be with Him and contemplate His glory.' But how could this happen physically since He himself was no longer bodily present after His ascension into heaven?

Even in our times this light is given to those who are obedient to our Lord. But today, since our Lord ascended into heaven, this light is perceived by the nous when it passes 'beyond the heavens' and is united to God, when it goes even beyond what is written by the saints and becomes aware of the unearthly visions and immaterial knowledge that come with the higher noetic light. Then the nous turns away from symbol and scripture, as it is *made beautiful by the creative and original Beauty, and illumined by the light of God.*

Like such men, the spiritual beings described by Dionysius in this passage are related hierarchically depending not only on their relation to the original experience and knowledge, but also on the light first seen in the sublime Trinitarian initiation. Not only do they participate in and contemplate the glory of the Trinity, but they also behold the light which Jesus revealed to the disciples on Tabor. Palamas says next: *Judged worthy of this vision, they receive a true initiation, for that light is also a deifying light. They truly come closer to Him and receive their first communion from his deifying radiance. This is why the truly blessed Macarius called this light the 'food of supra-celestial beings'. And here is what another theologian says: 'In spiritually celebrating this light, the whole divine order of heavenly beings gives us clear proof of the love which the Word bears towards us.'*

It was at this point that Paul was 'ravished' beyond the heavens, although his nous did not need to change its position. This noetic illumination, received and reported from their experience by those who have purified their hearts, is quite different from knowledge, although illumination can produce knowledge.

3.6 Signs are more than symbols

In modern terms, we should say that there are symbols or representations, and there are signs. Signs are perceptible outer events representing imperceptible things that are occurring but are themselves invisible.

In the Greek of Palamas, the idea of a 'symbol' is broader than its usual modern usage, and includes written descriptions that describe something outward which occur as a sign of something inner, perhaps a sign that takes figurative form. For example, the apparently physical illuminations in the Old Testament symbolise and tell of true holy illuminations that manifested in a symbolic way. As St Nilus describes it: *The first of these illuminations is known as 'the Place of God'.* The sign is experienced as a sapphire-blue light. This light is visible when the eyes are closed, although it is not the deep violet that is more commonly experienced when we close our eyes, but a much lighter colour which is only perceived when the passions are temporarily in abeyance. Thus Saint Nilus teaches that most of these Old Testament events are symbols of the illumination: *When the nous, after it has put off the old man, has clothed itself in what is born of grace, then, during prayer, it will see its own state like a sapphire or the colour of the sky; Scripture calls this 'the Place of God,' which the ancients saw at the foot of Mount Sinai.'* Similarly, Saint Isaac is also quoted in this context: *The nous, when grace acts on it, sees its own purity in prayer, like the heavenly colour which the community of Israel called the Place of God when it appeared to them on the mountain.*

Palamas continues: *Do you not see how these illuminations are symbols of what can happen now in pure hearts? And John Chrysostom explained these words of the Apostle: 'For God, who commanded the light to shine out in darkness, hath shined in our hearts.' According to him, the Apostle shows that the glory of Moses shone in us even more strongly, for it has shone in our hearts as it did on the face of Moses.' He also says: 'At the beginning of creation, He spoke and there was light. Today He did not speak, but he Himself has become our light.' So, if the light at the beginning of creation, or that which shone on the face of Moses, was a limited kind of knowledge, the illumination which occurs in our hearts would also be knowledge, but greater because it has been developed. Thus, since the light was not knowledge, but a radiance appearing on his face, the radiance it produces in us is also not knowledge, but a radiance of the psyche appearing to the purified nous. So there is one light that is visible to the eyes and necessarily sensible, and another which is noetic since it acts within us, where it can only be seen by the eyes of the nous.*

3.7 Illumination is light and knowledge

The end of illumination is not just light, but a form of knowledge that is not given in words, nor by the senses. As we are accustomed to obtaining knowledge in outward ways, we do not notice it when we acquire it inwardly, and we have to be taught to recognise it and trust it when it manifests in our lives. So now Palamas draws on the illumined Fathers to give us the testimony of their experiences of the uncreated light and the knowledge that comes from it. He begins by making it clear that the 'symbolic' light on the face of Moses was not merely sensory. It was the same light, the 'glory of Christ,' that even today shines in the psyche of modern saints, and the same inner light which – however it is named – first calls so many people to the labour of Christ.

Palamas then tells us that Macarius made a small addition to St Paul's words about this to make it clear that this light was not a light of the senses and to show that when we perceive this divine light of the Lord, our nous becomes transparent and so our own light gets brighter. *All of us who, with face uncovered, contemplate the glory of the Lord, that is to say, his noetic light, as if in a mirror, are transformed in the same image from glory to glory, that is to say by the increase in the light which is in us and which, under the influence of the divine light, becomes ever more distinct.* Palamas quotes the testimony of Saint Diadochos: '*You should not doubt that when the nous begins to regularly feel the action of the divine light, it becomes so completely translucent that it sees the abundance of its own light vividly. When the strength of the psyche makes it mistress of the passions, it becomes all light.*' While the divine Maximos says: '*A human nous would never have the power to raise itself to apprehend the divine radiance if it were not for God himself who draws it up and illumines it with divine brightness.*'

At this point Palamas refers to the two kinds of knowledge, human and divine, and quotes St Basil to confirm that divine knowledge does not come as a result of study and practice, but as a consequence of purifying the nous. *All human knowledge is simply study and practice, while the knowledge coming from the grace of God is justice and mercy. The first of these can be acquired by the passionate, while the second is only received by those who have conquered the passions and who see the radiance of their nous illumine them even outside the time of prayer.* So it is when the psyche becomes strong enough to control the passions that the nous becomes filled with divine light and so acquires the divine knowledge. Palamas himself says about this: *Do you understand clearly, brother, that the nous freed from passions as it prays sees itself as a light, and shines with divine light?* He then he quotes Macarius to show that this illumination is more than a light of the nous, it is also a light in the psyche: *The perfect illumination of the Spirit is not only a noetic revelation, but a certain and continuous illumination of hypostatic light in the psyche.* Palamas supports this further by quoting from St Paul and several of the Psalms: *He who commanded the light to shine in the heart of darkness has shone in our hearts* (2 Corinthians 4:6); *Enlighten my eyes, lest I sleep the sleep of death* (Psalm 13:3); *Send out thy light and thy truth, let them bring me to thy holy mountain* (Psalm 43:3); *The light of your countenance is come upon us as a sign* (Psalm 4:6). These are just a few of many similar passages confirming that the human nous does not have the power to participate in this divine illumination except when God draws it up to Him.

Man is the learning animal and the human is distinguished from the other mammals by the fact that, as Palamas says, human knowledge is the result of study and practice. The circus horse that dances, or the seal that balances a beach ball, do so because it has been trained by man. Modern neuroscience distinguishes between a layer of experiential knowledge in some way developed or organised by developing the structure of the brain, and a semantic layer of coded information, which is more quickly formed and more easily communicated, but is of very little practical use until its meaning has been understood, that is, until we know what it describes clearly in terms of actual experience. In addition to this, Saint Paul described a process of training which involves both the experiential and semantic levels. Training is, of course, different from intellectual education in that it concerns teaching the experiential level and, in terms of modern neuroscience, more directly informs the brain. True understanding is therefore an alignment, an agreement between these two, described as 'direct and semantic knowledge.'

When Palamas says a little earlier that *human knowledge is obtained by study and practice*, he is speaking of these two levels, the semantic and the experiential. One of the key principles of the psychological method is based on an understanding of the active relationship between these two levels. What is not generally understood is that, because of the character of this relationship, certain forms of learning are indirect; we learn experientially but, in many cases, the need for practice in learning at the experiential level involves clearly distinguishable semantic processes. With the benefit of modern experimental observation added to the insights of the tradition that Palamas represents we can define the following principles in the learning process:

1. The communication of experience to the semantic level occurs only when we give attention to the experience.
2. Both the experiential and the semantic levels have the ability to control our bodies, but with different degrees of facility.
3. The semantic level can inhibit the so-called 'voluntary' actions of the experiential level in order to take control of the actions, yet the experiential level may also inhibit the semantic level due to the influence of habitual behaviour, or other involuntary actions.
4. The experiential level learns new movements through iteration, that is, by repeated trial and error.
5. That repeated iteration (repetition) of the training process in a particular movement or group of movements or skills eventually leads to the process being assimilated at the experiential level.
6. Although the semantic level carries out actions less skilfully than the trained experiential level carries out exactly the same actions, it leads eventually to the assimilation of practical experience with greater capability than that demonstrated during the practice phase.

The individual successfully trained in this way then proves far more able to work with speed and precision than is possible to the experiential level alone, which is nothing more than a 'trial and error machine'.

7.   This process applies not only to the learning of physical skills, but to inner skills such as prayer and meditation, and to certain inner processes ranging from self-observation to self-control.

This is the important element in Palamas's view. Because of it this method plays an important part in the struggle against habits, particularly against the instinctive processes still acting in the untrained mind, as well as against unwanted habits of thought, feelings and action. Among other things, it forms the basis of ways of dealing with negative emotions, and with what the early church called the passions. It is this struggle that makes possible the achievement of *apatheaia* (dispassion), which opens the nous to the third, or spiritual level of experience and life.

The training process

The inner tradition distinguishes between inner and outer processes – one part of the brain is concerned with sensing and governing the inner world of the body, another large part with relating to the outer world. The thoughts and feelings of the psyche also possess both of these two relationships, but in varying degrees. In all complex creatures, most inner physiological processes are properly understood as instinctive, that is, they work without need for learning and without conscious attention, although in man a small degree of training and regulation is possible with special knowledge. In man, as a general rule, outer movements are learned by experiment or imitation and are then refined by practice. Even something that seems as instinctive as walking has to be learned at the start of our lives. In 'other animals', a vastly greater number of outer movements are instinctive, in the sense that they can be begun without an initial learning period and with little or no practice. However, the most complex animals show some ability to learn skills or modified behaviour. Chimpanzees, indeed, pass on tool-using skills to other members of their troop. Other higher animals, such as horses, can also learn additional movements under human supervision, showing that they have a capacity similar to man to acquire skills, but that man possesses an additional capacity which makes it possible to learn new skills or even to teach them to other creatures. The implications of this situation for spiritual growth are considerable.

In Palamas's understanding, human knowledge is distinguished by its development through practice. It can be obtained by the passionate, he says, but in the words of St Basil, divine knowledge is only received by those who have conquered the passions. It is the practice of dispassion which purifies the nous that gives us the possibility of receiving divine knowledge through the noetic light. When the nous is freed from passions, it sees itself during prayer as a light, and shines with divine light.

3.8 The nous is covered by a veil of impure feelings

We perceive our nous when it sees itself by its own noetic light, but most of the time it is hidden from us by what has been called a 'veil' of impurities. The knowledge obtained from the senses is not called 'light', because we use this term for another kind of knowledge, which comes from the activity of the nous. Where there is an active nous, there is a noetic light. Palamas says: *We do not see any being gifted with reasoning activity who lacks a noetic light.*

God is beyond even the noetic light, and as He is beyond essence, He transcends all beings. *God himself, who surpasses all noetic light and transcends essence upon essence, is called 'fire' by the holy theologians.* The ancient theologians called Him 'fire' because He seems like a faint fire when seen apart from everything else. But when He is seen in purified matter, He appears as a noetic light. *He possesses this mysterious and invisible character in himself, like a faint image of what fire is among sensory things, whenever there is no matter to receive the divine appearance. But when it takes hold of suitable matter that is undisguised, for example, any purified noetic nature not bearing a veil of evil, then it appears as a noetic light.*

We now have this sequence: the Divine light seen as a faint fire; the Divine light seen in the purified nous as a noetic light; the noetic light in itself; the noetic light appearing as a sensory light; sensory light.

3.9 The veiled nous can only perceive knowledge of the world

The nous is an organ of contemplation, that is, it 'sees' as an 'eye of the psyche', but whenever it is veiled by corrupted feelings – which is for most people almost all the time – it can only receive knowledge, but not the noetic light. In order to restore our connection through the nous to the spiritual level, these impurities have to be removed. *Just as fire, if it is hidden by opaque material, may give heat without light, so the nous likewise may get knowledge but not light, as long as it is covered by the veil of evil passions. Nous is not only contemplated by nous as a light, the last light seen in this way, but at the same time it is contemplation itself, like an eye in the inmost centre of the psyche. It is said, in fact, that 'the nous is the eye of the psyche.' The eye of the senses cannot become active unless it is illumined by an exterior light, so the nous cannot act as the organ of noetic sense, nor activate itself, unless the divine light illumines it.*

Palamas compares the action of the nous to that of the eye, which: *When active, itself becomes light, confuses itself with the light, and first sees this same light flooding onto the objects which it sees. In the same way the nous, when its sense perception is activated, is itself entirely like light. Then it is in the light, and with the aid of the light it sees the light clearly, in a way that is not only superior to the bodily senses, but also to everything we know, and, simply, superior to all created things.* As the eye of the senses only sees what is illumined by external light, the light of the nous only sees noetically when illumined by the divine light. But when it awakes its sensibility on the noetic level, it becomes a light above all sensory light.

The beatitudes tell us: *Blessed are the pure in heart, for they shall see God.* John says: *God is light and He makes His home in them, and shows Himself to those who love Him and are loved by Him, according to the promise that He gave them.* Palamas then explains how this happens: *He shows Himself to the purified nous as in a mirror, while all the while He Himself remains invisible. This is how an image appears in a mirror – it appears in reflection while the object remains invisible in itself. It is almost impossible to see at the same time both the image reflected in the mirror and the object which the mirror reflects. So God is light, and He lets us glimpse Him in the purified nous as if in a mirror, while being impossible to see face to face.*

3.10   The light brings us knowledge from beyond the senses

God by His power shows Himself to us through His energies that manifest as a non-sensory light within us. It is this uncreated light which brings us knowledge of things beyond perception.

This is how God appears now to those who have been purified in love, but one day, it is said, He will appear to them 'face to face.' But those who see the divine fire without love will not see it as light, but as a darkness which is not a sensory darkness, nor ignorance. In the words of Palamas: *Those who do not believe that God appears as a light beyond light, because they have no experience of divine things and do not see them, and those who believe that reason alone can contemplate the divine, are like blind people who only receive the warmth of the sun and do not believe those who also see its rays. And if these blind people undertake to give lessons to those who see, saying to them that the sun, the most luminous of the objects of the senses, is not a light, those who possess receptive eyes can only laugh.* It is not that we have in our nature the power to perceive God as he is: *God, who transcends all things, who is incomprehensible and indescribable, nevertheless consents, in a surfeit of goodness towards us, to become accessible to our nous and invisibly visible in his indivisible power beyond being.*

Even though this is so, says Palamas, the opponents of hesychasm: *Remain without love in regard to this purely spiritual love seen within. Moreover, they do not wish to follow the saints who, in their love towards men lead them with words towards that light. Instead, they bring themselves to the edge of the abyss and drag down with them those they persuade to accompany them.* Indeed, this light is not sensory and it is not knowledge, as the darkness that is its opposite is not ignorance. On the other hand, people who respond with love to love, even though they find themselves cut off from it again and again, will begin to pursue the 'will o' the wisp' of that love.

But this same light, which is neither knowledge nor sensation: *Brings with it the mystical and hidden knowledge of the mysteries of God . . . to those who have purified their hearts . . . and is itself an intelligible and noetic light, or rather it is spiritual – spiritually present, and spiritually visible.* It is this light, says Palamas, which transcends all knowledge and all virtue. It conveys to us the accomplishment that is brought only by revelation and the grace of the Holy Spirit.

3.11 Christ came to offer us this light

Christ came to lift the darkness from our psyches and make the divine light accessible to us. It is His light, shining from the 'immortal countenance of the interior man', which transforms and glorifies us. Quoting Macarius, Palamas relates how the perfect mystery of Christianity shown by St Paul is a ray of heavenly light. It is revealed by the power of the Holy Spirit to show people that the illuminations that reach them through the Spirit are something other than intellectual conclusions based on conceptual knowledge. The revelation is given this way to protect people from the danger of mistaking ordinary intellectual processes for the indescribable effects of God's grace.

Macarius adds this comment about the revelation of St Paul: *In effect, he is saying if what is transient is glorious, then what endures is even more glorious. He spoke of it as a transient thing because the glory shone round the mortal body of Moses. But he showed that this immortal glory of the Spirit, which appeared in a revelation, and today shines on the immortal countenance of the interior man, shines permanently for those who are worthy of it.* That countenance (Gr. *prosopon*, face) is the psyche, and the immortal countenance is the individualised psyche for which the veil between it and the eternal Lord has been removed. This link to the eternal is the immortality of the psyche. Our mortality is a result of the veiling of this countenance that occurred for mankind with the fall. Our immortality is the result of its unveiling. This is explained in perhaps the most difficult passage in the whole book. Present attempts to translate St Paul's words on this give us as many translations of this passage as there are versions of the New Testament. So we have tried yet another translation, as follows: *But all of us, that is to say, all those who have been unveiled to face the glory of the Lord, behold the same image as if in a mirror, so that they are transmuted from glory to glory even as the Lord who is the Spirit.* (2 Cor. 3.18) That seems to be the sense of it. It fits with the basic theme of Palamas's text, which is that Christ came into the world specifically to remove the veil of the psyche and so allow us to communicate with that immortalising ray of divine light.

3.12 The visible light of the Old Testament foretells the inner light of the New

Palamas tells us that the visible illuminations described in the Old Testament were a foretaste of the spiritual illumination which occurs in the psyches of those who 'in truth and practice believe in Christ'. Those who depend on their reason alone cannot experience this illumination and gain true knowledge. *The sensory illuminations that occurred under the old covenant prefigured the illumination of the Spirit which occurs in the psyches of those who in truth and practise believe in Christ.* Those who see them simply as symbolic should be led by those who know this inner experience through faith and by their own inner search, for as yet those without this experience and search are still 'men of the psyche', and 'do not receive the things of the Spirit.'

But when these people try to use the unaided psyche to teach other people about the true Goodness which cannot be described in words, they are simply behaving like madmen in their pride in their own cleverness. Palamas, in referring to St Paul, adds this commentary: *'But he that is spiritual judgeth all things, yet he himself is judged of no man. For who hath known the nous of the Lord, that he may instruct him? But we have the nous of Christ.'* So *whoever has faith in his own reasoning and the problems which it poses, who believes he can discover all truth by distinctions, syllogisms and analysis, can clearly neither know the things of the spiritual man, nor believe in them. He is a natural man, and 'the natural man', said Paul, 'does not receive the things of the Spirit'.* So 'the things of the spiritual man' are not gained by simply thinking one's own thoughts.

3.13 Self-knowledge on the path of prayer

Those who want to know themselves should study under those with true experience. But people who trust an intellectual education – even today – will more often pass judgement on those taught by the Spirit, and imagine that scientific or logical thought will lead them to perfection. This is an ancient untruth. Palamas tells us: *Those who can judge everything, that is to say, the spiritual men, for according to the Apostle 'the spiritual man judges all things', should bring under their authority those who cannot judge, so that this judgement may permit them to know themselves with certainty. But to the contrary . . . these people try to judge and correct spiritual men who are judged by nobody. 'The spiritual man', says the Apostle, 'is judged by nobody.'* In fact, Palamas, and with him probably most of the Fathers of the church, agreed with these words which define the exact character of the inner tradition. The true doctrine is not what is known through words and arguments, but through what is demonstrated in people's works and lives. That is not only the truth, but the only certain and immutable truth. Palamas then quotes the proverb, familiar in his time, *every word, argues with some other word. But,* he adds, *what word can argue with life?*

This definition of the doctrine is most important. It tells us how we can come to understand the meaning of the doctrine. Only those who have worked on themselves by struggling with themselves (for non-monastic seekers, by struggling against habits in thought and action) and by repentance, will obtain self-knowledge and so will understand the teaching correctly. Secondly, it allows us to distinguish with greater certainty between true and false – in our own interior monologue, as well as in the words of others. This is the way to begin the search for self-knowledge, or as Palamas expresses it: *We would even state that it is impossible to know yourself by the methods of distinction, syllogism and analysis; to know yourself one must free the nous from pride and evil by laborious repentance and active asceticism. One who has not worked his nous by these means will not even know his own poverty in the domain of knowledge. So this practical way is the beginning of self-knowledge.*

A form of self-knowledge

The psychological method depends on more than one kind of self-knowledge. When we begin to know ourselves, not in the deepest of all senses, but in the sense of knowing our character, at first we 'do not know that we know.' Later we will begin to become aware of this kind of self-knowledge. But what is it, how does it differ from the deepest levels of self-knowledge, what is its importance, and how is it formed?

We can accumulate experiential knowledge about ourselves and our life, about how we act and react to life and about what effect we can have on life, but for many years this knowledge will remain unknown, unrecognised by us. This is a kind of self-knowledge that often remains almost inarticulate. For many years it can remain as silent as a shy child. At first we meet it mostly in the back-corridors of our psyche. When it does appear in public we do not recognise it, do not trust it, and are somewhat embarrassed by its presence. Because it is not built either on ordinary thought or on recognisable forms of logic, we do not think it can be relied on. We are continually surprised when other people seem to recognise it as a voice of truth. It is one of the things about ourselves that puzzles us. But how is it that this knowledge remains unknown for so long? Is it perhaps because it does not belong to what modern neuroscience calls the 'semantic' level of the mind, but is in some way more directly 'written to' the brain? Subject to the need for further confirmation of what is at present simply a 'subjective' statement, it has certain characteristics which appear to be those of non-semantic brain learning. For example:

1. It appears to be inarticulate, yet it can be expressed. That is, it does not have the form of thought, so that we cannot trace its formation, development or expression in semantic terms.

2. It is built up very slowly, with large numbers of almost identical observations in the way that skills are built-up by long practice, or in the way that the experiential knowledge of the brain is reported to be built-up.

3. It can be observed to have the quality of 'recognition', in that we recognise the repetition of certain patterns in ourselves and in life.

4. The ways in which it is learned are similar to those in which we learn skills and such characteristics as intonations and accents.

5. It has the basic qualities of so-called subjective observations, but when first experienced it often seems to be without the added element of imagined conclusions or judgements, which appear to be added later at the semantic level.

6. This form of self-knowledge is the product of a particular kind of experience: of what happens inside us in response to certain kinds of outside events and knowledge of what happens in the world as a result of certain actions or certain states that come into being within us.

Self-knowledge such as this is laid down, like good wine, only by taking care, only by careful self-observation. That is, it comes into being only to the degree that we are able to observe both inner and outer world at the same time. This knowledge becomes articulate, only after it hits a certain threshold which appears to be quantitative, involving a certain number of multiple iterations of similar events, although we have not yet found any way of measuring it. This threshold appears also to have been recognised by neuroscience in as much as it becomes articulate only when we have learned to communicate it to and through the semantic components of the psyche; it becomes articulate only when the ordinary intellect learns to trust it and believe its conclusions.

3.14 The role of inner knowledge on the path of salvation

One kind of knowledge teaches us about the world and gives us ways of dealing with it. This knowledge dies when we die. The other kind of knowledge, which can only be apprehended within, is needed if we want to obtain salvation. Modern man does not understand what salvation is, and so he thinks that it is purely mythical or meaningless, and does not try to learn about it. Palamas quotes St Basil the Great, where he says: *Truth has two forms. There is one which it is absolutely necessary to possess and to communicate to others, as it contributes to our salvation. Regarding the earth and the sea, the sky, and all that is in them, even if we do not know the truth about these things, this is nothing that will prevent us acquiring the promised beatitude.* Palamas defines our aim like this: *The goal before us is God's promise of good things to come – adoption, deification, revelation, the possession and enjoyment of heavenly treasures.*

But words are not enough to awaken us to spiritual life. It is the awareness possessed by the purified psyche which gives us true knowledge of God. We cannot find God through secular education alone: *If the language of the senses were able to establish reality in the age to come, the wise men of this age would become heirs to the kingdom of heaven. But according to the true philosopher, Maximos: 'If it is the purity of the psyche which sees, then those sages will be far from the knowledge of God.' What need do we have of knowledge which does not bring us closer to God? How could we possibly acquire perfection and holiness with it?* To understand these words in such a way that they do not seem simply 'unrealistic', we also need some understanding of ourselves.

3.15 We cannot 'see' God unless He shows Himself to us

The divine is not only invisible to human scrutiny, it is also incomprehensible. For this reason God is unknowable by the exercise of human effort alone.

However, He can be known by the type of contemplation once known by the Greek word *theologia*, which then pointed to the practical daily exercise of addressing God (in contrast to the modern 'theology' with its abstract and overly intellectual implications). *The natural activity of the psyche and body brings about a transformation of our mental imagining* (images in our thoughts, mental reflections – *logike eikonos*). *But this is not at all the perfect beauty and virtuous state that comes from above. It does not bring the supernatural union with the light beyond radiance, which is the unique source of reliable theology, and whose effect sets in motion the inner powers of psyche and body according to nature.*

Since, as the Bible says, nobody has ever seen God, the rationalists claimed that people were wrong when they said that they had seen God, even in the form of noetic light seen within. *They say, in effect, that God is invisible and incomprehensible: 'No man hath seen God at any time; the only begotten Son, which is in the bosom of the Father, he hath declared him'*

On this basis they then reason: *'How then are they not obviously deluded, they who claim to see God as a noetic light in themselves?' Any one of these men whom they attack can refute them with the Word, the only Son of God, Who said: 'The pure in heart will see God' and, 'he that loves me, my Father will love him, and we will come and make our abode with him.' But then they will reply that their contemplation is knowledge, without noticing that they are contradicting themselves.*

In fact, the divine is not only invisible but is also incomprehensible. So those who teach that because God is invisible, so the noetic vision of God in the light is the fruit of a wandering imagination and daemonic activity, should also reject all knowledge described in similar language, because God is also incomprehensible. In fact, there is knowledge about God and His doctrines, a divine contemplation which we call theology. But this is not the dawn of the perfect beauty of the noble state which comes to us from above. It is not the supernatural union with the most resplendent light, which is the unique source of reliable theology, the effect of which is to organise the inner powers of psyche and body, and to make them move in conformity with nature. In rejecting this, they have rejected all virtue and all truth.

So although God is invisible, the supernatural union with the uncreated light is the unique source of certainty in theology, and it is this which also organises the interior powers of body and psyche. In our times, this inner reorganisation is one proof that this seeing is true!

3.16 The conditions for contemplation

Because God is invisible, He cannot be contemplated in sensory and intellectual terms. The higher and mystical contemplation does not belong to that domain; it belongs to those who are watchful, who have stabilised their hearts by dispassion and who have received the Holy Spirit within themselves.

Palamas tells us that he learned this when he was with those who participated in true contemplation. They speak of a different kind of knowledge, obtained in a different way. To say that God is invisible means that he cannot be perceived by the senses, nor known by sensory knowledge. But God is known by contemplative knowledge, *theologia*. Only with the help of the Holy Spirit can we see the pure light of God. Palamas poses the question: *Do you think that the Holy Spirit does not see what concerns God? For it is He who 'searches out the deep things of God.' If someone pretended to see the pure light without the help of the Holy Spirit, you would be right to confront him and to say to him: 'How could one see the invisible?'*

Palamas continues by describing certain conditions which enable the one who fulfils them to see that which eye has not seen, which ear has not heard, and which has never arisen in the heart of man. Here we will list them as a kind of 'spiritual checklist,' each step of which must be understood and put into practice in our lives:

If a man rejects the spirit of the world,
If he purifies himself of all self-will,
If he also ignores human traditions which weaken his faith,
If he gathers the powers of his psyche together properly, and maintains the eye of his heart in watchfulness,
If he then lives meditating in his nous on what is true to nature and what pleases God,
Then he may transcend himself and receive the Spirit which comes from God, and which knows the things of God just as the spirit of man knows what is within a man.
If he receives this Spirit in order to know the things which God has given him mystically by His grace,
Then how would such a man not see the invisible light by the help of the Spirit?

Such men receive spiritual eyes and have the nous of Christ, so they can: *See the Invisible and noetically think of the Incomprehensible, for it is not invisible to them, but only to those who think and see only with their natural and created eyes and thoughts.* This contemplative knowledge is not gained by study. God gives it to those who allow Him to direct their lives. The labourer is worthy of his hire!

3.17   The eyes of love perceive a different world

Divine Contemplation lies beyond the abstraction of apophatic theology. Palamas shows one way in which this occurs when he tells how David uses the language of theology in the *Song of Songs* to describe the beauty of God seen by the eyes of love.

See that you are beautiful, he says to Him, *you who are close to me; your eyes are like the eyes of doves.* Here the physical eye is an analogy for the spiritual vision of the 'eye of the psyche.' *Just as when radiance in the eyes acts as light when it is united to the radiance of the sun and so sees sensory things, in the same way the nous, having become 'one Spirit with the Lord,' sees spiritual things clearly.* But nobody has ever seen the fullness of this beauty. We do not see the true measure of the beauty except to the measure that our own capacity for seeing has been made receptive by the divine Spirit. And when we are initiated into a knowledge of the future, experience the eternal, and understand the incomprehensible, we still do not understand just how we understand it. Dionysius explains: *The union of someone who has been divinised to the light which comes from above occurs when all noetic activity ceases.* The union is a result of stopping all activity, but we cannot produce it in ourselves simply by ceasing to act.

Contemplation is not simply cessation or abstraction: *It is a union and a divinisation which occurs, mystically and inexpressibly by the grace of God, after we have separated ourselves from all that has come from below to write on the nous. In fact, it happens after the cessation of all noetic activity. This is more than mere separation, and the inner separation is no more than the sign of that cessation. This is why every believer should consider God as separate from all His creatures, for the cessation of all noetic activity and the resulting union with the light from on high is an objective state, and part of the accomplishment of divinisation. It happens only to those who have purified their hearts and received grace.* It occurs in a union granted by the grace of God once the nous is freed of all lower impressions. It depends on purity of heart, and on the grace of God acting in a nous that has been made clean of sensory and noetic impressions and activity. Those see truly who no longer see, and who obey without first knowing, and the faculty of this vision is neither sense nor nous.

3.18 In the stillness of hesychia, we perceive by the Holy Spirit

In the stillness of God we enter a new kind of life. Once all noetic activity has ceased, then nous, eyes, and ears are replaced by the Holy Spirit, and through Him they see God. Palamas says: *For if all their noetic activity has come to rest, how could the angels and men like angels see God except by the power of the Spirit?* He also tells us that this vision is not received through the senses, or in the thoughts, or in the knowledge that comes from them, nor is it a product of imagination, nor an opinion, nor a conclusion of logic. It happens when all these activities cease. On the other hand, the nous does not acquire this simply by raising itself up by means of negation. Palamas then tells us that: *Every divine command and sacred law aims at purity of heart. Every mode and aspect of prayer is crowned by pure prayer.* Every upward thought comes to an end beyond created things.

Yet even this is not an end. Beyond these things are many others: *There is the pledge of things promised in this age. There are also the blessings of the age to come. . . Then, beyond prayer, there is the vision that cannot be spoken of, the ecstasy in the vision, and the hidden mysteries. . . After the cessation is the unknowing that is greater than knowledge. There is a cloud, but is more than radiance ... it is in this radiant darkness that divine things are given to the saints.* Beyond abstraction from the things of earth is participation in things divine. Beyond what can be said are things which cannot be spoken of, except in images and analogies.

Palamas concludes the chapter: *Thus the most perfect contemplation of God and divine things is not simply interior abstraction. Beyond this abstraction there is a participation in things divine, which is more a gift and a possession than a process of abstraction. These possessions and gifts are indescribable. If one says anything about them, one must use images and analogies, not because these things are seen only as images and analogies, but because one cannot show what has been seen in any other way. When we talk about things that are indescribable, we must describe them in an imaginative way. Then those who do not lend an attentive ear to it consider that this knowledge which surpasses all wisdom is simply foolishness. They trample the noetic pearls underfoot with their criticisms. As far as is possible with words, they also strive to destroy those who have shown them these pearls.*

3.19 The idea of unwritten tradition is simple but exact

The idea of an 'unwritten tradition' points to the question: how can we speak about the unspeakable? How do we deal with the fact that ideas are inadequate to express these truths, just as studying the tree cannot tell us the taste of its fruit? *It is because of their love of men that the saints speak of indescribable things, as far as that is possible. They reject the error of those who, in their ignorance, imagine that beyond abstraction from created things there remains only total inaction, when that inaction actually transcends all activity. But, I repeat, these things remain impossible to describe by their very nature.* Dionysius the Areopagite says that after abstraction from created things, there is no language, but only *an absence of words.* He also tells us that beyond the ascent is silence, union with the inexpressible.

In his *Mystical Theology* Dionysius tells us this: *The higher we rise, the more our words are confined to the ideas we are capable of forming; so that now as we plunge into that darkness beyond intellect ... we find ourselves speechless and unknowing. But my argument now rises from what is below up to the transcendent, and the more it climbs, the more language falters, and when it has passed up and beyond the ascent, it will turn silent completely, since it will finally be at one with Him who is indescribable.* (*Mystical Theology*, 1033) Since it is inexpressible, negation alone (i.e. recognising what God is not) is not enough to enable the nous to attain things that are beyond the nous. The way of negation is simply a way of grasping the difference between Creator and His creation. It is: *An understanding of what appears to differ from God. It merely gives an image of the inexpressible illumination and of the realisation of the nous in that illumination. The way of negation is not in itself that realisation.*

The experience of transcendence is in the power of the divine light seen by those who have purified themselves in obedience and consecrated themselves to immaterial prayer. But the realisation is more than speaking about the realisation, says Palamas: *Those who, like angels, have been united to that light, sing of this using the image of total abstraction. A mystical union with the light beyond essence teaches them that this light transcends all things. Moreover, those judged worthy to receive the mystery, and even those who have a faithful and prudent ear around these initiates, can also sing of the divine and incomprehensible light that comes when we are abstracted from all things. But they cannot unite themselves to it and see it unless they have purified themselves by taking care to fulfil the commandments, and by consecrating their nous to pure and immaterial prayer, thus receiving the supernatural power of divine contemplation.*

3.20 The mystery of contemplation is neither sensory nor noetic

Theoria (divine contemplation) is neither purely sensory nor purely noetic. Palamas calls the power of contemplation a 'noetic sense', and defines it as a form of union, not of knowledge. It brings blessed purity in its train. Solomon described it as a *sensation that is both noetic and divine*. Palamas comments: *By combining those two adjectives, he urges his audience to consider it neither as solely sensory nor as simply a noetic activity, for neither is the activity of the nous sensory, nor is that of the senses noetic.* He tells us that Dionysius distinguishes between a *noetic power*, which allows us to see noetic things, and a *power of union* which goes beyond the nous and joins it to what transcends it.

In theosis, says the same saint, when the psyche becomes godlike, the noetic powers as well as the senses become superfluous. In this way the final purification is an act of the divine light itself: *The noetic powers as well as the senses are no longer needed when the psyche becomes divinised, and they concentrate sightlessly and through an unknowing union on the rays of 'unapproachable light.'* St Maximos also speaks of this union: *In beholding the light of the hidden glory which cannot be put into words, the saints too, like the celestial powers, become capable of receiving the blessed purity.*

3.21 Dispassion leads to a vision of the invisible

Negative theology, on its own, does not lead to union. Purification of the psyche may free the nous, and this opens us to the vision of the invisible during prayer, as a noetically perceptible reality. Then the nous no longer prays any definite prayer but finds itself in ecstasy amidst incomprehensible realities. This unknowing is *higher than knowledge*.

The negative or apophatic method helps us to free our thoughts from outside influences by distinguishing all experiences as being something other than God, but it does not lead to union. The purification of the psyche is the method that leads to dispassion, which effectively then liberates the nous. And this in turn allows the nous to be united in prayer to the grace of the Spirit, and opens it to the divine light, so that it appears angelic or god-like.

It is this state, in which man sees directly by the Spirit, which the Fathers called spiritual sensation – a most exact description of it as a mystical and hidden contemplation. *At such times,* says Palamas, *man truly sees neither by the nous, nor by the body, but by the Spirit. Then he surely knows that he sees supernaturally a light that is beyond light. Yet at that moment he does not know which instrument allows him to see this light, nor can he discover the nature of that instrument, for he cannot follow the traces of the Spirit. This was what Paul said when he heard the inexpressible words and saw invisible things, of which he said: 'Whether in the body or whether out of the body, I cannot tell'. In other words, he did not know whether he saw through his nous or through his body.*

We perceive through the Spirit when in this state, and are aware that we see a light which is beyond the light that we ordinarily know. Even St Paul did not know how he saw this. Yet this sight is as clear as the sight of the senses, but with a great sweetness added, as Palamas tells us. This is ecstasy, from the Greek word *ecstasis*. In this state the nous transcends the activity of prayer by achieving through grace the aim of all prayer: *The end of prayer is in an ecstasy of the inmost heart.*

Under the influence of this ecstasy, writes Palamas, commenting on St Paul, *he even forgot prayer to God. It is this of which St Isaac speaks, confirming the great and divine Gregory: 'Prayer is the purification of the nous, which is brought forth by the light of the Holy Trinity in the midst of astonishment. Purity of nous is what allows the light of the Holy Trinity to shine at the moment of prayer. The nous then transcends prayer, and this state should not properly be called prayer, although it is a fruit of the pure prayer sent by the Holy Spirit. Then the nous no longer prays any definite prayer, it finds itself in ecstasy amidst incomprehensible realities. This is the unknowing that is higher than knowledge.'*

This was what ravished St Paul, and about which Palamas said: *Paul was returned to wholeness and his nous stepped back from every created thing when he was ravished in that most joyful reality, which he beheld as a light, a light of revelation, although it did not reveal sensible bodies. It was a light with no limit either in depth, or in height, or to either side. He saw absolutely no limit to his vision, or to the light which shone on him, as if it were a sun infinitely brighter and greater than the universe. He held himself at the centre of it, having become all eye.*

Notice the qualities of this vision: a revelation but not sensory; withdrawn from all created things; unlimited in space; a light of limitless brightness; and viewed from the centre.

3.22 We recognise the true light by its effect on us

The light of the infinite appears endless, and this makes us aware that our own finite ability limits our capacity to comprehend it. We recognise its truth by the effects it has on us.

Palamas relates how Macarius describes this light: *Infinite and beyond the heavens.* Palamas comments, *another saint, one of the most perfect, saw the whole universe contained in a single ray of this noetic sun, even though he himself did not see the full nature and the measure of that light, seeing it only to the measure that he was fit to receive it.* If we are eventually able to see it, we too will perceive it only to the degree that we have been made receptive. The limit of such a vision, says Palamas, is in our nature, not in the nature of what is seen. What will we learn? We will not learn what it is, but will learn with certainty that it does exist. This distinction is important. Palamas says: *This vision of the Infinite cannot permanently belong to any individual, nor to all men together. He who does not see this light will understand that it is he himself who lacks the capacity to see because he is not perfectly adapted to the Spirit by complete purification, it is not the Object of vision that falls short. When the vision comes down to him, the seer knows with certainty that it is the light, even if he only sees it faintly.*

We know that this is the true light by the effects it has on us – by the calm it brings into being in our nous, by the passionless joy it arouses in us, by the fire of love it awakens in our heart. As we draw closer to God and further from the world, this contemplation becomes ever richer: *In proportion to his practice of what is agreeable to God, in his rejection of everything else, in his attentiveness in prayer, and to the degree of elevation of his psyche towards God, so he experiences an ever more luminous contemplation.*

The more we recognise our vision is infinite, because we are contemplating the Infinite and cannot see an end to its radiance, the more we recognise how limited is our own capacity to perceive that radiance.

3.23 The psyche, as the living soul, finds its true life in God

The Greek language uses the word 'psyche' for the life that enlivens the body, and the same word is the root of the word psychology. As psyche brings life to the body, God by His light brings the life of *theosis* (deification) to the psyche.

But the important thing, as Palamas re-iterates in different ways, is that even though the vision of the light is an important revelation of reality to us, it is not an actual perception of God's nature. What happens is that, just as the psyche communicates life to the living body, so God, Who dwells in the God-bearing psyche, communicates a light of *theosis* to the psyche. It is the light and the splendour of His greatness which is communicated to us, not His actual nature. As Palamas says: *This light is thus divine, and the saints rightly call it 'divinity' because it is the source of deification. So it is not only 'divinity' but 'deification-itself,' and the rule of God.* He tells us that the light is the light of theosis, and that it has been called many wonderful things, in particular divinity, because it is divine in origin and is the source of theosis ;deification itself,' and 'the Kingdom of God.' Paradoxically, this divine light seems to manifest as distinction and multiplicity within the one God, but it is nevertheless a sign of the one God who is the divine source, more than God and more than source, the One who remains undivided in space or time.

Following Dionysius the Areopagite, the Fathers of the church called the deifying gift that comes from God 'divinity.' Dionysius explained how God could even be beyond *thearchia* (divine authority): *If you regard the substance of the gift which deifies us as 'Divinity', and this gift is the source of deification, then He who transcends every source, including the Divinity spoken of here, also surpasses the source of Divinity.* And in terms of expressing this reality, this is what Peter had to say: *Which things also we speak, not in the words which man's wisdom teacheth, but which the Holy Spirit teacheth; comparing spiritual things with spiritual.* (II Peter 1, 16-18) It is this one God who deifies man and brings every noetic reality into being. Palamas again sums up: *So the fathers say that the divine grace of the light that is beyond the senses is God. Yet God in his nature is not identical with this grace, because He is able not only to illumine and deify the nous, but can bring out of non-being every noetic essence.*

3.24 The noetic light described in the New Testament is confirmed by the teachings of the Old

Our perception of the noetic light can be distinguished by the fact that its qualities go beyond our ordinary knowledge. By this light contemplatives discover that the New Covenant, the teaching of grace in the New Testament, confirms and is confirmed by the teaching of the Law in the Old Testament.

However logical they are, even those who see this light think of it as an 'invisible light'. Contemplatives know that they see it by a noetic sense, and that our limited knowledge does not limit its reality: *They know that this light is God who, by his grace, makes luminous those who participate in the mysterious union. And if you ask them how they see the Invisible, they will answer you: 'not in the words which man's wisdom teaches, but through those by which the Holy Spirit teaches.' In effect, they lack nothing, they have no need of human wisdom, since they possess the teaching of the Spirit.* They know that what they learn is not in any way limited by what they already know: *Because they behaved in the world with simplicity, purity and Godly sincerity, and not with fleshly wisdom.* (2 Corinthians 1:12) Those who have received the light will say: *'Things divine, O man, are not in the least limited by our knowledge. On the contrary, many things of which we are ignorant have their origin in God'. Thus, following the Apostle, it is by 'comparing the spiritual' to the spiritual in this way that we establish that the grace of the New Covenant is in agreement with the Old. The Apostle called this demonstration from the old covenant 'comparison,' for after having established the new things in this way, we can also show that the gifts of grace are superior to those of the law.*

To those who ask, 'how can an invisible light be seen?' Palamas offers this response: *Those who live and see by the Spirit will reply thus: 'How did Elijah, the prophet of God, see the light: the cloak in which he wrapped his face showed that he was not seeing in a sensory way. Moreover, the surname by which all knew him clearly announces and testifies that he really had seen God, even though his sensory eyes were hidden by his cloak. Everybody called him 'Theoptes' and even 'Theoptikotatos', 'the greatest seer of God'.*

3.25 Signs confirming the reality of the inner light

The authenticity of the inner light is confirmed by other signs, it affects the body, warms the heart or fills us with a cool and utter stillness. The light that brings these signs is the 'bread of angels', the grace which makes man immortal. This light is given to those who continually ask God for it.

There are other signs of grace and of effective prayer besides the inner light. It is important to understand this, as they are valuable confirmations for us on our way. Palamas tells us if you question the divine contemplatives thus: *'Why do you say that prayer resounds mystically in your innards, and what sets your heart in motion?' they will point to the earthquake Elias felt which preceded the noetic manifestation of God. They will also refer to the sounding of the stomach described in Isaiah. And if you then ask them why prayer produces warmth in us, they will speak of the fire which the same Elias named as a sign of God before His appearance, a sign that then becomes like a light breeze when close to being clothed by the divine radiance, which is named the Invisible by he who contemplates it. They will speak again of Elias who appeared and really was like a fire when he physically ascended in a chariot of fire. They will also speak of the other prophet whose innards were burned as if by fire; the words of God had become fire in him. And they will say always and to everyone, 'have you not heard, that a man has eaten the bread of angels?'* (Psalm 78:25)

The 'bread of angels' is the light of union beyond the heavens. The Old Testament symbol for this was manna, given to the Israelites in the desert as a promise of the illumination to come. It was finally manifested by Christ in the

Holy Gifts of communion, themselves a pledge and sign of the indescribable communion with Jesus in the age to come. Men unite to this light, says Palamas, 'either directly or by transmission.' And he then adds: *Did you not hear the Lord say that he will give the Holy Spirit to those who ask Him night and day?* (Luke 11:13 and 18:7)

The events of the Old Testament pre-figure the graces of Christ, noetic illumination and the graces beyond knowledge. *Do you see,* ends Palamas, *that these symbolic illuminations are the outer manifestations of noetic illumination, and of mysteries other than knowledge?*

3.26 The Transfiguration on Tabor as a glimpse of our own salvation

The Transfiguration of Christ on Mount Tabor pre-figured His Coming Again. Today we understand that most often He returns within us as an inner light that testifies to us of the Kingdom to which we are called – in this life or the next! Palamas tells us that this experience was *theologia* – in the sense that it conforms to the ancient principles of the theology of direct experience, not those of the reason, logic and assumption of modern theology.

Both St Mark, in his gospel, and St Peter testify that Peter saw the majesty of Christ shining on Mount Tabor. St Chrysostom calls this the 'radiance of divinity', while Dionysius calls it *divine manifestation and the vision of God*. Gregory the Theologian says: *The Divinity manifested to the disciples on the mountain was a light.* Symeon wrote that the apostle John *saw the very Divinity of the Word* unveiled on the mountain.

All these witnesses agree that the most perfect vision of God takes the form of a light, says Palamas. Yet the vision revealed to the apostles was neither symbolic nor transient. It did not appear and then disappear; it was identical with the Second coming of Christ, and the same light will illumine those who are worthy in the age without end, for it is an eternal light. Basil the Great speaks of it as a prelude to the Second Coming, and Christ in the Gospels calls it *the Kingdom of God*.

3.27 The light of the Transfiguration was seen through the eyes by means of the nous

The light of the Transfiguration was seen by sensory eyes, but only because there was a nous behind them, because it was not seen by animals. In addition, it could be seen to have an infinite nature, so this was no ordinary sensory light: *The saints do not say that this light is a light of the senses, but call it 'noetic,' as Solomon said of the Holy Spirit.* Even today, people object if we speak about seeing God, whether as a sensory or as a noetic light. Palamas states that those who oppose noetic prayer claim that: *The divine vision of God they see in prayer is simply sensory light, while on the other hand they oppose any sensory reality in the divine gifts of grace! How then, forgetting themselves, can they heap scorn on those who say that the divine light is not sensory? Do you see their inconsistency and their inconstancy?*

But it seems probable that any animals nearby during the Transfiguration of Christ were not aware of this light. If humans saw this with the eyes of their senses, it would have been because they act differently from eyes that lack the backing of the human nous. Apart from the Apostles, nobody else nearby saw this brilliant light, so it was not in any way a sensory light. And we know that this light of divine glory has neither beginning nor end. Since nothing sensory is eternal, this light was not sensory.

3.28 The meanings of words extended to describe the inner life

In this passage we add an explanation of the extended meanings given to outer words when they are used to describe inner experiences. It also develops the idea of the light of transfiguration more fully, and again drives home the fact that this was a noetic light and not merely sensory.

Palamas says: *The radiance of Jesus' face was indescribable, unapproachable, and timeless – because it acted through an inexpressible reality.* It was a glimpse, a foretaste and preview of the light which shines on the saints in heaven. So although it sometimes appears in a strange way to become accessible to the senses, it is nevertheless part of a reality which transcends the nous itself, and the names which are given to it are extended from their ordinary meanings. To deal with the problems of describing inner experiences to those who have not met them before, the Fathers frequently used familiar words in unfamiliar ways. Words that already had a meaning in ordinary external experience would be used with new or extended meanings to describe unfamiliar interior experiences.

So, given that when we pray for the dead, we pray for God to keep their psyches in a place of light, Palamas then poses the question: *What need have these psyches of a sensory light, and why would they be afflicted by the darkness that was the opposite of this light, if it was simply a sensory darkness? Do you see that none of these things properly belong to the domain of the senses? We also showed earlier on, when we mentioned the dark fire prepared for the race of daemons, that this is also not simply a matter of ignorance or knowledge.* This logic will seem flawed, and in fact, Palamas says, we do not need to make statements based on ordinary reasoning about this experience of the light on Tabor. We should rather have followed the instruction of the Fathers who tell us to wait until we obtain exact knowledge through experience we have gained in purity of heart. It is this latter kind of knowledge that leads to union with the light. This is a light that cannot be described in ordinary language, for this light cannot be compared to any being, because it transcends all created things: *How could the radiance of God be as that of a created being?*

3.29 Inner experience of the light of the Transfiguration

The light of Christ as seen by inner experience is the same light as that of the Transfiguration. It is His action, freely given to us when the time is right, in order to sustain our transformed psyche in a state of righteousness. This experience still happens today, and in those who give enough time to the search it happens fairly early on the path. Macarius says that when the psyche turns back to God in remorse, filled with fear, love and shame, God ignores its transgressions, and immediately clothes it in a 'robe of glory' – the light of Christ. This light is the same as that seen by Peter on the mountain. But if this simply belonged to the domain of the senses, it could not form a garment for the psyche.

In fact, says Palamas, this is really spiritual food, the food of the angels and of the just. He then continues, quoting Macarius: '*The Lord made the composition of human nature that was assumed by Him sit on the right hand of the divine majesty in the heavens', in a fullness of glory, visible, not on his face alone as with Moses, but on his whole body. If nobody perceives this light, does it shine in vain? Yes, if the light is sensory. Is it not actually the food of the spirits, of angels, and of the just? This is why, when we pray for the dead, we ask Christ to place their souls where they are watched over by the light of His face.*

In this way, the saint indicates to the hesychast how to recognise the state of light that shows when he or she obtains the right results in their spiritual practice. The noetic light is given by God to the righteous as a spiritual food that sustains the life of the spirit. When we pray for the dead to be placed in that light, we pray that they should be fed on spiritual food. How would the dead obtain joy from sensory food? And if, as he says, *Christ on the mountain appeared as infinite light*, then *how could a sensory light be infinite?*

3.30 Symbolic language is one way to describe inner experience

Symbolic language is totally unnecessary to convey sensory experiences in themselves, but it can contain and convey inner meanings, the meanings of inner events and the deeper meanings of sensory perceptions that cannot be explained in any other way. Here, an example from the life of St Stephen explores the relation of sign to symbol and the place of symbolic ideas in language. It also describes how the true spiritual vision is more than the symbolic. According to the Acts of the Apostles, while Stephen was standing on the earth he saw: *The heavens open and the glory of God, and Christ standing at the right hand of God.* This could not have been perceived with the ordinary senses, so the description here contains a symbolic content. Palamas enquires: *Is it then possible to reach with our senses as far as realities beyond the heavens? Yet this man saw such realities while remaining here on earth. What is even more marvellous was that he not only saw Christ, but also His Father. How, could he have seen that the Son was on His right, if he had not also seen the Father?* Palamas talks about the vision itself as something separate from its symbolic content: *The invisible allows itself to be seen by those whose hearts are purified, but by a mysterious power, in a manner which is neither sensible, nor noetic, nor apophatic, for the sublime majesty and the glory of the Father cannot be in any way accessible to the senses.*

The nature of symbols

Symbolic language describes experiences which cannot be seen outside us. The same passage also refers to a more direct experience of an inner light which is simply referred to as light, but here we need to take care to avoid confusing it with external light.

The position on the right was symbolic, although the vision was not. Although the position itself was only a symbol standing for Him Who is fixed and immutable, like the absolutely unchangeable permanence of the divine nature, yet Stephen saw it in an mysterious way. For the position to the right was not a trick by the Only Begotten, intended to show a different reality, but by being always to the right of the Father, He clearly wanted to show His own glory to someone who was still in the flesh but had surrendered his very psyche for that glory. This example speaks of Christ as standing on the right of His Father. This is a figurative way of describing something that was actually not in any way like a sensory image. We should not attempt to interpret it literally, it is analogy. It is its deeper meaning which is true. The vision was not a sensory image, and the symbolic image used was not a true visual description of the experience, but an analogy for its meaning. So here the idea that Christ was on the right of the Father symbolised his close relationship to God the Father by taking as an analogy the 'place of honour' to the right hand of a king, since it is this, through the ages, which has been known to represent the closest relation to the king Himself.

If Stephen's vision of the glory of God was a noetic vision, or the result of deduction or analogy, that would mean that we should be able to see what he saw. Palamas writes: *We too are able to represent the God-become-man by analogy – showing Him standing or seated in heaven on the right of the divine Majesty. But why was this vision not already or even always in the nous of the disciple of the Evangelist? Why did he grasp it only at that exact moment? 'Behold', he said, 'I see the heavens opened and the Son of Man standing on the right hand of God.'* (Acts 7:56)

Why did he need to 'turn his eyes to heaven' asks Palamas: *What need had he to turn his eyes to heaven, and for heaven to open, if this vision had been no more than knowledge obtained noetically? Yet in what way did the first martyr have this vision if he saw it neither noetically, nor with the senses, nor by negation, nor if he conceived these divine things by deduction nor by analogy? I will dare to tell you – spiritually! Those who see the pure light through revelation, said the fathers, see spiritually. The divine Luke also teaches this, saying that: 'He, full of faith and the Holy Spirit, turning his eyes to heaven, saw the glory of God.' And you too, if you are full of faith and the Holy Spirit, will be able to contemplate spiritually things which are invisible to the nous. But if, on the other hand, you remain devoid of faith, you will not even believe those who bear witness to what they have seen.*

So this vision of the pure light was a spiritual vision and, as Palamas says, if you have even a small amount of real faith, you will listen attentively when people speak of such things. You will not try to interpret what they say in sensory terms, nor will you reject the grace of God simply because it is difficult to describe it adequately.

3.31 The uncreated light is spiritual food

Because it serves as food of the spirit, as well as a source of contemplative knowledge, this contemplation of the pure or uncreated light was described by one of the Fathers as *especially true*. Within contemplation, *prayer energises the heart with spiritual warmth, and delight, and the joyful tears of grace.* Palamas continues: *It is of course the noetic sense that is responsible for grasping all this. I say 'sense' because the perception involved is manifest and clear, free from delusion and imagination. Furthermore, in a certain way the body also participates in the grace that acts through the nous. The body harmonises with this grace, and it too becomes sensitive to the hidden mystery occurring in the psyche. Grace then communicates a perception of what is being produced at that moment through the senses of anyone who looks from the outside on those who possess this grace.*

Thus the radiance of the nous within Moses or Stephen, as it took angelic form, became brilliantly visible on their faces, as can happen even today. (see *On Acquisition of the Holy Spirit*, St Seraphim of Sarov) *This is also how Mary of Egypt, or rather Mary of Heaven, rose bodily into the air when praying, perceptibly and actually changing her position. For as her nous rose, her body also rose and, leaving the earth, was seen as a flying body.*

3.32 The warmth of grace, voluntary suffering and joyful dispassion

Palamas here deals with three important elements in the path: the warmth that is communicated to the body in intense prayer, when the heart wakes with joy from the power of its love for the Lord; the fact that this warmth is not daemonic but holy and beneficial; the nature of voluntary suffering and the fact that by overcoming passions it leads to this joy.

When the psyche is powerfully moved by an irresistible love for the true object of desire, the heart begins to move, leaping in a spiritual way. This shows that it is in communion with grace. Palamas said of this: *When the psyche is inspired as if aroused by the ardent beloved, the only desirable one, the heart arises and spiritually leaps, and marked by grace for communion, it is hence urged on towards that Body in the clouds which announces the coming of the Lord. And so when, in unceasing prayer, the noetic fire appears and the noetic torch is lit, and when the nous awakens its desire through the heavenly fire of spiritual contemplation, then, in a mysterious way, the body too becomes light and warm. To those who see it, according to the writer who described the spiritual ladder, it appears to come from a furnace visible to the senses.* The rationalists of his time believed that the physical warmth that comes from prayer is daemonic, while Palamas says that prayer can generate physical heat, and that there is nothing wrong with this. Prayer that avoids this does not lead to transformation or improvement.

Then he teaches the importance of affliction (*thlypsis*) or *voluntary suffering* in overcoming passions. In breaking the divine commandments we have developed preferences for certain physical pleasures, which since then have ruled our lives. We experience pain when we voluntarily surrender these bodily pleasures, but after this experience, during prayer we taste with our noetic sense a divine joy unmixed with pain. This is the inner asceticism of the psychological method. The prophet David experienced this joy and it transformed his very body to make it accessible to dispassion and divine love: *Your words are sweet to my palate, sweeter than honey to my mouth and also my psyche shall be satisfied as with marrow and fatness, and my mouth shall praise thee with joyful lips.* (Psalm 63:5) Dionysius the Great called this experience *the visitation of divine enlightenment.*

3.33 Transformation of the body by remorse

Then there is a divinely purifying remorse that transforms the body itself. In those who struggle for purity, this remorse is not only sensed in their psyche. Their tears of remorse show that it also acts in their bodies and affects their physical senses. For instance, when the signs of divine joy given by the Spirit are manifested by the faltering senses of the body, the Lord says: *Blessed are they that mourn, for they shall be comforted.* Palamas continues: *The body also participates in many different ways in this consolation. Those who have experienced this know it. In fact, it is not only the psyche which receives the promise of good things to come, but also the body, which runs the race of the Gospel with it.* This is why this saint says that these experiences are received by the senses, then adds 'but by the noetic senses,' because our nous is closer to the divine Nous and receives these influences first. *In this way,* says Palamas, *it shows and prefigures the absorption of the flesh by the Spirit in the age to come. It is not the eyes of the body but the eyes of the psyche which receive the power of the Spirit that allows them to see these things. We therefore call this power 'noetic,' even though it is above the nous.*

3.34 If we think of these energies as physical, we delude ourselves

In this chapter Palamas says that we must not think that these indescribable spiritual energies are physical or corporeal, or we will delude ourselves and act wrongly as a result. Those who think this have heard the pure teachings of the saints in an impure way, and so they have misunderstood them and gone against those who gave these teachings.

Perhaps, says Palamas, such people, *do not even know that the Great Macarius said: 'The spiritual soul of those without trial remains untouched, but for those with apprehension of holiness and faith, who have been tested and tried, comes communion with the Holy Spirit from whom alone they receive the heavenly treasure of Spirit and are made known and come into a new state of being. The profane can in no way contain this power within their nous.'* Palamas says that we should ponder this passage so as to become filled with faith, and this will make us worthy to experience these wonders. Then the true experiences of the 'eyes of the psyche' – a name for the nous – will show us what inner experiences are possible for the Christian psyche even in life. But we must not confuse these 'eyes of the psyche' which experience the heavenly treasure with ordinary reason.

Ordinary reason is as capable of dealing with physical things as noetic; Palamas offers this analogy: *Think of this in the same way that you would think of a city you had not yet seen – you cannot experience it simply by thinking of it. So it is with the things of God and things Divine, you cannot acquire experience of them simply by thinking or talking about them. If you do not possess gold in a tangible way, if you do not hold it visibly in your two hands, if you do not see it with your own eyes, you do not grasp it, you do not see it and you do not possess it, even if the thought of gold passes through your head ten thousand times – the same is true of thinking ten thousand times of divine treasures. Without confirming the divine things by experience, and without seeing them with the noetic eyes that transcend reason, you see nothing, you have nothing, you do not truly possess any of the divine things.* We see such things through *noetic eyes,* yet they originate from a point even 'above' these 'eyes of the heart'.

3.35 The light of the age to come can be seen on earth, but is visible to few

Because it is so far from ordinary, says Palamas, only three chosen disciples were called to the Transfiguration on Tabor which was invisible to sense and impossible to describe. But it is part of the New Covenant for all Christians who persevere and so enter the age to come.

Dionysius said that in the age to come we will be illumined by *the visible theophany of Christ* in communion through the nous, just as were the disciples at the Transfiguration, and furthermore: *We will participate in noetic illumination with a passionless and immaterial nous and in a union transcending the nous in a more divine imitation of the supra-celestial Minds.* Our nous will then be made dispassionate and immaterial: *Even then, we will not come to conceive that the light shining from the beloved Body is a sensory radiance, perceived by the senses without the power of a reasoning psyche. Indeed, only this last power can receive the power of the Spirit, which in its turn can contemplate the light of grace. The radiance which cannot be perceived by these means cannot be perceived at all.*

Palamas then poses this question: *How could a sensible light not be visible through the air? We would then see the light more or less distinctly, not as a measure of each individual's virtue and the purity resulting from that virtue, but as a measure of the purity of the air! 'The just will shine like the sun.' So each of them would appear brighter or darker not in proportion to their good actions, but merely depending on the purity of the air around them! What is more, in this case the good things of the age to come would be accessible to the eyes of the senses, now and forever. Everyone would see those good things which not only has 'eye not seen and ear not heard', but also which 'have not entered into the heart' of the man who tries to penetrate incomprehensible things by verbal reasoning. If it is sensory, how could this light be invisible to sinners? Or, according to these people, would there be a barrier formed of shadows and cones, of conjunctions resulting in eclipses, and of cycles of light in various forms? Will we need the vain activity of astronomers in a life of ages without end?*

3.36 The resurrection body perceives the light

In ordinary life, for the senses of the physical body to perceive a light which is not sensory it must first overcome the passions which have brought into being a veil of impure feelings, thoughts and imaginings around us which obscures our more subtle noetic senses. But in the age to come, the dispassionate nous will perceive directly, no longer veiled by the body. The light we may glimpse briefly today is the light of heaven that illumines the age to come.

Notice the faith in Palamas's words, in which, although he is aware that in most cases when he speaks of the Old Testament he is speaking of parable or analogy, here, on the basis of his own experience, he takes the Biblical account as a description of observed fact. So he states that the bodily senses will apprehend a light that is not truly sensible: *By the power of the all-powerful Spirit, the power by which the chosen apostles themselves saw it on Tabor, when it blazed out not only from the flesh which carries the Son within it, but also from the cloud which carries within it the Father of Christ.*

In the age to come, on the other hand, the body will no longer be a natural body, it will have been replaced by a spiritual body. In the words of the Apostle: *It is sown as a natural body, it is resurrected as a spiritual body.* This of course links with Our Lord's saying: *Truly, truly, I say to you, unless a grain of wheat falls into the earth and dies, it remains alone; but if it dies, it bears much fruit.* (John 12:24) It is because the body will be spiritual that it will be able to perceive the divine ray. It is important to understand that, as we are now, through the effect of the passions on us, our psyche is clothed with mortal, fleshly thoughts, of the life of the body, so that it becomes 'fleshly', and is dragged deeper into imagination. It is this veil that makes our nous unaware of spiritual things.

When humans are alive on earth, says Palamas, their psyches are hidden and obscured within their bodies. In the 'sons of the resurrection', who live in the age to come, it is their body which will be hidden within them. It is clear by this that whether this is merely a 'symbolic statement' or has a physical equivalent, either way it tells us that their relation with life will be conducted through the nous. Palamas ends by saying: *With the triumph of the nous ... they will enjoy the divine light in their body and their senses.*

3.37 In inner stillness the body participates in deification

Palamas says that it is not only the relationship between body and nous which is important. The body which has ceased all noetic and sensory activity will be divinised at the same time. God Himself acts through that inaction, and when He looks through our bodily eyes we will see the divine light as if it was physical.

To explain how not only the nous but even the psyche and the body are brought into the divine life, Palamas quotes Saint Maximos: *The psyche becomes God by participation in divine grace after it has itself ceased all noetic and sensory activity, as well as having ceased from all the natural activities of the body; for the body is divinised at the same time as the psyche, through its own corresponding participation in the process of deification. Thus God alone is made manifest through the psyche and the body, because their natural properties are overcome by the superabundance of God's glory.* In this state, we do not perceive by our own abilities, but through God, who 'sees through us.' Although He is invisible to His creatures, He is 'visible' to Himself. It is He who lends us the ability to see the inaccessible divine light as if with our bodily faculties. Finally, Palamas enquires: *Do you now understand that, in the proper sense of the term, the light that illumined the apostles on Tabor was not a sensory light?*

3.38 Our bodies communicate with the body of Christ

As He illumined those who approached Him on Tabor properly prepared, He now inwardly illumines the psyches of those who approach Him properly prepared for communion. This means that from the liturgical viewpoint the psychological method can be regarded as a method of *preparation for communion.*

Since the divine light has been seen through the eyes of the senses, there is agreement between spiritual men and their noetically blind opponents that there was a vision on Mount Tabor. So why, asks Palamas, if someone accepts that the divine light can be seen by bodily eyes, could they not accept that it can also be seen by spiritual eyes? And here he is speaking of psyche as that which contains the nous, asking if any psyche could be so veiled by evil it cannot perceive the light, or should be more dense than the physical body which, on occasion, is able to perceive the light. For even if the body sees the divine light through the mediation of the psyche, how could we regard the body as closer to God than the psyche? And if the Transfiguration of Our Lord was a preview of 'the Glory which is to come', then just as the apostles were given the privilege of contemplating this light with physical eyes, why could not those whose hearts are pure today be given the same privilege of previewing it in their nous? Thus when the Son of God in His love for us unites in communion of His substance with our nature so that He becomes a body containing a psyche which in turn contains a nous, in order *to appear on earth and live as a man*, He makes of our bodies *a temple for the whole Divinity*. For in the very Body of Christ dwells all the fullness of the Divinity.

3.39 The age to come can be experienced now

In the age to come we will see the Invisible face to face, so those whose hearts are pure are given a foretaste of this, seeing the invisible noetic reality within them while they are still alive. It is this which is known as the 'white stone'. Those with pure hearts receive the pledge of this now, and through their senses they see the invisible noetic formation within them. For the nous is as immaterial as the light, and is also similar to the First and sublime Light in which all things participate, although that Light is transcendent to them all.

By turning entirely toward the true Light in ceaseless prayer, the nous is purified and ascends toward God. Without turning back, the nous is then deemed worthy and divinely transformed, becoming like an angel, and is illumined with the angels by the divine splendour of the first light. This appears by participation in which the archetype is the cause, revealing itself as a hidden and irresistible beauty, resplendent in unapproachable radiance. David, the divine musician, noetically sensing that radiance in himself, rejoiced in it and shared with the faithful that great and mysterious gift 'The glory of our God is upon us'.

In this regard, St John wrote in Revelation that: *To him that overcometh, I will give him a white stone, and in the stone a new name written, which no man knoweth saving him that receiveth it.* (Revelation 2:17) Those who neither possess this 'white stone' which nobody ever explains, nor trust the words of those who have had these experiences, will assume these things cannot exist, and so they will think that these experiences are invented. Unable to verify the true teachings, they may invent false teachings about this light.

3.40 The true light is truly light as well as truth

The light of truth is not merely knowledge or virtue because it turns the night of the psyche to day and raises us above our petty everyday concerns, turning us away from the world and towards the inner sources of light and joy in a contemplation that 'goes beyond all works.'

Truth must exist if it is imitated, says Palamas, so if the devil imitates an angel of light, it is because there really is an 'angel of light'. So Palamas says: *God is the light, and the angel of God is the angel of the light.* God is called light because he illumines our psyches, not simply because he overcomes the darkness of ignorance. And this illumination is not merely knowledge or virtue because it causes us to transcend all human concerns. Palamas quotes St Nilus: *The nous which is brought into itself no longer contemplates anything sensory, nor any form of thought, but only the unveiled nous and the divine radiance. From these flow peace and joy.*

Saint Isaac of Nineveh (Isaac the Syrian), who said earlier that he *saw his own nous clothed in a celestial colour*, shows the way that leads us to experience this blissful vision. *When attention seeks prayer it finds it. For if anything follows the train of attention, it is prayer, and so it must be cultivated.* Palamas continues: *Those who have truly prayed, applying their nous to divine prayer, are illuminated by the radiance of God.* And Maximos says: *He who has made his heart pure not only knows the causes of lesser and secondary things and their relation to God, but he sees God Himself.*

3.41 The commandment of Christ is found within the pure heart

The commandment of Christ is written within us, and it is found by introspection in an ever-increasing purity of heart, altogether empty of forms and images. But it must then be able to retain the impression of the divine signs, including the light.

None of this happens by accident or chance, it is best to consider that all of it is the result of effort as well as grace, that grace follows effort, and that although 'for God nothing is impossible,' even so, no exceptions to this rule will occur if we become quiescent and wait for God to do our work for us. The contemplation we call knowledge of God, *theologia*, is only found within us, so that Palamas tells us that when God becomes present in the heart, he writes his own message there by the action of the Holy Spirit. Paul tells us that: *The law of grace will be written not on tablets of stone, but on tablets of flesh.* That is to say, on our hearts. This is important, because, as Macarius said: *The heart directs and governs all other organs of the body. When grace endows the heart, it rules over all the members and all the thoughts. For there, in the heart, the nous abides as well as all the thoughts of the psyche and all its hopes. It is there that grace inscribes the laws of the Spirit.*

All of this is a development of the Christian model of memory, which is found in pre-Christian form in Plato's wax tablet image from the Theaetetus, and in slightly different form in the gospel parable of the sower. (Matthew 13:3-23) But this happens only when the heart is in a properly prepared state. Palamas quotes Maximos: *The pure heart is one that has presented to God a nous altogether empty of all forms, so that it is ready to be imprinted only by the signs of God, by which means it becomes visible.* Palamas then tells us that God said, through one of the God-bearing Fathers: *Do not enrol in the school of a man or a book, but that of My rays and My radiance within you.* If the nous is a blank slate and can hold the imprint of the divine signs, he adds, in words which will be echoed by anyone who has faith: *How can it fail to be superior to knowledge obtained from created beings?*

3.42   There are two great stages in the ascent to God

Palamas now writes about what we might describe today as different methods of effective theology. There are those which are accessible to us as we are, or little changed, and there are those which are accessible only to those whose hearts are pure. We ascend to the second by means of the first.

First of all, the saint tells us there are different ways or stages of learning of God. There is apophatic theology – the negative way which turns our thoughts towards God; there are the signs which have been imprinted on the nous by the Holy Spirit, but which have to be remembered. Beyond that is the vision of God in light, beyond even that is intimate conversation with God. Then there is subsidiary knowledge which makes us able to use the knowledge of the above methods in our lives or to communicate it to others. But we cannot possess God (and be possessed by Him in a spiritual sense) until we purify ourselves by virtue to the point where we are no longer concerned for ourselves. As Palamas tells us here: *We cannot associate with*

God in purity – and immerse ourselves in light without mixture to the limit of the possibilities of human nature – unless we rid ourselves of passions, and, turning our back on sensations and all that is sensory, ascend above thoughts, reasoning, and the knowledge they procure, and so abandon ourselves entirely to the immaterial and noetic activity of prayer. Then, says Palamas, we will find: *The unknowing which surpasses all knowledge,* so that: *We can be filled with the resplendent beauty of the Spirit and so invisibly contemplate the rewards of the nature of the immortal cosmos.* Worldly philosophy is based on the senses and seeks to know different forms of sensation. It does not lead naturally to purity, but at the same time without purity it will be subjectively biased and relatively incoherent. The basis of spiritual contemplation is the Good, which is reached through purity of life. There is also a true and authentic knowledge of created things and of reality which 'does not come from study, but appears with purity.' This is the only thing which can distinguish 'what is truly good and useful from what is not.' Palamas ends here by writing: *The end toward which spiritual contemplation leads is the promise of the age to come, the unknowing which surpasses all knowledge, and the knowledge which surpasses all thought, the secret communion in the hidden and inexpressible vision, the divine contemplation, and the mystical taste of eternal light.*

3.43 no commentary

3.44 The irrationality of our nature

The light that was physically visible at Christ's Transfiguration can now be seen by the eyes of faith by those who turn away from the pull of the world and seek God above all things. When we experience this, we begin to discover the irrationality of our actions and of our psyche, until we discover that: *The natural man does not receive the things of the Spirit.*

Even today, the light that transfigured Christ can be seen by the eyes of faith, so that Palamas tells us that David said: *'I believed, that is why I have spoken'.* We should add that the Apostle said 'we too believe, this is why we speak'. (2 Corinthians 4:13) He then defines someone who will have this experience by saying: *He who has detached himself from material possessions, from human glory and carnal pleasure, in order to embrace life according to the Gospel; one who is confirmed in this renunciation, submitting to those who have come into their measure and stature according to Christ; one who thereby sees the dispassionate, sacred and divine love flare up vividly within him: such is one who desires God above all nature, and seeks union with Him that transcends the very cosmos. Entirely possessed by that desire, he finds it necessary to carefully observe the activities of the body and the powers of the psyche in the hope that he might find in them a way to unite himself to God.* It is then, through observing our activities and powers of the psyche, that we discover how irrational we are.

Even our most rational actions are influenced by what happens around us. Our thoughts and opinions are tainted by imagination and sensory images. All in all, it is understandable that at this point the individual begins to search for a life that truly goes beyond all this, a life that is filled with noetic experience, and not filled with unnecessary concerns for the everyday. Evagrius, in a text ascribed to St Nilus, is clearly speaking of the interior life when he says: *Even if the nous should rise above the contemplation of corporeal nature, still it does not as yet see the perfect place of God. For it might well be engaged in the contemplation of intelligible things and share in their multiplicity.* And again: *Consideration of real things impress a certain form on the nous and draw one far away from God.* Which can be re-stated as 'the nous is very far from God when it functions in a conceptual way'.

3.45 The conceptual capacities of the nous

Here we learn that when it returns to itself, our nous regains certain possibilities. The ability to see conceptual things that exist remains mere theory until we learn to conceive them by the nous, and after that a power of union is given, by which that nous can transcend its own noetic nature and attach itself to what is higher even than the nous. It is by this and in this way that we can know God, and can maintain this while giving necessary attention to everyday life.

If we study this nous, this higher faculty of ours that is the singular perfect essence of our humanity, we will discover that this faculty sets the boundaries of thought on which scientific certainty depends, and is the basis of all forms. Palamas writes: *It is this that defines and unifies the windings of the nous, as being the form of all forms, through which it possesses the certainty of rational knowledge, and which progresses, like a creature that creeps, by dividing and contracting.* This faculty is therefore the form of all forms. This use of the nous is the root of the capacity to divide concepts, it defines and unifies, which is so important to the correct understanding of things.

When the attention of the nous descends into these forms, and through them into the multiplicity of life, it also possesses a higher activity. Just as a knight may act in one way but also possesses a higher level of activity which is different from what ordinarily guides his behaviour, so the nous which is not entirely involved in worldly life can also 'enjoy a higher and sublime activity.' This proper activity of the nous is to turn to itself and watch itself, and when it transcends itself in this way, it can be united with God.

3.46 From total concentration comes transformation

One who wants to live the life of God turns away from the life that leads nowhere and gathers his attention totally into himself, joining his nous to God through unceasing prayer. Totally concentrated within himself, says Palamas, he finds: *A new and indescribable way of ascending to heaven through what we might call the elusive darkness of silence.* In this path the primary choice for the seeker is the monastic life. If he must live in the world, he follows the psychological method in which he strives to be an individual and not to be dependent on others, but in this case he needs to have periods when he can free himself from outside pressures.

This concentration takes time to build up for someone who most of the time is busy with worldly things. He turns away from all material ties, and seeks to turn his attention to the silence by constant prayer, concentrating himself within. Once this is achieved, says Palamas, he joyfully seeks to live *without trouble or care in the sanctuary of hesychia.* In terms of the psychological method, he remains in deep inner stillness while outwardly taking his place in the world. By this, in either form – monastic or lay – he goes beyond his personal self, giving himself entirely to God, and enjoys the glory of the light of God which is perceived directly by pure psyches. And, as Palamas then says: *When the noetic sense is used for union with what is beyond it, the nous cannot see without this divine light, just as no bodily eye can see without the light of the senses.*

3.47 The condescension of God

The nous unites with God by going out of itself. To make this possible, God also in a sense 'goes out of Himself' to unite with the nous in *gracious condescension.* This condescension is how Our Lord, having humbled Himself to come down to the point of death on the cross to be able to reach us, has been able to communicate His light to us as we are. Palamas here quotes Dionysius, who wrote: *He who is above everything and transcends all things, in a superabundance of loving care goes out of Himself, yet remains within Himself, as if drawn by our love and by our desire.* Palamas makes it clear that: *In this very union, which transcends the nous, He unites Himself to us.* Saint Macarius tells us: *In His infinite kindness the Great-One-beyond-being made himself small so that he could mingle with His noetic creatures, by which I mean with the psyches of the saints and the angels, so that through His divinity they too can participate in the immortal life.*

3.48 Guarding against delusions

We need to guard against delusion and be careful what we trust. We should not be moved by argument either into or out of some belief, but should keep an open mind until we have the appropriate experience, accepting that there may be genuine experiences which are still hidden from us. If we are still unsure about experiences of the light, we should pray to God that either it is made clear to us that the light is true, or the delusion be removed.

Only if we listen to the words of the Fathers with faith will we avoid becoming like those blind people who try to encourage others to ignore the lesson of faith. When people call the light 'darkness' simply because they themselves cannot see it, they place themselves out of reach of the divine condescension. The term 'father' is properly applied only to people from whom we would accept truths that we would question if we were told by someone else. If we want to avoid these dangers, it is certainly important to keep an open mind. Indeed, Palamas suggests an approach which may help us to keep the mind open, reminding us that Saint Mark said: *There exists a grace which the infant does not know, which we should neither deny, as it may be true, nor accept, as it may lead to error.* This I see as a timely reminder that we should not close our minds to something just because we have not already had evidence that it is true. Palamas adds: *It is not good to assume that grace which has not yet been put to the test is therefore illusion.* He tells us that Nilus (whose writings are now ascribed to Evagrius)) counsels us to ask God to clarify phenomena of this kind: *At that moment, pray with fervour for God Himself to enlighten you, as soon as possible, on whether a vision comes from Him, and if it does not come from Him, that He will drive the delusion far from you.*

As an additional aid, Palamas points out something that follows automatically from the gospel principle that such things are 'known by their fruits', saying that we can know whether the light in our psyche comes from God or Satan by its effects on us. He has already quoted the Fathers in saying that: *A delusion, even if it imitates the face of goodness, even if it clothes itself in colourful appearances, will not cause a good action. It will not lead us to hate the world, nor to despise the glory of men, nor to desire heavenly things, nor to repress harmful thoughts. It will not obtain for us spiritual rest, joy, peace or humility. It will not bring pleasures and passions to an end, nor put the psyche in a good disposition.* All the virtues, he adds, are produced by grace, while delusions lead to their opposite.

3.49 The reward of humility

In this life, even humans who have seen the light are not infallible. When we work towards *apatheia* it must be for the dispassion that is possible for humans in this life. At the same time, we can recognise the true light, and will understand the doctrine when we reach it. But union is the reward of humility.

In our times, says Palamas, even to be aware of this light that is free of illusion does not make any of us infallible. St John Climacus tells us that as a result of sin, no human being can avoid making mistakes. But he also says that some people become humble as a result of their mistakes and then when they are forgiven their sins they are re-united with the Mother of graces.

However, we should not aim at the perfect dispassion of the angels as our objective, says Palamas, but the dispassion possible to human beings. He tells us that Climacus says that we would recognise without any mistake when this is reached. We will know it by the fact that: *You will feel an indescribable abundance of a light, and an inexpressible desire for prayer.* Then he draws from Climacus an exact definition of what state this is: *Only the psyche which is liberated from every bad predisposition can contemplate the divine light. But many are they who possess a knowledge of the divine doctrines while they still have predispositions.* And, again from Climacus: *Those whose psyches are weak recognise the watch that the Lord keeps over them by other signs, while the perfect recognise it by the presence of the Spirit.* And the same saint then itemizes a series of steps: *Among those who are at an elementary stage, it is the growth of humility in them that gives them certainty that they are progressing according to God's will; in those who are midway, it is the ending of inner conflict; among the perfect, it shows in the increase and great abundance of divine light.*

3.50 Stages in the action of the light

There are stages in which the effect of grace within us changes as we change. The divine light continually increases the humility of the 'perfect', but at the same time God's love for humanity allows it to illumine even people like ourselves who – by the standards of that time and place – are still spiritually young. This grace is first obvious to us, then unnoticed, and then it enters a third stage. The noetic light does not only give knowledge, it is itself a kind of knowledge, as its presence is proof of an inner state which is pleasing to God, and which is described as perfection. The following teachings of the Fathers were quoted by Palamas to clarify this. Diadochos tells us: *At the beginning, we usually feel very strongly that the psyche is illuminated by its own light through grace, while in the middle of our struggles this generally acts within the psyche, for the most part without our recognition.* Evagrius says this: *The Holy Spirit takes compassion on our weakness and comes to visit us even though we are impure. If He should find our nous praying to Him out of love for the truth, He then descends and dispels all the legions of thoughts and reflections that besiege it.*

Saint Macarius said: *God is good, in His Love for men He satisfies the petitions of those who pray to Him. The divine grace sometimes comes to dwell in those who exhaust themselves in prayer, even if they have not manifested equal zeal towards the other virtues. Prayer is given to such a person in proportion to grace, in joy according to what he has asked from God, even if he lacks all the other virtues. This is not to say, however, that he should disregard these other virtues, but that, by perseverance and practice in this struggle, he strives in his heart to become obliging and obedient to God, thus seeking to acquire all the virtues. Thus, indeed, the grace of prayer granted by the Spirit will go on to bear fruit, bringing with it true humility, a real love, and the full array of virtues that he asked for at the beginning of his struggle.*

3.51 Humility opens us to grace

The kingdom of heaven starts small and grows in us slowly. We are not immediately 'rebuilt' as soon as we enter the path, but in time there will be inner space in us for all the truths of heaven. But when we become too full of ourselves and cut ourselves off from good guidance we may lose our access to grace. This should serve us as a reminder that our early experiences of grace are not proof of our perfection. God rebuilds what needs rebuilding without first uncovering the 'foundations'. He does not knock down the whole building, as it were, because He knows it is not yet finished. He knows that our growth will be slow. We must understand that the Kingdom of Heaven when it is first sown in us is the smallest of all things. But in time it grows so great that it fills the whole psyche and makes space for 'the birds of the sky' ... for all the truths that can be learned through the nous. But when we begin we get so full of ourselves that we refuse to follow others and instead become like these people, the rationalists who, because of their lack of spiritual experience, feel that they themselves can judge who is spiritual. Because of this they generally lack good guidance and so lose the grace which would bring them to the same state. So Palamas quotes Saint Paul where he says: *Who are you, you who judge the servant of another?* (Romans 14:4)

3.52 Awakening of the heart

Someone who does not believe in the great mystery of new grace, who is blind to the hope of deification, cannot disdain the pleasures of flesh, money, riches, or human glory. If he does so for a brief moment, it is immediately superseded by pride at having attained perfection, so that he falls back into the ranks of the impure. Someone who desires this hope, even someone who has accomplished all the good actions, seeks for a perfection that is more than perfect, and even infinite. He does not think about what he has already acquired and so he progresses in humility. He sometimes thinks of the superiority of the saints who preceded him and at other times of the great abundance of divine love towards men. In sorrow he weeps and cries out, like Isaiah: 'Woe to me! I am impure, I have unclean lips, for my eyes have seen the Lord Sabaoth'. But this sorrow brings progress in purification, and the Lord of grace adds consolation and illumination. This is why John Climacus, who teaches from experience, says to us 'the depth of sorrow has seen consolation and purity of heart has received illumination'.

Only a purified heart can receive this illumination, although even an impure heart can take in what we can say or know on the subject of God. Because it is given to the nous by the Holy Spirit, this illumination actually goes beyond all words and all knowledge, even if we call it 'knowledge' or 'thought'. It happens through another kind of perception which, because impurities in the heart restrict the sensitivity of the nous, cannot be experienced by us until our hearts are made pure by good actions. Thus He who produced the vision and is Himself its object, that is to say, God as the Christ, the light of the pure heart, says: *Blessed are the pure in heart, for they shall see God.* (Matthew 5:8) They are blessed with a knowledge of a kind that the impure cannot obtain.

Since we do not 'see' it through the senses, illumination is not a kind of knowledge, it is a hidden energy, which we see without seeing, and since it is not in the domain of reason, we conceive it without knowing. Why is it indescribable? Because: *He who wants to describe in words the perception and action of divine illumination to those who have not experienced it, is like someone who tries to use words to describe the sweetness of honey to those who have never tasted it.* Even in our times, the only way to an understanding of this path is through direct experience!

*The nous
then transcends prayer,
and this state should not properly
be called prayer, although it is a fruit
of the pure prayer sent by the Holy Spirit.
Then the nous no longer prays any
definite prayer, it finds itself in ecstasy
amidst incomprehensible realities.
This is the unknowing that is
higher than knowledge.*

AFTERWORD

Lillian Delevoryas Amis

When a man as multi-faceted as Robin has departed this life and I, as his wife, am faced with the task of presenting the record of this remarkable man as truly as I can, I realise that no matter how accurate they are, words are hopelessly inadequate in conveying the reality and substance – the essential nature – of the person and his contribution to the world.

Nevertheless, more than anything else, I think that my husband's life and what he stood for could best be described as a bridge, spanning the gap that existed between the Christian Tradition and all the other alternatives which appeared with the rise of the New Age in the 50s and 60s, a bridge which made it possible for seekers after truth in the West to find their way back to their own tradition.

Robin's childhood in the 30s had been marked by the effects that the first World War had on his father, who was a pilot and had been shot down, gassed, and then imprisoned. The damage he suffered in consequence was unrecognised and untreated back then and left him in a condition that in later years would be diagnosed as post-traumatic stress disorder. As a result of the effects of this on his family life, Robin could see that the world was not what it appeared to be, and so his long search for meaning began. Robin had seen glimpses of what lies beyond the ordinary from an early age and later he tried to reflect as exactly as possible in his writing what he had understood from his own experience. He described some of these formative experiences in *Cornerstones*, a short pamphlet that he wrote around 1960, in which he described three experiences which had happened quite close together and which he named *Compassion*, *Fire*, and *Light*. Here are some excerpts:

from *Compassion*:

'Forgetting myself I was not myself. The barrier between I and they dissolved and I became all those people on the street – and all the thousands round about for a radius of a mile or more. In some way now dimly remembered, dimly understood, I experienced for every human being, each *was myself.* I knew where each was in relation to the others, and sensed the strange web of connections which binds human to human, sometimes over great distances.'

from *Fire*:

'The same life is within and joining all things, creatures and men. Before we can trust ourselves to live with this flaming inner life we must have achieved a certain order or balance in our own life, namely in the mind and emotions. Lack of this balance makes the mind fearful of the forces of life, and by this fear our awareness of the inner life is brought to an end.'

from *Light*:

'Learn that the truest and greatest happiness, the greatest fulfilment, is not to be found in anything outside one: not in possessions, not in good friends, not in health or wealth or a job well done – although those things can many of them help one come nearer to the true joy within. Learn that the source of joy is Love, and that of the greatest joy is the greatest Love.

'Learn that the labour of love is to unite all things and bring an end to separation, that in the light of this love all that is shall function as a single whole. And that man's work is to destroy the barriers to this love and, in part, to carry some of this love to others, both men, creatures and the things of the world.'

These seminal experiences gave him the certainty of things unseen, which was to form the touchstone of all his teaching and writings thereafter. Because he had experienced these realities, he could speak with the certainty of somebody who had lived them. However, with this gift he had been given – of seeing the world beyond the senses – he was now faced with the responsibility of opening it up for others as well. This was the payment. Seeing the sorrow all around him in the world of post-war Britain, he could no longer be content until he had made the effort in sharing with others what he had discovered, to find ways of making it accessible to those who were desperately in need of such knowledge and especially to those who were actively seeking it.

By the mid-twentieth Century there was already a general disillusionment with Christianity among many; there appeared to be a great divide between the Word and the reality to which it points and seekers after truth were not prepared to accept apparently empty rules in its place. At that time, most churches seemed to be concerned with the outer forms of faith, the 'what' of religious observance and not the 'how' of personal practice: the inner way seemed to be missing. Who amongst us can really turn the other cheek and how do we acquire the wherewithal to do this?

Back then, the world of ideas, especially regarding the life of the spirit, was in the midst of massive change and possibilities were opening, bringing as many alternative routes to heaven, or even nirvana, as there are mushroom after the rain. One avenue Robin explored was within the Anglican church of which he was then a member. However, his suggestion that working on oneself towards attaining these experiences was not one that went down too well, and he found himself on the outside of acceptable practice. When it became clear that the church he encountered in that period (he hadn't yet visited Mount Athos) was unable to give him answers to his burning questions, he began to look elsewhere, as did so many other serious seekers in the West.

During the 1960s Robin explored various traditions, such as the Sufis, Kabbala and Indian Advaita, and connected with various groups, including the Fourth Way, based on the teachings of Gurdjieff and Ouspensky. As his studies gradually deepened he discovered that he had a gift for conveying these teachings and this ability began to attract people to him, at first individually, and then in small groups. Over time these grew into larger groups and soon he began giving public talks and hosting workshops where he taught what was called the psychological method and the vital role attention played in it. The role of attention was a key aspect of Fourth Way teachings and it was this aspect which would link these early explorations with the tradition he subsequently encountered on Mount Athos.

The focus of Robin's life was to find a teaching that worked in practical terms, a means of working on oneself (or what he later understood as a form of ascesis) that can be used within the course of everyday life. In order to be effective, the method had to combat our contemporary 'demons' – the incessant distractions of modern life, the constant racket in our heads – which veil our inner life and prevent higher spiritual influences from entering. This is the battle in which modern man has to engage, the unseen warfare that has to be fought at every minute, every hour of the waking day and silently, without the support of a sheltered environment, and often with the subtle opposition of one's own family or friends ('a man's enemies will be the members of his own household').

Through his numerous talks and seminars Robin gradually made connections with seekers who had long since turned their backs on the possibility that there might be a Christian alternative to all the various paths which either Eastern religions or Fourth Way Schools had presented. Over time, his work thus became focused on showing that within our own tradition there are methods and techniques of working on oneself that, although they may appear similar to the disciplines of Zen or Yoga, are nevertheless very different. Robin often said that because the origin of our culture is in the Christian tradition, the cure for the illness and decay of our culture and us could only be found in its roots.

One particular method from the Christian tradition which he introduced into his teaching was Ora et Labora – prayer and work – an exercise in which one would perform everyday tasks and then alternate the task with prayer. In the 70s he began to hold weekend study groups in the Forest of Dean in Gloucestershire, when days were set up to incorporate this way of working on physical tasks combined with prayer and contemplation. Robin used to quote one of the Early Fathers on the Beatitudes as a way of linking the Gospel teachings with the ascesis of the psychological method:

He who does not have attention in himself and does not guard his nous
can not become pure in heart, and so cannot see God.
He who does not have attention in himself
can not be poor in spirit,
cannot weep and be contrite,
nor be gentle and meek,
nor hunger and thirst after righteousness,
nor be merciful, nor a peacemaker,
nor suffer persecution for righteousness sake.

St Symeon the New Theologian

The knowledge that Robin had gained from the various disciplines up to the 80s had taken him as far as the 'door'. Although he had penetrated it for himself, he had yet to find a key to unlock it for those he was guiding. Then, in 1982, through a series of 'coincidences', he learned that there still exists a form of Christianity on Mount Athos in Greece where the monks had maintained spiritual practices which were virtually unchanged from their beginnings in the fourth century. His joy at meeting the Tradition was reflected in something he once said about his first experience there. In the past he had often had the sense while praying of being present in a large cathedral, but that it was solitary and very lonely. Following his first visit to Athos he said that at last he found that this cathedral was populated with many others.

The years of training in the disciplines he had practised for over 20 years prepared Robin well for meeting the Tradition on Mount Athos, which he immediately recognised as genuine. From his first visits it appeared that the recognition was mutual – in 1982, on his second visit, the late Abbot George of the Monastery of Gregoriou issued him with a letter citing him as a *Synergatis,*[1] a 'fellow worker'. This document allowed him to come and go as often as he wished and to stay as long as he was able, by-passing the usual bureaucracy of getting and extending a diamonitirion (the 3-day 'visa' which all visitors, lay and clergy, have to apply for to gain entry to Mt Athos). This unusual recognition gave Robin the freedom to fully share in the Tradition that has been practised there for over a thousand years and to immerse himself in that 'living water'. Thus began his pilgrimages to the Holy Mountain where, to his great joy, he discovered that the experiential aspect of Christianity was very much alive and available to those who went there as pilgrims, seeking God with open hearts. Shortly after this first encounter with the Holy Mountain we converted to Orthodoxy and from then onwards his teaching would be grounded by the Tradition still existing in the monasteries.

On an early visit to the Mount Athos, Robin was fortunate to make contact with a true elder who, until his death in 1994, would become his guide and teacher. This was the blessed Father Paisios, recently canonised as one of the contemporary saints of the Orthodox Church. Robin's relationship with this holy man developed over the next ten years and his steps were guided by the wisdom of a remarkable Saint. He once asked Saint Paisios: how could one know the will of God? The answer was: "You already know it. Do what you know to be right". It seems incredibly simple, yet to follow this through can take one far beyond one's own limitations.

In seeing the benefits that monastics gain through obedience and ascesis, Robin felt that lay people in the world needed a way that parallels this and which is more suitable to a life that includes a job, marriage and a family. A way of working on oneself had to be found that could be incorporated in a life outside the shelter of a monastery, which protects a monk or nun from the decisions and distractions that form a normal part of life in the world. Whenever he would ask the monks if there was a text or guidebook that was used by the monks for this purpose, he was always given the same answer: "It's the Tradition".

On one of Robin's early visits to the monastery something happened to him at his departure: the abbot gave him a blessing, on receiving which he turned icy cold and was enveloped by a great stillness. This state remained, albeit partially, after he returned to England. A week or two later he had to visit his acupuncturist who, on examining him, asked where all this new energy had come from. Robin told him of his experience on the Holy Mountain, on hearing which the practitioner put him in touch with an Egyptian who had been working on the translation of a body of work, written in French by a Russian emigré. A few days later a large package arrived in the post containing a type-written bundle of papers – representing the first volume of a book by Boris Mouravieff titled *Gnosis: Study and Commentaries on the Esoteric Tradition of Eastern Orthodoxy* [2]. In this work Mouravieff presented a blueprint for working on oneself while following a normal life as a layperson outside a monastery. It amplified the Fourth Way teachings in a more systematic fashion, with the addition of copious scriptural quotations. This pointed towards the Fourth Way having many commonalities with Christian practice [3], and introduced the dimension of the divine to the teachings. Robin recognised the similarities between some of the teachings of Gurdjieff, Ouspensky and Mouravieff and the tradition of the monks of Mt Athos. He also recognised that effective teachings need not only an elder, or 'master' to guide one, but also a living tradition to feed one's practice.

The task of preparing a proper translation of *Gnosis*, which took over six years, led Robin to found the Praxis Research Institute which he also developed into a publishing house. *Gnosis* was eventually published in three volumes, followed by other books on the Inner Tradition, including *The Path of Prayer* and *The Heart of Salvation* by St Theophan the Recluse and *The Eros of Repentance* by the late Abbot George Kapsanis of Gregoriou Monastery. Robin's first book, *A Different Christianity*, was published by the State University Press of New York in 1995. Within this work he gathered the different strands of his own researches and experience, in such a way that the book would go on to attract many seekers to the Christian faith – including many who had given up seeking in that direction. The work acted as a kind of funnel, drawing people of diverse backgrounds to the living heart of Christian practice, a heart that many had either never knew existed, or had presumed to be dead.

Several years after publishing *A Different Christianity*, Robin came upon *In Defence of the Holy Hesychasts* by St Gregory Palamas, in the French translation of John Meyendorff. This text, more than many any other he had seen, formed the interface between the Early Fathers and the modern world. It was through this work in particular that he could see the means by which the gap between methods of work in the world and of work in the monastery could be bridged. Although *In Defence of the Holy Hesychasts* was written against the attacks of the westernising scholastics, it is also a textbook par excellence for those working on themselves through prayer, attention and inner stillness. Since the full text was not available in English, Robin prepared a translation and first published the work in 2002 as *The Triads: Book One*. He subsequently worked on revising the translation and in writing the Commentary until his death in 2014.

This book is thus presented posthumously as the summation of Robin's life work, in the hope that the reader may reap in their own lifetime the practical benefits of this remarkable text and find the path to *holy hesychia*.

NOTES

NOTES to INTRODUCTION

1. For instance, see 1 Corinthians, 9:24-27
2. G.K. Chesterton, *What's Wrong with the World*
3. e.g. Plato's analogy of the straight stick appearing to be bent when seen in water.
4. Jean Meyendorff, *Defense des saints hesychastes,* Louvain, 1959
5. Nicholas Gendle, *Gregory Palamas, The Triads,* Paulist Press, New York and SPCK, London, 1983
6. Meyendorff, *A Study of Gregory Palamas*, p134, SVS, Crestwood, New York, 1998
7. This issue has also been addressed by the monks of the Holy Monastery of Gregoriou, Mt Athos, in a paper entitled *A Study of English Orthodox Theological Terms Compared to the Original Greek* (2004), in which they comment on the state of the psyche (ψυχή) in Western civilization: 'This fragmentation is both systematic and indicative of a deep spiritual malady, which shows little or no sign of abating, and whose consequences reverberate throughout the whole world. As Robin Amis, who to our knowledge is the first person to highlight this rift, says, 'this is indicative of the dislocation of the psyche that Western civilisation is now subject to'. This psychic dis-functionality of Western civilisation has only been diagnosed recently, and has as yet had no impact on either the health care system or theology.'
8. Saint Anthony the Great, *On the Character of Men*, from *The Philokalia*, Vol.1, Faber, London, 1981
9. Robin Amis, *A Different Christianity*, SUNY, 1995
10. St Isaac the Syrian, *The Ascetical Homilies*, Homily 3
11. In the *Catholic Encyclopedia* of 1909, Simon Vailhé described the teaching of Palamas that humans could achieve a corporal perception of the Divinity, and his distinction between God's essence and his energies, as 'monstrous errors' and 'perilous theological theories'. Furthermore, he bizarrely characterized the Eastern incorporation of Palamas's teachings into doctrine as a 'resurrection of polytheism'.
12. The clergy were authorised by the Catholic Church to absolve penitents both from the guilt of sins and from punishment in hell, but it did not absolve them from doing penance on earth. The sale of indulgences, which 'absolved' the sinner for a fee, became a common practise in the Middle Ages. An indulgence, therefore, was the remission, by the church, of part or all of the temporal penalties incurred by sins whose guilt had been forgiven in the sacrament of penitence. (see Will Durant, *The Story of Civilization,* The Reformation)
13. *In Defence of the Holy Hesychasts*, 3.17
14. *The Eros Of Repentance*, Archimandrite George Kapsanis, Pleroma, 2016
15. *In Defence of the Holy Hesychasts*, Book Three, 1.32
16. Macarius the Great, *Homily* 15.20. Palamas quotes this passage twice in the present text, at 2.3 & 3.41.

NOTES to PART ONE

1. Greek *agnoia*, which, for Evagrius and others of the spiritual tradition, is the opposite of gnosis, and is said to represent a state of spiritual and noetic emptiness which can be filled only by grace. (See *In Defence of the Holy Hesychasts*, 3.3)

2. Gr. *paedeia*. The Greek word for education, which originally referred to an education that included philosophy, aesthetics and physical exercises, but in this context describes it as referring to a Hellenic form of education of Palamas's time. In the approach of those who supported this, the intellectual and speculative elements of classical Greek thought as applied to theology that had been eliminated by the Fathers of the church were then being reintroduced. 'Hellenic', 'Hellenes' and 'Hellenists' refers to the intellectual culture and its proponents that were then prevalent in the eastern Mediterranean sea-board, the Baltic states and around the Black Sea, and is not identical with Greek nation.

3. Barlaam, *Letter 3 to Palamas*

4. Gr. *gnosis*: knowledge

5. According to the Fathers, noetic knowledge was of the nous, and nous was the highest power of psyche: the 'eye of the psyche.' But it appears that the intellectuals of the period we are studying regarded the nous as intellect in the modern sense, discursive and logical, whereas the nous of the Fathers of the church was something different from this.

6. Gr. *psyche*: means life or vitality, soul

7. These methods are taken from Barlaam, *Letter I to Palamas*

8. I Peter 3:15

9. Hebrews 13:9, 'Be not carried about with divers and strange doctrines. For it is a good thing that the heart be established with grace; not with meats, which have not profited them that have been occupied therein.'

10. This idea that the hesychast tradition is founded in experience is important in the teaching represented by Palamas.

11. A proverb of the times, which appears to have been a favourite with Palamas.

12. Gr. *hoi sophoi*: those wise ones, Palamas's ironic phrase for the intellectuals.

13. Meyendorff, in his French translation, notes that according to Barlaam the main value of the Greek philosophers was to affirm the un-knowability of God and so define the limits of human knowledge.

14. Gr. *demiurgiko no*: Divine Creative Nous

15. Romans 11:34

16. Gr. *logois*: reasons in the sense of reasons why; causes or purposes.

17. I Corinthians 1:17-25

18. I Corinthians 8:1

19. Gr. *nous sarkos*. cf. Colossians 2:18

20. I Corinthians 1:26

21. Gr. *logon ai eikones*. According to some sources, if we become aware of these images of *logoi* within our hearts and learn to live by them, this will lead us toward salvation. Sin is what obscures them and prevents their playing their proper part in our lives.

22. Gr. *alethous theorias*: seems to refer to contemplative truth.

23. Gr. *sundiaioniseis*: 'together through the ages'

24. Romans 16:27, 'To God only wise, be glory through Jesus Christ for ever. Amen.'

25. The phenomenon of over-oxygenation has no spiritual significance.

26. Gr. *mellontos aionos*, the age to come. According to certain of the Early Fathers, the age to come can be found not only at some far future time after death, but it can also be reached by sufficiently purified individuals in this life. That is to say, it is a state, not a place.

27. Palamas links the idea of becoming perfect (cf. Matthew 5:48) with I Corinthians 14:20 'Brethren, be not children in understanding: howbeit in malice be ye children, but in understanding be men.'

28. Philippians 3:15, 'Let us therefore, as many as be perfect, be like-minded: and if in any thing ye be otherwise minded, God shall reveal even this unto you.'

29. I Corinthians 2:6

30. Dionysius the Areopagite, *The Ecclesiastical Hierarchy*, 2

31. John the Baptist

32. Matthew 11:11, 'Verily I say unto you, Among them that are born of women there hath not risen a greater than John the Baptist: notwithstanding he that is least in the kingdom of heaven is greater than he.'

33. John 8:58

34. John 18:37

35. Christ as the image or icon of God in humanity.

36. As Barlaam and the intellectuals had said.

37. Matthew 19:21

38. cf. Matthew 16:24, Mark 8:34, Luke 9:23

39. I Corinthians 1:27

40. I Corinthians 1:20

41. Christ as the image or icon of God in humanity, cf. 1 Corinthians 1:21.

42. ibid.

43. I Corinthians 1:30 – but perhaps not quite as we know that sentence, given in the King James version as: 'But of him are ye in Christ Jesus, who of God is made unto us wisdom, and righteousness, and sanctification, and redemption.'

44. John 1:9

45. II Peter 1:19

46. A wick: perhaps an image of a way of feeding a clear and steady light in the psyche.

47. Meyendorff points out that St John Climacus recommends the opposite to this, not to allow ourselves to grow old in our studies. (*Ladder of Divine Ascent,* 26)

48. Genesis 2:15

49. The nous was often described by the Early Fathers as the eye of the psyche.

50. Meyendorff reports that Palamas's attitude towards profane studies agrees exactly with the official decisions of the Byzantine church and with the condemnation, made in 1082, 'against those who practice the Hellenic sciences, not with the aim of educating oneself, but in complying with its hollow views.' i.e. science is not itself condemned, but only inasmuch as it usurps theology as the measure of man.

51. Saint Gregory Nazianzen

52. Gr. *iuggas* : charm, passionate yearning

53. Proverbs 1:7

54. Compunction: Gr. *katanuxei*, pricking (of the heart)

55. Deuteronomy 6:5, 'And thou shalt love the Lord thy God with all thine heart, and with all thy soul, and with all thy might.'

56. Meyendorff links this image to Evagrius, Macarius, and Maximos and the images of purification to Gregory of Nyssa.

57. Exodus 5:17

58. Acts 17:21

59. In St Basil's *Homily on Psalm XLV*. We can see here that it is easy and probably correct to assume from this that the term wicked spirits refers to the corrupted spirits of the individuals who act in this way, not to creatures of the air, in any superstitious sense.

60. Proverbs 1:2

61. In St Basil's *Homily XII*, on Proverbs 1:6

62. Romans 1:22

63. I Corinthians 2:6

64. St Basil the Great, *Epistle* 223

65. Matthew 16:3. But the Greek does not translate exactly. For Palamas, the Kingdom is not simply a place, but the coming of divine authority into our lives.

66. James 1:5, 'If any of you lack wisdom, let him ask of God, that giveth to all men liberally, and upbraideth not; and it shall be given him.'

67. Romans 2:13

68. Luke 12:47-48

69. St John Chrysostom, *Homily IV*, 4

70. cf. I Corinthians 1:17, 'For Christ sent me not to baptise, but to preach the gospel: not with wisdom of words, lest the cross of Christ should be made of none effect.'

71. cf. I Corinthians 2:4, 'And my speech and my preaching was not with enticing words of man's wisdom, but in demonstration of the Spirit and of power.'

72. I Corinthians 2:2, 'For I determined not to know any thing among you, save Jesus Christ, and Him crucified.'

73. I Corinthians 8:1

74. cf. Ephesians 4:22, Colossians 3:9

75. James 3:17

76. I Corinthians 1:21, 24 etc.

77. James 3:15

78. I Corinthians 2:14, 'But the natural man receiveth not the things of the Spirit of God: for they are foolishness unto him: neither can he know them, because they are spiritually discerned.'

79. For this important theme of the two kinds of knowledge, see St Maximus, *Four Centuries*, 1.22.

80. Gr. *proseche seauto*. cf. Deuteronomy 15:9. The English rendering of the phrase is usually 'beware'. *Proseche seauto* (attend to yourself, or take heed) is a formula adopted by all Christian spirituals in preference to *gnose seauton* (know thyself). The phrase is particularly significant for Palamas, see Part 2.9 of the present work.

81. Gr. *gnose seauton*. A key element in this part of the book, which strives to distinguish clearly between the attentiveness of the spirituals and the 'know yourself' of the philosophers.

82. Acts 16:17

83. II Corinthians 11:14

84. II Corinthians 11:15

85. Numenius of Apamea

86. I Corinthians 2:16

87. Isaiah 55:9

88. James 1:17

89. Jeremiah 10:11

90. John 1:9

91. A summary of the image and terms in the *Second Letter to Barlaam*.

92. I Samuel 17:26, also ibid, 17:36

93. I Corinthians 1:20

94. Dionysius the Areopagite, *The Divine Names*, 4.19

95. The concept of angels as second lights – perhaps reflected lights – is found particularly in Gregory Nazianzus.

96. John 1:9

97. Romans 3:31

98. John 5:39

99. John 5:46

100. The Greek has unspeakable, which is to be taken literally.

101. cf. I Corinthians 2:14

102. cf. Romans 1:25

103. I Corinthians 1:21

104. Romans 1:21, 'Because, when they knew God, they glorified him not as God, neither were thankful; but became vain in their imaginations, and their foolish heart was darkened.'

105. Romans 1:28, 'And even as they did not like to retain God in their knowledge God gave them over to a reprobate mind, to do those things which are not convenient.'

106. Romans 1:25

107. I Corinthians 1:25

108. Plato, *Phaedrus*, 245a

109. Plato, *Timaeus*, 27cd

110. As the oracle of Apollo apparently said about Socrates.

111. Homer, *The Iliad*, 1.5.1

112. The *Theogony* is a poem by Hesiod describing the origins and genealogies of the Greek gods, composed c. 700 BC.

113. Pieria is the birthplace of the Muses; Mt. Helicon is a location favoured by the Muses, a place associated with poetic inspiration.

114. Wisdom 1:5

115. I Corinthians 10:21, 'Ye cannot drink the cup of the Lord, and the cup of devils: ye cannot be partakers of the Lord's table, and of the table of devils.'

116. I Corinthians 1:21, 'For after that in the wisdom of God the world by wisdom

knew not God, it pleased God by the foolishness of preaching to save them that believe.'

117. Dionysius the Areopagite, *Letters*, VII

118. Dionysius the Areopagite, *The Divine Names*, 4. 23

119. Dionysius the Areopagite, *Letters*, VII. Alternatively, 'irreligiously opposes itself to divine things'.

120. I Corinthians 1:21

121. I Corinthians 2:7, 'But we speak the wisdom of God in a mystery, even the hidden wisdom, which God ordained before the world unto our glory.'

122. I Corinthians 2:6

123. I Corinthians 2:8

124. I Corinthians 1.30

125. Romans 1.21

126. Refers to the doctrine of the 'world soul' in Plato's *Timaeus*.

127. Matthew 7:18.

128. cf. Gregory of Nyssa, *On the Making of Man*, written against the doctrine of the transmigration of souls.

129. I Corinthians 2:13

130. I Corinthians 2:4, 'Where is the wise? Where is the scribe? Where is the disputant of this world? Hath not God made foolish the wisdom of this world?'

131. I Corinthians 1:26

132. Romans 1:22

133. I Corinthians 1:20

134. Colossians 2:8

135. I Corinthians 2:6

136. Dionysius the Areopagite, *The Divine Names*, 7.2

137. Gr. *anoun*: without nous, or without understanding.

138. James 3:15

139. This image was used by Palamas in his second letter to Barlaam.

140. Meyendorff says that this is a reference to Genesis 4:7, in the Septuagint version, which says: 'If you make your offering correctly without dividing correctly, do you not sin?'

141. St Isaac of Nineveh (Isaac the Syrian.) *Homily 72*

142. I Corinthians 2:9

143. But how can one remove the 'extremities' of an idea while keeping the meaning? This depends on a subtle understanding of the ancient idea of antinomies that provides a method of distinguishing the worldly from the divine.

144. I Corinthians 1:26

145. Gregory the Theologian, *Sermons*, 41.14. Palamas also quotes these passages at 2.12 of the present work.

146. cf. Acts 13:9

147. II Corinthians 12:2-4

148. Gr. *theosophia*

149. I Corinthians 1:6

150. I Corinthians 2:6

151. I Corinthians 1:18

152. John 10:5
153. St Gregory of Nyssa, *Epistle 8*
154. Dionysius the Areopagite, *The Ecclesiastical Hierarchy*, 2
155. St John Chrysostom, *Homily 1*, 4-5
156. St Cyril, *Commentary on the Psalms*
157. St Gregory of Nyssa, *Commentary on Ecclesiastes*, 1.18

NOTES to PART TWO

1. Luke 10:16
2. Barlaam says in his *Fifth Letter* that the nous enters and leaves through the nostrils in time with the breathing.
3. I Corinthians 6:19
4. Hebrews 3:6
5. II Corinthians 6:16
6. Meyendorff states that this is a Manichean survival of the Messalian heresy, after Barlaam had earlier accused the hesychasts of being heretics like the Messalians and Euchites.
7. According to the Fathers and Orthodox tradition, body and psyche form a unity given by God. The view that the body is evil in itself has its roots in gnostic dualism.
8. Psalm 63:1
9. Psalm 84:2
10. Isaiah 16:11. Palamas quotes the Old Testament from the Greek Septaguint (LXX), which dates from the 2nd century BC and is based on the Tanakh as then preserved in the Temple at Jerusalem. Most modern translations of the O.T. (except the Douay-Rheims, from the latin Vulgate of St Jerome) are from the Masoretic text which was compiled following the destruction of the Temple in 70 AD and edited into its present form by the 10th century AD. The edition on which the KJV translation is based is the Bomberg edition of 1525, published in Venice.
11. Isaiah 26:18. This should be taken almost literally.
12. Romans 7:24
13. Romans 7:14
14. Romans 7:18
15. Romans 7:23
16. Romans 8:2, 'But I see another law in my members, warring against the law of my nous, and bringing me into captivity to the law of sin which is in my members.'
17. Gr. *episkopen*: oversight; this word is related to the word for Bishop.
18. Gr. *somatos*: the physical body itself.
19. Gr. *egkrateia*: self-control, or temperance
20. Gr. *agape*: unselfish love
21. Gr. *nepsis*: watchfulness, or sobriety. The practise of watchfulness, or guarding one's thoughts, is of central importance to the hesychasts.
22. II Corinthians 4:6
23. II Corinthians 4:7
24. See reference to Macarius at note 27 below.
25. Matthew 15:11
26. Matthew 15:19
27. Macarius the Great, *Homily* 16:20
28. The heart is the seat of thought, and attention is an action of the nous. So to bring attention to thought, ultimately we bring the nous into the inmost heart.
29. Macarius the Great, *Homilies,* 15, ibid.

30. Gr. *hesychia*

31. Psalm 45:13. Meyendorff says that the application of this text to the spiritual life probably goes back to Origen.

32. Galatians 4:6

33. Luke 17:21

34. Proverbs 27:21, from the Septaguint. This phrase is not included in traditional English versions and is noted as 27:21a in some translations of the Septaguint. 'Fire is the trial for silver and gold; and a man is tried by the mouth of them that praise him. The heart of the transgressor seeks after mischiefs; but an upright heart seeks knowledge.' (Brenton Septaguint Translation)

35. St John Climacus, *Ladder of Divine Ascent*, 26

36. II Corinthians 1:22

37. 1 Timothy 6:20. 'O Timothy, keep that which is committed to thy trust, avoiding profane and vain babblings, and oppositions of science falsely so called.'

38. St Basil the Great, *Homily XII*, on Proverbs 7

39. I Corinthians 2:14 -15. 'But the natural man receiveth not the things of the Spirit of God, for they are foolishness unto him; neither can he know them, because they are spiritually discerned.'

40. Dionysius the Areopagite, *The Divine Names*, 4, 9

41. ibid.

42. St Basil the Great, *Letter Two*, to St Gregory Naziansus: 'Thus the mind, saved from dissipation without, and not through the senses thrown upon the world, falls back upon itself and thereby ascends to the contemplation of God'. This concept of the faultless action that draws the pure nous to God is also found in Indian philosophy in the idea of the Method of Cause and Effect.

43. Dionysius the Areopagite, *The Divine Names*, 4.9

44. See Barlaam's Letter to Ignatius.

45. St John Climacus, *Ladder of Divine Ascent*, 27.6

46. For Meyendorff, this implies union with Christ. For the translators of The Philokalia into English, it is the union of the nous with the matter of the body. As Palamas says later, the matter of the body finds its life in Christ.

47. It sometimes seems from usage that this originally implied not just one who lives alone but a unified, self-sufficient person.

48. Symeon the New Theologian, *The Three Methods of Attention & Prayer*, in *The Philokalia* Vol.4, Faber, London, 1995

49. Dionysius the Areopagite, *The Divine Names*, 4.9

50. Gr. *enoeide suneliksin*: 'only one gathering-in' or 'singular recollection'. The phrase 'single-pointed concentration', as used by the schools of Gurdjieff and Ouspensky, is similar though perhaps not the same.

51. I Corinthians 13:7

52. The fall, as a transgression against God's commandment.

53. Macarius the Great, *Homilies*, 16.7. This might also be rendered 'the inner man naturally adapts to outer forms'. See also St John Climacus, *The Ladder of Divine Ascent*, 25.28, 'The soul becomes like its bodily occupations. It conforms itself to its activities and takes its shape from them.'

54. Dionysius the Areopagite, *The Divine Names*, 4.8

55. Symeon the New Theologian, *Three Methods of Attention & Prayer*, ibid. Palamas used the same description in his second letter to Barlaam.

56. Gr. *noeton theros*

57. This is the area which Japanese tradition calls the hara.

58. Romans 7:23

59. Titus 3:5, 'Not by works of righteousness which we have done, but according to His mercy he saved us, by the font of regeneration, and the renewing of the Holy Spirit.' In this text, this refers to baptism.

60. Luke 11:26

61. Gr. *proseche seauto*, 'be aware', 'be careful', 'take care' in standard Bible translations; in the Septaguint, 'Take heed to thyself'.

62. Deuteronomy 15:9

63. This crucial directive might also be rendered: 'Take heed of yourself, oversee yourself, observe yourself, or rather take command, examine and master yourself.'

64. Deuteronomy 15:9

65. Ecclesiastes 10:4

66. Psalm 7:9; cf. Jeremiah 17:10

67. I Corinthians 11:31

68. Psalm 139: 11-13

69. A reference to Genesis 6:1-6

70. Romans 8:11, 'But if the Spirit of Him that raised up Jesus from the dead dwell in you, He that raised up Christ from the dead shall also quicken your mortal bodies by His Spirit that dwelleth in you.'

71. I Kings 18:42

72. cf. Matthew 23:25, and Luke 11:39

73. Luke 18:13, 'And the publican, standing afar off, would not lift up so much as his eyes unto heaven, but smote upon his breast, saying, God be merciful to me, a sinner.'

74. Literally, 'navel-souls', (as if their brains were in their navels); perhaps the origin of the English term 'navel-gazers'.

75. Barlaam advised his associate Ignatius to abandon the sobriety of the hesychasts and find another method.

76. A recapitulation of Psalm 40:8, 'I delight to do Thy will. O Lord: yea, Thy law is within my heart.'

77. Isaiah 16:11

78. Jeremiah 1.18

79. Palamas is here using Barlaam's logic against him: if it is right to say that the hesychasts, who by their outward appearance in their approach to God can be said to be 'omphalopsychics', then the prophets, by the words they use to describe their approach to God, must similarly be said to be 'coeliopsychics', i.e. belly-souls. Of course, no one with any respect for Scripture and the prophets could say such a thing. The argument points to the need for discernment between the inner and outer. Acquiring such discernment is achieved by those who 'observe and purify the interior of ... their hearts'. cf. *Part Two*, 2.8.

80. Barlaam himself referred to the unknowability of God and never pretended to see

anything more than shadows and images.

81. *Hesychia* is stillness, the fruit of keeping watchfulness on the activities of the nous in order to still harmful passions, thereby cleansing the heart and psyche.

82. Philotheus Kokkinos, in his *Life of St Gregory Palamas*, reports that Palamas was himself initiated into the hesychastic life by Theoleptus.

83. A play on the meaning of his name, Theoleptus.

84. Psalm 103:1

NOTES to PART THREE

1. Variation on Colossians, 2:18

2. Gr. *gnosis*

3. Delusion as a state, not an item of misinformation, Gr. *planes*, wandering. Used to describe the state of the nous when it wanders, when it is unstable because disturbed by the activities of the psyche.

4. On 10th October in 351 AD at Nike in Thrace the Arians obtained from a delegation of Orthodox bishops the signing of a formula which disowned the decisions of Nicea, the most important of the seven Ecumenical Councils of the early church and which had first defined the faith of the church in 325 AD.

5. II Timothy, 2:15

6. Gr. *monologisto proseuche*: 'prayer of a single thought' i.e. prayer whose aim is to keep the mind on the single thought of God. A phrase often used to refer to the Jesus Prayer, or Prayer of the Heart, 'Lord Jesus Christ, Son of God, have mercy on me, the sinner'.

7. Gr. *dianoian*

8. Gr. *arche*, cause, beginning, fundamental principle. A key word that was developed progressively in classical Greek philosophy, and fills a key position in Genesis and in the first verse of St John's Gospel: 'In the beginning (*arche*) was the Word.'

9. Gr. *logikes psyches*

10. This refers to Peter 2:4, 'God spared not the angels that sinned, but cast them down to hell, and delivered them into chains of darkness.'

11. II Corinthians 4:6

12. Dionysius the Areopagite, *The Divine Names*, 4.6

13. Gr. *noeton*

14. Gr. *noeron*

15. Macarius, *Homily V*. When the light visibly radiates from the body of an individual, it is said that this is evidence of the resurrection of the body. If we understand Palamas's teaching we will understand this statement.

16. Dionysius the Areopagite, *The Divine Names*

17. Palamas is here referring to the apophatic way, the 'negative theology' that describes God only in terms of what He is not, since language, as something created, cannot in any way encompass the Uncreated.

18. Judges 13:17

19 Gr. *hieroi andres*: sacred, or holy men.

20. John 17:22, 'And the glory which thou gavest me I have given them; that they may be one, even as we are one.'

21. Dionysius the Areopagite, *The Ecclesiastical Hierarchy*, 1.4

22. The light revealed to the eyes of the disciples when our Lord was transfigured on the mountain. cf. Matthew 17:1-3, Mark 9:2-13, Luke 9:28-36

23. St Andrew of Crete, *Homily VII*

24. II Corinthians, 12:2

25. Many of the writings attributed to St Nilus in the time of Palamas are now attributed to Evagrius of Pontus, as is this.

26. Exodus 24:9-11

27. Evagrius, *Thoughts,* 1, (in *Evagrius of Pontus: the Greek Ascetic Corpus*)

28. St Isaac the Syrian, *Homily 32*

29. II Corinthians 4:6

30. St John Chrysostom, *Epistle II*, On Corinthians

31. Macarius the Great, *Homilies* 5.10

32. Diadochos of Photiki, *On Spiritual Knowledge and Discrimination*, (in *The Philokalia*, Vol.1)

33. Maximos the Confessor, *Four Centuries on Love*, 1.31 (in *Early Fathers From the Philokalia*)

34. The Nilus Palamas refers to here is probably Evagrius; the source of his quotation is uncertain.

35. Corinthians 4:6

36. Psalm 12: 3

37. Psalm 42:3

38. Psalm 4:6

39. In our times, this figurative use of the word light has become commonplace so that the original meaning of an inner light is obscured.

40. Gr. *logou dynamin*

41. Gr. *theoreton*: contemplated, referring to non-sensory awareness.

42. St Isaac the Syrian and many others have used terms like these, which describe the nous as the eye of the soul.

43. Gr. *noeran echon aisthesin horoe*

44. Matthew 5:8

45. John 1:5

46. John 14:21

47. I Corinthians 13:12

48. Malachi 4:2

49. Gr. *hyperanidrumenon*

50. Gregory the Theologian, *Homilies,* 21.2

51. Matthew 25:41

52. Philippians 2:11

53. cf. II Corinthians, 1:22; Ephesians 1:14

54. Perhaps in the modern sense of 'in the now'.

55. Gr. *pneumatikon*

56. Gr. *teleiotetos*

57. Gr. *phroneseos*

58. II Corinthians 3:11. 'For if that which is done away was glorious, much more that which remaineth is glorious.'

59. Gr. *to athanato tou eso anthropou prosopo*

60. II Corinthians 3:18. 'But we all, with open face beholding as in a glass the glory of the Lord, are changed into the same image from glory to glory, even as by the Spirit of the Lord.'

61. Gr. *epistrepse*
62. Macarius the Great, *On Freedom of the Mind*, 21
63. I Corinthians 2:15-16
64. Gr. *psychikos*: natural, or material-minded man: one whose psyche has not woken to the pneumatos, or spirit. A psyche wakes to the Spirit when the nous is cleansed of the veil of passions.
65. I Corinthians 2:14
66. Gr. *nepsis*: the practice of watchfulness, vigilance of the nous and thus the passions. The essential practice of the hesychast in the exercise of repentance and self-purification.
67. cf. Romans 1:22; I Corinthians 1:20
68. I Corinthians 2:10.
69. I Corinthians 2:13-16. Normally translated as the 'mind of Christ'.
70. I Corinthians 2:12
71. Habakkuk 2:15
72. I Corinthians 2:15
73. ibid.
74. Literally, 'But what about life?'
75. Gr. *metanoia*: change of nous, or mind, i.e. a re-orientation towards God.
76. St Basil the Great; source uncertain
77. John 1:18
78. Matthew 5:8
79. John 14:23
80. Gr. *logikes eikonos*; can also be translated as 'thought forms'.
81. I Corinthians 2:10. 'But God hath revealed them unto us by His Spirit: for the Spirit searcheth all things, yea, the deep things of God.'
82. St Basil the Great, *Second Letter to Gregory of Nazianzus*. Alternate translation: 'stabilises the eye of his heart in watchfulness.'
83. I Corinthians 2:11
84. I Corinthians 2:9
85. I Corinthians 2:16, 'For who hath known the mind of the Lord, that he may instruct him? But we have the mind of Christ.'
86. Gr. *noousi*
87. Gr. *igoumeni*, same root as *igoumenos*, the term used for an abbot.
88. Song of Solomon 1:15
89. I Corinthians 6:17, 'But he that is joined unto the Lord is one spirit.'
90. Gregory of Nyssa, *Homilies on the Song of Songs*, IV & VII
91. Dionysius the Areopagite, *On the Divine Names*, 1.5. Transcendence is not caused by activity but by a cessation of the activity of the nous. Theoria (contemplation) is not just loss, but gains the extraordinary when it loses the ordinary in the meeting of passionlessness and the nous in *apatheia* and divine grace.
92. Gr. *apharaisin*: abstraction. In this context, inner separation of the nous from activities in the psyche. The Aristotelian background of Palamas shows here. The alternative rendering of stripping-away is arguably neo-Platonist and perhaps not Christian in implication.

93. St Isaac's statement relates to the traditional Christian doctrine that admission to the divine presence is by the grace of God, not by the will or choice of man.

94. In the computer sense of writing data & hence of storing information in memory.

95. Gr. *gnoseos*

96. Gr. *phantasia*

97. Gr. *dianoia*

98. Gr. *doxa*

99. Gr. *logos*

100. Dionysius the Areopagite, *Letter 1*; cf. *The Mystical Theology*, 3

101. Gr. *gnophos* – perhaps a play on words combining *gnosis* and *pho*, knowledge and light.

102. cf. Matthew 7:6

103. Dionysius the Areopagite, *The Mystical Theology*, 3

104. ibid.

105. Gr. *apopleroseos*, related to pleroma, fullness

106. The uncreated light

107. Dionysius the Areopagite, *The Divine Names*, 7.1

108. Dionysius the Areopagite, *The Divine Names*, 4.11

109. 2 Corinthians 12:2

110. Gr. *ekplexeos*; related to *ekplexis*, striking with a sudden shock, panic or fear

111. St Isaac the Syrian, *Homily 32*

112. ibid.

113. Gr. *ekstesan*: related to the word ecstasy

114. Gr. *thearchia*: thearchy or divine sovereignty

115. Dionysius the Areopagite, *Letters*, 2

116. I Corinthians 2:13, 'Which things also we speak, not in the words which man's wisdom teacheth, but which the Holy Ghost teacheth; comparing spiritual things with spiritual.'

117. II Corinthians 1:12

118. I Kings 19:13

119. Gr. *Theoptes*, 'seer of God', 'one who sees God'. Palamas refers in many places to Elijah as one of the prototypes of hesychasm, following a well-established patristic and liturgical tradition.

120. I Kings 19:12

121. Isaiah 16:11 'Wherefore my bowels shall sound like a harp for Moab, and mine inward parts for Kir-haresh.'

122. II Kings 2:11

123. Jeremiah 20:8-9

124. Psalm 78:25

125. Luke 11:13 & 18:7

126. Dionysius the Areopagite, *The Divine Names*, 1.5

127. Mark 9:2-8

128. II Peter 1:16-18

129. St John Chrysostom

130. Gregory Nazianzen, *Homilies,* 40.6

131. Symeon Metaphrastes, *Life of St John the Evangelist*, 1
132. cf. Matthew 16:38; Mark 9:1; Luke 9:27
133. Wisdom 7:22
134. Gr. *photophaneias*
135. Luke 2:8-10
136. Macarius the Great, source uncertain
137. II Peter 1:16-18
138. cf. Hebrews 1:3
139. Acts 7:55-56. Given almost exactly as in the Greek New Testament.
140. Acts 7:56
141. In Greek thought, this idea of witnessing or confessing to the truth of the faith is one of proving what you witness to by sacrificing yourself for it. The implication here is that without faith you will believe neither words nor even the testimony of self-sacrifice.
142. Gr. *aplanes*: without error; literally, without wandering.
143. Exodus 34:35
144. Acts 6:15
145. see *The Life of St Mary the Egyptian*
146. Matthew 24:30
147. St John Climacus
148. Luke 22:44
149. Psalm 118:103
150. Psalm 63:5
151. Matthew. 5:4
152. Song of Songs 4:11
153. Gr. *noeran*
154. Gr. *hyper noeran*
155. Meyendorff suggests that this is taken from an unpublished text of Macarius and so cannot be traced exactly.
156. Dionysius the Areopagite, *The Divine Names*, 1.4
157. I Corinthians 15:28
158. It can be seen externally through the senses augmented by nous, it can be seen now, in moments, again by the nous, and it can be seen in the age to come.
159. Matthew 13:43
160. I Corinthians 2:9
161. I Corinthians 15:44
162. Luke 20:36
163. Matthew 22:30, 'For in the resurrection they neither marry, nor are given in marriage, but are as the angels of God in heaven.'
164. St Maximos, *Four Centuries*, 2.88
165. Baruch 3:38. The book of Baruch is included in the Greek Septuagint but only in the Apocrypha of the King James Bible.
166. Colossians 2:9
167. I Corinthians 13:12, 'For now we see through a glass, darkly; but then face to face: now I know in part; but then shall I know even as also I am known.'

168. Psalm 90:17

169. Revelation 2:17, 'He that hath an ear, let him hear what the Spirit saith unto the churches: To him that overcometh will I give to eat of the hidden manna, and will give him a white stone, and in the stone a new name written, which no man knoweth saving he that receiveth it.'

170. II Corinthians 11:14

171. cf. St Maximos, *Scholia on The Divine Names*, 13

172. cf. St Gregory Nazianzus, *Homilies* 40.5

173. cf. Evagrius, *Practikos*, 66

174. Evagrius, *On Prayer*, 149

175. S. Maximos, *Four Centuries*, 2.80

176. ibid.

177. II Corinthians 3:3, 'Forasmuch as ye are manifestly declared to be the epistle of Christ ministered by us, written not with ink, but with the Spirit of the living God; not in tables of stone, but in fleshly tables of the heart.'

178. Palamas quotes this same passage from Macarius at 2.3 of the present work.

179. St Maximos, *Four Centuries*, 2.82

180. Gr. *aneidos*, imageless, or a 'blank slate'.

181. Gr. *dianoias*

182. Dionysius the Areopagite, *The Divine Names*, 1.4

183. Macarius, *On Freedom of the Mind*, 24

184. Psalm 116:10

185. II Corinthians 4:13

186. Ephesians 4:13, 'Until we all come in the unity of the faith, and of the knowledge of the Son of God, unto a perfect man, unto the measure of the stature of the fullness of Christ.'

187. Gr. *eroti*

188. Gr. *tas somatikas energeias*

189. Gr. *tas psychikas dynameis*

190. I Corinthians 2:14. 'But the natural man receiveth not the things of the Spirit of God, for they are foolishness unto him; neither can he know them, because they are spiritually discerned.'

191. Evagrius, *On Prayer*, 57

192. Evagrius, *On Prayer*, 56

193. Gr. *ta noeta*

194. Dionysius the Areopagite, *The Divine Names*, 7.1

195. Gr. *eidos ousa ton eidon*

196. Possible source of the description of the personality type of the same name in Boris Mouravieff, *Gnosis*, Volume 2.

197. St Maximos, *Four Centuries*, 1.31

198. Dionysius the Areopagite, *The Divine Names*, 4.13

199. Macarius the Great, *Peri Ipsoseos Toi Noos (On the Elevation of the Nous)*

200. Romans 7:24

201. Philippians 2:8

202. Matthew 15:14

203. St Mark the Ascetic, *On Those Who Think They Are Made Righteous By Works*, (in *The Philokalia*, Vol. 1)

204. Evagrius, *Chapters On Prayer*, 94

205. Macarius the Great, *Peri Ipomonis kai Diakriseos* (*On Patience and Discernment*)1.3

206. St John Climacus, *The Ladder of Divine Ascent*, 4

207. St John Climacus, *The Ladder of Divine Ascent*, 26

208. St Diadochus of Photiki, *On Spiritual Knowledge and Discrimination*, 69 (in *The Philokalia*, Vol. 1)

209. Evagrius of Pontus, *Chapters On Prayer*, 62

210. Macarius the Great, *Homily* 19

211. Matthew 13: 31-32

212. Romans 14:4

213. Isaiah 6:5

214. St John Climacus, *The Ladder of Divine Ascent*, 7

215. Matthew 5:8

216. St John Climacus, *The Ladder of Divine Ascent*, 7

217. St John Climacus, *The Ladder of Divine Ascent*, 25

NOTES to AFTERWORD

1. The document was issued in May 1985 'from the entire community of the Monastery of Gregoriou' and designated Robin as a *synergatis* (fellow-worker and equal to the monks), requesting 'that he be given free access, both coming in and going out of the Holy Mountain'. The document is reproduced in the appendix of Robin Amis, *Views From Mount Athos*, Praxis Institute Press, 2014.

2. Gnosis is the Greek for knowledge; unfortunately it has become confused in the minds of some with 'gnostic' or 'gnosticism', terms that now relate to an heretical form of Christianity from the 2nd Century.

3. Some correspondences between terms employed by the hesychasts and proponents of 'the psychological method' are as follows: *ascesis* – conscious labour; *thlypsis* – intentional suffering; *nepsis* – self-observation; *nous*, *psyche* and body – mental, emotional and physical; *nous* as 'eye of the psyche' and the veiled nous – essence and personality; *attention* (as activity of the nous) – attention; *circular attention* – self-remembering (doubled attention).

FURTHER READING

St Basil the Great, *Homilies*: many versions available online, worth seeking out.
Pseudo-Dionysius, *The Complete Works*, Paulist Press , New York, 1987
(Dionysius the Areopagite is styled 'Pseudo-Dionysius' in the West)
Evagrius, *Practikos & Chapters on Prayer,* Cistercian Publications, 1972
Evagrius, *Evagrius of Pontus: the Greek Ascetic Corpus*, tr. R. Sinkewicz, Oxford, 2006
St Gregory Nazianzen, *Homilies,* available online.
St Gregory of Nyssa, *Homilies on the Song of Songs,* Soc. of Biblical Lit., Atlanta, 2013
St Gregory of Nyssa, *From Glory to Glory,* SVS Press, New York, 1979
St Gregory of Nyssa, *On the Making of Man,* Createspace, 2013
St Isaac the Syrian, *Ascetical Homilies,* Holy Transfiguration Monastery, Boston, 2011
St John Climacus, *Ladder of Divine Ascent,* Paulist Press, New York, 1982
Pseudo-Macarius, *Fifty Spiritual Homilies,* tr. A.D. Mason, SPCK, London, 1921
(Macarius the Great is styled 'Pseudo-Macarius' in the West)
St Maximus, *Four Centuries* (in *The Philokalia,* Vol. 2, Faber and Faber, London, 1982)
Jean Meyendorff, *Defense des saints hesychastes,* Louvain, 1959
Early Fathers From the Philokalia, Faber and Faber, London, 1954
The Philokalia, Vol. 1, Faber and Faber, London, 1979
The Philokalia, Vol. 4, Faber and Faber, London, 1999

Please visit
www.praxisresearch.net
to explore the work of Robin Amis
and ways in which the teachings of tradition
can be applied in daily life.

The page ornaments on pp iii, 105 & 207 are by Andrew Gould,
at www.newworldbyzantine.com and supplied by the
Orthodox Arts Journal. Many Thanks!

Milton Keynes UK
Ingram Content Group UK Ltd.
UKHW020900151024
2179UKWH00018B/107

9 780995 510302